Corporate Property Management:
aligning real estate with business strategy

Dedication

To all the men in our lives:
Adam, Zary, Rufus and Basil Shaljean and Rick and Dylan Taylor

Corporate Property Management:
aligning real estate with business strategy

Victoria Edwards

Department of Property Resource Management
University of Portsmouth

and

Louise Ellison

School of Surveying
Kingston University

Blackwell
Science

© 2004 by Blackwell Science Ltd
a Blackwell Publishing Company

Editorial Offices:
Blackwell Science Ltd, 9600 Garsington Rd, Oxford
OX4 2DQ, UK
  Tel: +44 (0)1865 776868
Blackwell Publishing Inc., 350 Main Street, Malden,
MA 02148-5020, USA
  Tel: +1 781 388 8250
Blackwell Publishing Asia Pty Ltd, 550 Swanston
Street, Carlton, Victoria 3053, Australia
  Tel: +61 (0)3 8359 1011

First published 2004

Library of Congress
Cataloging-in-Publication Data
Edwards, Victoria.
    Corporate property management: aligning real
estate with business strategy/Victoria Edwards
and Louise Ellison.
    p. cm.
    Includes bibliographical references and index.
    ISBN 0-632-06051-4 (pbk.: alk. paper)
    1. Commercial real estate–Great Britain–
Management.   2. Real estate management–Great
Britain.   3. Real estate investment–Great
Britain.   4. Strategic planning–Great Britain.
I. Ellison, Louise, 1967–   II. Title.

HD1393.58.G7E39   2003
333.33′87′0684–dc21

                                    2003010429

ISBN 0-632-06051-4

A catalogue record for this title is available from the
British Library

Set in 10/12.5 pt Palatino
by DP Photosetting, Aylesbury, Buckinghamshire
Printed and bound in Great Britain on acid-free
paper by MPB Books Ltd, Bodmin, Cornwall

For further information on Blackwell Publishing,
visit our website:
www.blackwellpublishing.com

Contents

Preface

In 1989, we began to teach a different approach to property management in our own department at Portsmouth Polytechnic, now the University of Portsmouth. This assumed, among other things, that a property manager must understand the *users'* requirements for any property under her care.

This is a concept that has always been inherent in the training of land agents for the management of landed estates. Students of rural estate management have traditionally studied agriculture and agricultural valuations, forestry, recreational land management, and, more recently, other contemporary land uses, from fish farming to theme park management. As such, they have been equipped to manage the diverse nature of their landed estates by having a full understanding of an estate's potential and by being able to build relationships with neighbours, tenants and other users who are likely to realise that potential for the estate.

Without a proper understanding of the businesses that the estate can support, the land owner cannot properly identify and exploit opportunities, calculate and reduce the risks involved with any new ventures, and ensure that the potential is fully achieved. He can only do this by maintaining good working relationships, which are based on sound understanding of other peoples' businesses.

At Portsmouth we believed that a similar approach should be adopted in the urban environment. We viewed the property manager not as a technician or clerk, but as a strategic partner. However, we recognised that partnerships must be based on shared understanding. Thus, if our students aspired to managing real estate within the breweries, they needed a grounding in the brewing industry, from top to bottom (something students have been known to take very seriously). Similarly, if they were to manage a retail estate, they must understand the way in which the retail world operates and, specifically, what a particular occupier needs from its shop premises.

Clearly, there is only so much one can squeeze into an estate management course, but with the help of outside experts, we believe that we managed to provide some insight into an occupier's relationship with a property. Whether students then went on to act as agents for investors, managing portfolios of different types of property, or as managers for occupiers, such as large retail chains, they understood the value of property to the occupier's business in more than simply financial terms. As a consequence, they did not automatically separate the corporate business from property management. We hope that they graduated with an understanding that their role should be one of facilitation: where the landlord–tenant relationship is viewed as a business partnership for mutual gain.

This book has been written as a result of this approach to teaching, and as a text to support it. While there are a number of excellent property and investment management textbooks available, we have never found one that takes the sort of strategic approach that we feel is so important. This is our attempt to fill that gap within the market.

The book focuses on the strategic management of property held as a corporate asset, i.e. the management of the operational portfolio of an organisation. The aim is to enable the reader to take a strategic approach to this management function, regardless of the type of property with which they are involved. To achieve this the book aims to equip the reader with an understanding of:

- the different roles that property plays within society and the economy
- the different roles that property plays within an organisation
- the value that property can add to an organisation
- why it is important to take a strategic approach to the management of property.

The analytical framework presented and discussed in Chapter 2 is a generic tool that should be capable of application to most organisational circumstances. It is not a model, it is simply a means of reducing the strategic property management approach to its component parts, thereby allowing problems that potentially underlie the operation of a real estate portfolio to be explored.

When we studied estate management, we did so in a world where all hypothetical scenarios in books, lectures and examinations involved landowners, landlords, tenants who were exclusively men, invariably with English names. Occasionally a female tenant would appear in the story, more often than not to cause a nuisance or renege on an agreement. When we began our teaching careers, we quite quickly managed to convince our male colleagues that such practice does nothing to help build diverse role models in surveying. As in our lectures and assessments, we have tried to adopt a non-sexist language policy in the book, randomly using male and female pronouns. We hope that this does not make for an awkward or irritating style and that some of our female readers will be uplifted to discover, albeit subconsciously, that they too can be corporate property managers.

Acknowledgements

We are indebted to several people and organisations in helping us write this book, some of who have been involved in the course at Portsmouth for over a decade.

First, we would like to thank our case study contributors, who have provided much help and inspiration in bringing our theory to life:

- Geoff Robotham of Borders Books UK Ltd
- Andrew Raven of Ardtornish Estate
- Roger Clark and Jake Chalmers of the Youth Hostels Association
- Keith Toms and Jeff Wagland of Clifford Chance
- Paul Winter of Corpra.

Second, we would like to thank Professor Bill Seabrooke of Hong Kong Polytechnic University, who, while Head of Department at Portsmouth, introduced the concept of Strategic Property Management to our courses.

Third, we would like to thank the following people who assisted in the book's execution:

- Isobel Kilgallon, for years of superb librarian support
- Nobby Clarke, Rick Taylor, Adam Shaljean and James Ellwood, for painstakingly commenting on early drafts
- Madeleine Metcalfe for being such an encouraging editor.

Of course, it would not have been possible to complete this project without the support of our respective Departments; the School of Environmental Design and Management at the University of Portsmouth and the School of Surveying at Kingston University.

Victoria Edwards   Louise Ellison
University of Portsmouth   Kingston University

Section I
Strategic Corporate Property Management – an analytical framework

Chapter 1
Introduction to Strategic Property Management

Introduction

Many books and papers have been written on the valuation of property, but few focus on how to add value through sound strategic management. Strategic management is crucial for both investors in, and occupiers of, property. Investment objectives can only be met through management that maximises the value of a property portfolio. Similarly, the value of any business can be enhanced through strategic management of the property that supports the business.

Much of what is written on property management is preoccupied with the day to day operation of managing a portfolio. Similarly, facilities management literature has tended to focus on maximising the value obtained from the specific use of facilities, rather than adopting a strategic perspective on property occupation overall. The management of property held for investment purposes has also been the subject of substantial works, alongside those dealing more generally with portfolio management.

This book focuses on property as a *corporate* asset. However, the inherent value of property makes it impossible to study it as a corporate asset without having regard to the management of its investment potential. This is reflected within the text and investment issues are explored where necessary. However, it is important to stress that the main focus here is the strategic management of property as a corporate asset.

The aim of this first chapter is to provide a general introduction to strategic property management and to the principles which underlie strategy formulation and implementation for property portfolios. It identifies the role of the property manager in all property scenarios – whether managing investment property, corporate property or property occupied by the non-profit sector – and emphasises the need for a strategic approach that seeks to maximise the 'value' of property.

First, it is worth concentrating on why strategic property management is important.

The importance of strategic property management

Let us consider property as being held (in any type of property right) for one of two purposes:

- as an investment asset
- as an operational asset.

Property held as an investment asset, like any other investment asset, is expected to earn a rate of return on capital employed for the holder and, particularly in the case of freehold or other long-term ownership (such as a long leasehold), appreciate in capital value.

Property held as an operational asset serves to support the activities of the business occupying the property. This type of property is sometimes referred to as 'corporate property'.

Maximising value

In both these cases, the objective of property management should be the same – to maximise the value of the property. By this, we do not necessarily mean financial value – all properties are capable of being assessed in terms of different types of value (including social, ecological, cultural, etc.). Thus 'value' is the universal currency of property resource management and it needs to be maximised in whichever form or forms is most appropriate for the property in question.

It is extraordinary how valuers in the property world often command the highest respect in their work place. It is extraordinary because valuers' jobs are, in some ways, very simple – they have to assess the financial value of the future flow of benefits that a property can produce. They take a snap-shot view of a property, from a single perspective, using a heavily prescribed methodology. A property manager, in contrast, has to enhance value by seeing property from a number of different perspectives, recognising changing values to different stakeholders, with no prescribed formula.

'Property' as a concept is a social instrument, used to define a reservoir or flow of benefits. Property rights to land are social institutions which have evolved as a means of enforcing claims to that benefit stream. By attaching rights to property, we show the intention to enforce duties of a potential user to observe restricted (or prohibited) access to and use of the resource.

While a valuer's job is to place a value on the future benefits that a particular right to property can achieve, a property manager has to *realise* those benefits – she has to make the property work so well that the value is actually achieved. Perhaps the anomaly lies in the separation of the task of valuing and managing. For without an understanding of future management, how can a valuer anticipate the flow of benefits that the property might bring; and in the case of the manager, who would want to take on the responsibility of managing a property based on someone else's expectations of value? We know we would want to have made our own assessment of the property's potential benefit flow before committing ourselves to realising those benefits!

An article in the *Financial Times* in 1990 told the story of a public sector asset in Britain: Herstmonceux Castle, the former home of the Greenwich Royal Observatory. The article illustrated how two quite different values can be placed on the same property by two people who have quite differing expectations of what can be achieved in terms of a flow of benefits in the future. The valuer working for the vendor advised that they accept a bid of £8 million for the castle. The purchaser admitted that at the time he knew it was worth around £25 million. In this case, the difference in the values assigned to the property reflected the different approaches to management. The second, higher value reflected the more innovative approach by the purchaser, who was able to perceive additional benefits to be produced by managing the property well. His plan for the property was to convert it into a 120 bedroom luxury hotel, with a leisure club, 18 hole golf course and clubhouse and 60 corporate lodges for business entertaining. At the time of the article, the purchaser was ready to sell on without full planning permission, but at twice the price he had paid for it only two years previously. While managing the property for two years, the purchaser had discovered a useful income stream from it. A horticultural business came in every day to grow lilies on the pond, which they then sold to restaurants and hotels in London. They paid him up to £3,600 per week in the summer for the right to grow lilies on his pond (Hanson, 1990).

Property as an investment asset

Most large investment funds hold property at around 15% of their total investments. Smaller funds tend to hold property in unit trusts, which allows them to invest in diversified property holdings as relatively small investments. In the case of an investment property, the property manager wants to exploit the value of the property for her clients. This means achieving the best return on capital possible and, it is hoped, adding capital appreciation to the property. Let us assume that our investment property manager has in her portfolio a collection of freehold properties – some offices and some shops – all of which are let to business tenants.

Let us say that the property investment manager decides to buy another small office block to add to the portfolio at a cost of £1,000,000. The income received in rent each year is £60,000. Her return on capital (the 'yield') is therefore 6%

$$\frac{60,000}{1,000,000} \times 100 = 6\%$$

After a short time, she is offered £1,200,000 for the same office block and wonders why the capital value has increased. The rent the tenant is paying is still £60,000 p.a. However, if someone else were to buy the office block for £1,200,000 now, his yield would only be 5%. The fact that other investors are willing to buy and receive a lower return on their capital investment means that there has been some sort of change in the market.

Without knowing the specific circumstances, it would be difficult to anticipate what that change might be. Maybe the purchaser anticipates greater future rental growth. Maybe other forms of investment are offering even lower rates of return, sending investors towards property as a preferable investment. Maybe the property is seen as a less risky investment.

Whatever the reason for the increased value of the property, the investment manager still has to exploit the value of the property to its full. The 'value equation' for the investment manager is

$$\text{Capital value (a)} = (\text{Rent (b)} - \text{Operating costs (c)}) \times \frac{100}{\text{Yield(Y)}}$$

The components of this equation will be considered further in the section on Maximising the value of investment property later in this chapter.

Example 1.1 Current yields

Find out about the current rents and capital values of properties in your area. For example, you might look in the local newspaper to see what the average price of a 3 bedroomed house is in your area. Are similar properties available to let? What types of rents are they achieving each month? How much does this make the annual rental value?

Using the formula above, consider what yield you would achieve if you were to buy such a property to let. How does this compare with the interest rates being offered on a high interest account by a building society?

In order to compare the yields fairly, what costs do you think you might incur *after* receiving the rent from your residential tenants, in order to arrive at the *net* rent?

Lack of a strategic approach

The value of commercial property to the business community is rising. Currie and Scott (1991) estimated commercial property as accounting for around 20% of total assets of financial institutions. Nevertheless, many investment managers have been happy to sit back and collect the rents from their property portfolios, without using any strategic management that might add value.

To some degree, this approach to property is a product of the way the market is organised. Leases were designed to offer maximum security of income to the landlord. Fixed-term leases of 20–25 years, with 5-yearly 'upwards-only' rent reviews were common in the UK for office property. That is, as the rent was reviewed, it could only be increased; if the market had fallen since the last rent review, then the rent would remain the same.

During the prosperous 1980s, it was a landlord's market, with property investors able to attract high rents and enjoy security of income from reliable tenants. Such conditions did not encourage innovative or proactive property management. Management of investment property at the time involved selecting the best portfolio, securing the property through sound maintenance planning, serving the correct notices to review the rents, and then sitting back and watching the revenue flow in and the capital value increase.

It was not until the property slump of the early 1990s in the UK that investment managers started to look for ways to add value to their property portfolios by adopting more imaginative strategies. Some of those left with office space unoccupied were able to convert it to hotel accommodation. Others, instead of looking for long, secure leases, opted for more short-term arrangements. Unable to let on old terms, some investors converted large office blocks to 'serviced office suites'. Following the American example, they offered shorter contract arrangements rather than leases (in some cases, weekly contracts) and included in-house services (such as cleaning, catering, security, shared boardroom space, receptionists, etc.) as part of the deal.

Such a strategic approach to maximising the value of investment property should be part of any investment manager's role. However, it only really comes to the fore when problems arising from economic conditions highlight the downside of property as an investment, such as the following:

- *Illiquidity:* it is difficult to realise the financial value of property quickly, because sale of the property will take time.
- *Allocations of large portions of capital:* the high price of property means that large sums of capital are tied up in a single asset.
- *The potential for obsolesence:* changing needs of occupiers can render the property useless, as it fails to provide suitable space for occupiers' activities.
- *High transaction costs:* buying and selling property is not a cheap activity – high costs such as solicitors' fees, taxes and agents' fees mean that the transaction itself costs money.

Research has demonstrated quite clearly that once the market rises again, attention to proactive management strategies for operational portfolios slips way down the corporate agenda (Bon and Luck, 1999; Nourse and Roulac, 1993; Manning and Roulac, 1996).

Maximising the value of investment property

In order to exploit the property to its best value, the investment property manager has to 'work' at all of the components in the equation on p. 6.

Capital value (a)

Maintaining and enhancing the property's capital value is fundamental to the investment property manager. Most obviously, the manager must try to maximise the other components in the equation in order to do this. However, she must also look after the long-term interests of the property by:

- protecting the property rights
- monitoring the local environment (to ensure no encroachment, competition, etc.)
- adapting the property to changing occupier needs
- making appropriate acquisitions and sales (in relation to individual properties and the whole portfolio)
- restructuring the property rights to maximise value (more leaseholds/ licences/wayleaves, easements/contracts)
- valuing the property on a regular basis, to ensure that it is adequately valued (especially for insurance purposes).

Rent (b)

The investment property manager can increase the gross income received in the form of rent by:

- conducting market analysis and providing property that is best suited to the current demands of tenants
- targeting promotional activities to suit the marketplace
- diversifying income sources (offering a variety of leases and other contracts and services)
- achieving an optimum balance of tenants and risk.

Administration costs (c)

By reducing the costs of administering the property, the investment manager can increase the net revenue received from rental income. This might be achieved by:

- negotiating new lease terms
- employing new technology to reduce utilities (water, electricity, etc.) and maintenance costs
- managing rents for a better cash flow
- reducing the tax liability of the investor.

Yield (Y)

As we have seen above, the yield is largely outside the control of the individual property manager. The extent to which the manager can influence the yields achieved in a particular area depends on how much influence he can exercise on the local environment. In the case of a shopping centre, the manager may be able to increase the attractiveness of the investment over time, because he has control over the whole complex and can thus work to improve the overall environment and attractiveness of the collection of properties – retail units – to prospective tenants.

The same may be true, although to a lesser extent, of retail property in a town centre. Town centre managers (employed by local governing authorities, such as city or district councils) and local property owners and occupiers can work together to improve the local environment and so increase local economic activity and prosperity. In both cases, this might involve improved environmental features (car parking, street lighting, security, landscaping) and increased marketing (such as holiday promotional events, discount cards, etc.). Any improvement to the local economy will be reflected in rental growth and reduced risk.

Corporate property

For property experts, it is easy to assume that property is at the forefront of each corporation's mind. In reality, however, many corporations are barely conscious of the importance that property has in their business in spite of property routinely being the second largest business cost next to labour (Zeckhauser and Silverman, 1983, Bon and Luck 1999; Bootle and Kalyan, 2002). Such a haphazard approach to managing personnel would be accepted as serious folly.

Businesses need property in order to generate turnover and profits – every business needs some sort of property in which to carry on its activity. In this respect, property is functional and secondary to the main business activities. Of course, the degree of importance of this functional role of property in the business differs with each organisation. You might think of it as a spectrum of functional importance (Fig. 1.1).

Activities that directly use the property and its resources (primary industries, such as farming, forestry and mining), must be placed at the 'most important' end of the spectrum, since their activities depend very much on the nature of

Farming	Retail	Office Space	Industrial
Forestry	Leisure	Educational	Warehousing
Mining	Sports		

| Substantial $\longrightarrow$ | Important $\longrightarrow$ | Significant $\longrightarrow$ | Marginal |
| and direct | and direct | but indirect | and little connection |

$\longrightarrow$ Degree of importance of the property to the activities of the business occupying it $\longrightarrow$

Fig. 1.1   The corporate property spectrum of functional importance

the individual property concerned. Further along the spectrum come the service sector industries (leisure, tourism, retailing), which use the property to add value to their activities, by providing the customer with a particularly designed environment through the use of the individual properties involved.

These industries are closely followed by businesses occupying office space. Again, the individual offices can help to add value to the business, by providing the optimum environment to generate productivity from the occupiers. Nevertheless, the individual offices occupied have a much less direct link to the activities of the business (finance, insurance, professions, for example) than is the case in retailing. At the furthest end of the spectrum is warehousing, where the property simply provides a large area of secure shelter for the goods. It is recognised that the location of the individual warehouses is of paramount importance to the activity of a distribution business, but the function of the building adds little to the productivity of the business beyond shelter and access.

Example 1.2 Where are you sitting on the functional spectrum?

Think about the building or space you are currently in. Where would you place it on the functional spectrum? It might be a library, an office, a seminar room, a lecture theatre, a station. Each has a place somewhere on the spectrum.

You might like to consider other businesses and where the property that they occupy might be placed on the functional spectrum. Where, for example, would you place non-corporate property, such as a public hospital, university, or even a national park?

What is the relevance of the location of the building? Is it crucial to the building's proper functioning?

Lack of a strategic approach

Despite the importance of the role of property in corporate and non-corporate activity, many organisations continue to overlook the importance of property in their activity (Gale and Case, 1989; Pitman and Parker, 1989; Veale, 1989; Edwards, 1991; Teoh, 1993). This is surprising when one considers that commercial property comprises around 30–40% of the total assets in the balance sheets of most UK companies (Currie and Scott, 1991; Bootle and Kalyan 2002). Indeed, it is a significant issue, when considered within the context of around 75% of corporate borrowing in the UK being secured against property assets. That alone suggests that property ought to be managed effectively by businesses. In conjunction with the potential for property to add value to a business activity, then sound property management becomes imperative.

One of the problems with corporate property ownership is that corporations tend to view property as a liability, since the property does not appear to be contributing *directly* to the success of the business (Hurtt, 1988). A common response by senior corporate executives seems to be that they are 'not in the real estate business' (Teoh, 1993). In such circumstances, it is often seen as a (large) operational cost rather than an asset. It is seldom seen as a source of wealth creation and commercial opportunity. Research undertaken in the late 1980s by the University of Reading involved a survey of 50 corporate businesses in the UK and was designed to identify the approach that they took to their property management (Avis, Gibson and Watts 1989). The research found that few organisations:

- established objectives for their property
- assessed the importance of achieving those objectives
- measured the extent to which their property contributed to their organisation's overall performance
- established a decision-making structure which even allowed them to maximise the property's performance.

Since that research, further surveys of the public sector in the UK have shown similar results. For example, a survey of local authorities in England and Wales by the Audit Commission found that expenditure on property management was about £16 billion per year (about a quarter of total annual expenditure) (Audit Commission, 1988). However, despite the level of public funds being spent on property, few local authorities kept a register of even the most basic data concerning the physical, legal or economic attributes of their real estate. In essence, they did not even have proper information about what they owned. Research carried out as recently as 2000 shows the situation is more or less unchanged. Research by Gibson *et al.*, 2000, cited in Bootle and Kalyan 2002, examined the property cost information available in 48 organisations and still found a surprisingly low level of information routinely available to property managers.

Teoh's research (1993), which focuses on corporations in New Zealand, identifies primary and secondary factors that contribute to greater corporate real estate performance. Primary factors are:

- corporate attitudes to property
- the structure of the property unit
- the organisation of a property inventory record.

Secondary factors are:

- the property management staff
- the reward system for performance.

An inventory of property assets is fundamental to any strategic property management. Lack of such basic information can result in disastrous consequences for a commercial corporation. If the importance of the property in the total asset valuation of the corporation is underestimated by the owners, but recognised by those outside the corporation, then the result might be a hostile takeover bid. In some cases, where the property is more valuable to the purchaser than the core business, this might lead to a subsequent sale or transfer of the property assets and dissolving of the core business. We address this issue in Chapter 4.

In the case of public and non-profit organisations, lack of awareness of their property assets can lead to similar consequences, but is more likely to result in a series of missed opportunities and considerably reduced performance in delivering their services. A hospital occupying prime city-centre space might be better to realise the value of its valuable property assets for redevelopment and relocate to a suburban site, where ambulances can achieve quicker access to the hospital and a larger and more up-to-date facility can be built for the same value.

Maximising the value of corporate property

While sound corporate property management should always start with a good knowledge of the asset base, it does not always lead to sale and relocation. As well as a good knowledge of the property within her control, the corporate property manager needs a good understanding of the business, its implications for the property occupied and the contribution to the business that is both required and possible from the property.

It is the role of the property manager to provide options to achieve the overall business goals and to help solve business problems with property solutions. The property manager should be proactive and interactive, working with the board of directors to anticipate the business's needs, and planning ahead to translate those needs to property requirements. In addition, she should be identifying opportunities where property might add to the business performance, giving it a competitive advantage over other businesses by increasing the *net* value of its activities (i.e. increasing its sales and/or decreasing its costs).

Research by the property firm Strutt and Parker provides some worrying results in this respect. The research investigated the attitude of 100 corporate occupiers to their occupational property portfolios. It sought to identify whether commercial operators value their properties sufficiently and organised their portfolios efficiently. More than half of the respondents said that responsibility for property was designated as an administrative function and almost 60% of employees responsible for property management were categorised as junior administration or accounting staff, with no property background or qualifications (Elphick and Wright, 2002).

The corporate property manager must be involved in the overall strategic planning of the business and its activities and should provide the property expertise to help the corporation achieve its long-term goals. As such, the property manager must prepare a strategic plan for the property that flows from *and* feeds into the corporate business strategy. In this sense, it is an iterative process – the property strategy should not just follow from the strategic business plan; if this were the case then it would suggest that property cannot play a central role in improving the core business – it can.

Consider the example of a Second Division football team. To reach the First Division they knew that they had to improve the quality of their players greatly. This could be achieved in one of two ways: (a) training up their own junior team into better players and (b) buying talent in from another team. Both options would cost money, but the second seemed to be well outside the grasp of the small club, until, that is, the property manager suggested that they sell their city-centre football ground for redevelopment as a shopping centre. The club then relocated to the outskirts of town, where they were able to build a bigger ground, which would seat more fans and provide space for additional catering and retail units. As a result, the club had a higher weekly income from matches and had enough capital left over to purchase two First Division players. In this scenario, the property management strategy was an integral part of achieving the club's improved performance.

A similar example can be found in the supermarket chain Sainsburys. A newspaper article in 2000 reported on its future strategic plans and explained how Sainsburys intended to exploit its existing sites for leisure, residential, commercial and service sector property development, so freeing up some value from its £4.5bn property portfolio (Cohen and Hollinger, 2000).

Conclusion

It is clear that, whether a property is held for investment purposes or as an operational asset and whether for financial profit or for other objectives, strategic management of property is the only method of ensuring that it is managed for maximum value. Strategic management demands that the manager has a clear understanding of the owner's or occupier's objectives and the core activities that will take place in or on the property. It demands that the manager is able to understand the activities that the property supports and the competitive demands that it faces daily. The manager can then develop property action plans that are capable of balancing short- and long-term goals with respect to:

- capital value
- rents received
- operating costs
- security of income.

A manager must also appreciate that each of the above affects the others in this balancing act. The next chapter in this book sets out an analytical framework designed to assist the practitioner in exactly this process. This framework is discussed in some detail within the remaining chapters in Section 1 of the book, and applied to a series of case studies in Section 2. It is hoped that this will provide a generic, flexible but systematic approach that can be applied to the strategic management of any real estate assets.

References

Audit Commission (1988) *Local Authority Property: A Management Overview*. HMSO, London.

Avis, M., Gibson, V. & Watts, J. (1989) *Managing Operational Property Assets*. Department of Land Management and Development, University of Reading, Reading.

Bon, R. & Luck, R. (1999) Annual CREMRU–JCI survey of corporate real estate practices in Europe and North America: 1993–1998. *Facilities*, **17** (5/6) 167–176.

Bootle, R., & Kalyan, S. (2002) *Property in Business: A waste of space?* RICS Books, London.

Cohen, N. & Hollinger, P. (2000) Sainsbury in move to add value to sites. *Financial Times*, 12 September, p. 28.

Currie, D. & Scott, A. (1991) *The Place of Commercial Property in the UK Economy*. London Business School, London.

Edwards, V.M. & Seabrooke, W. (1991) Proactive property management (Briefing). *Property Management*, **9**(4) 373–385.

Elphick, R. & Wright, J. (2002) Assets that are leaking money. *Estates Gazette*, 2 February.

Gale, J. & Case, F. (1989) A study of corporate real estate resource management. *Journal of Real Estate Research*, **4**(3) 23–33.

Gibson, V. (2000) Evaluating Office Space Needs and Choices. Report for MWB Business Exchange, University of Reading, Reading.

Hanson. M. (1990) Estate doubles its asking price. *Financial Times*, 14/15 July.

Hurtt, S.M. (1988) Real estate: liability or asset? *Real Estate Finance Journal*. Winter, 61–71.

Manning, C. & Roulac, S.E. (1996) Structuring the corporate real property function for greater bottom line impact. *Journal of Real Estate Research*, **12**(3) 383–396.

Nourse, H.O. & Roulac, S.E. (1993). Linking real estate decisions to corporate strategy, *Journal of Real Estate Research*, **8**(4) 475–494.

Pitman, R.H. & Parker, J.R. (1989) A survey of corporate real estate executives on factors informing corporate real estate performance. *Journal of Real Estate Research*, **4**(3) 107–19.

Teoh, W. K. (1993). Corporate real estate asset management: the New Zealand evidence. *Journal of Real Estate Research*, **8**(4) 607–23.

Veale, P.R. (1989). Managing corporate real estate assets: Current executive attitudes and prospects of an emergent management discipline. *Journal of Real Estate Research*, **4**(3) 1–22.

Zeckhauser, S. & Silverman, R. (1983). Rediscovering your company's real estate, *Harvard Business Review*, **61**(1) 111–117.

Further reading

Brett, M. (1990) *Property and Money*. The Estates Gazette Ltd, London.

Brown, R.K. & Arnold, A.L. (1993) *Managing Corporate Real Estate*. Wiley, Chichester.

Brown, R.K., Lapides, P. & Rondeau, E. (1994) *Managing Corporate Real Estate: Forms and Procedures.* Wiley Law, New York.

Dubben, N. & Sayce, S. (1991) *Property Portfolio Management.* Routledge, London.

Evans, M. & Weatherhead, M. (1999) *Think Profit Act Property.* RICS Corporate Property Users Group, London.

Hines, M.A. (1990) *Global Corporate Real Estate Management: A handbook for multinational business organisations.* Quorum Books, London.

Hodges, N.W. (1996) *The Economic Management of Physical Assets.* Mechanical Engineering Publications Ltd, London.

School of Estate Management, Oxford Brookes University & Department of Land Management and Development, University of Reading (1993) *Property Management Performance Monitoring.* GTI, Oxford.

Weatherhead, M. (1997) *Real Estate in Corporate Strategy.* Macmillan, London.

Chapter 2
Formulation of Strategy – Adopting an Analytical Approach

Introduction

Real estate management is a multi-disciplinary subject that relies on theory and analysis from a whole host of disciplines, including economics, political science, law, sociology, and management science. As such, a consistent framework of analysis is needed to bring together the theories of the different disciplines and to underlie case studies, so allowing the development of more generic theories and observations.

This chapter introduces a metatheoretical[1] framework of analysis, to aid the understanding of property and the uses that it supports. The framework that we have developed for our work on real estate management is derived from political science and, specifically, work by Oakerson (1986; 1992). The framework therefore has a strong institutionalist perspective which we feel is particularly appropriate to strategic management of property. We endeavour to explain this institutionalist perspective and make clear its importance to our approach to the management of property in this chapter. The topic is then returned to in more detail in a later chapter. We hope that the analytical framework used in the book will help students decipher new sectors of the property market for themselves. This chapter sets the scene for the next eight chapters, during which the analytical framework will be explained in more detail.

Throughout this book, we will refer to the *institutional arrangements* of the property market. Institutional arrangements define choice sets within which individuals and groups operate. In this sense, they can help establish not only opportunities but also constraints for property managers. This is because the institutional arrangements provide a structure that governs how individuals will behave with respect to each other and with respect to the resources involved. In essence, they provide the rules of the game. Within the given institutional arrangements, the players can adopt different, individual strategies. A footballer taking a shot at a goal can choose to bend it like Beckham or head it like Shearer. What he can't do, without penalty, is play offside. Institutional arrangements provide the same purpose, they define our choices, but they allow us to adopt different strategies. For a full explanation of the institutional approach, see Chapter 7.

As rules of the game, institutional arrangements are a crucial part of our understanding of property and property markets. Yet in planning the management and use of property, little analysis is applied to the institutional arrangements governing this major resource (Bromley, 1985; 1989). We believe that the framework we present here provides a most useful tool in undertaking analysis of property and, in particular, the institutional arrangements *governing* property use.

A common framework of analysis

The framework presented in this chapter is based upon work by V. Ostrom (1976), Kiser and Ostrom (1982), E. Ostrom (1986), Oakerson (1986; 1992) and Edwards and Steins (1998; 1999). Our framework does not attempt to be a fully specified model. It is merely a conceptual tool for organising and analysing information about property and different types of users and uses. It does not set out to provide answers, rather to prompt a series of questions that distinguish the different characteristics of property and the relationships between the different characteristics. The relationships between the situational characteristics identified can then be specified in ways that will allow diagnosis and understanding of problems of a particular property or portfolio.

The analytical framework for property is constructed incrementally in this chapter. First, the chapter explains the basic framework, its component parts and their interactions. Second, the chapter provides some conclusions for the future development and testing of the framework and explains how each subsequent chapter employs the framework to study specific issues of strategic property management. The second section of the book provides a series of case studies where the framework has been used to explore the issues surrounding the management of operational property portfolios for a variety of organisations.

The framework

The framework (Fig. 2.1) helps to explain how property strategies are formulated. First, it distinguishes two categories of characteristics which have a direct influence on possible strategy formulation, and must be taken into account at the onset of analysis:

(1) the *property's* characteristics
(2) the property *users'* characteristics.

Both sets of variables form a set of opportunities and constraints with regard to possible strategy formulation. They start to form the choice set from which the

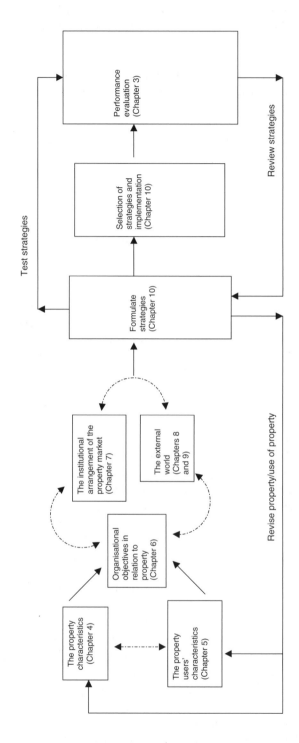

Fig 2.1   Strategic property management: an analytical framework to aid strategy formulation

property manager can develop strategies. However, three more influencing factors must be taken into account before specific strategies can be formulated:

(3)   the *objectives* of the property users
(4)   the *institutional arrangement* of the property market
(5)   the context provided by the *external world* in which the property manager must operate.

Once the strategies are formulated, chosen and implemented, effective management requires an evaluation of their performance; hence the final box in the framework:

(6)   *performance* evaluation.

Each component part is explained before the relationships between the variables are examined.

Performance evaluation

Performance evaluation, which is discussed at greater length in Chapter 3, is, necessarily, both the first and last thing you need to do if you are to effectively manage anything, particularly real estate. For example, information on performance will help you select a car. Your own evaluation of its performance during your ownership will inform your decision when you buy the next car. It is not entirely without logic then that performance evaluation is the first element of the framework addressed here, but is the last box in the schematic in Fig. 2.1.

The performance of property in its support of the operational activities of the business, as an investment asset, and as a cost base, all have to be explored and understood before any strategy can be devised. The performance of property in all these functions has to be explored and understood again once the strategy has been implemented, and during its operation, if the iterative processes of management are to be applied. Only if this happens will management of the operational portfolio become truly effective. Performance can be evaluated against a variety of criteria, such as financial, social, environmental and cultural.

Chapter 3 on performance evaluation therefore explores a variety of different measures of property performance. In doing so it highlights the importance of understanding the function of property within the operation of a business, *before* trying to evaluate it. Key tools of evaluation are explored. These range from space charging and the efficiency gains that can be made by making space costs explicit within the profit and loss accounts of different departments, to benchmarking and the savings that can be made by learning from other companies' experiences.

Research by Bootle and Kalyan (2002) estimates that UK businesses could improve the performance of the properties they occupy to the extent that they could increase their trading profits by up to 13%. If true, such a move could significantly improve the economic performance of the UK as a country.

Characteristics of property

In order to manage property effectively, it is essential for the manager fully to understand the characteristics of the property at her disposal. The most basic step in this process is to have thorough knowledge of what is in the property portfolio. Nevertheless, there are countless stories of large corporations that lack a comprehensive asset register, simply detailing their property ownership.

In Chapter 4 we present a taxonomy of property characteristics which must be identified for each sector of property – including physical, legal and financial characteristics. Different properties have different levels of relevance to the use that they support. There is a 'property use spectrum' (see Fig. 1.1, Chapter 1, p. 9). At one end of the spectrum is property that supports a particular use by merely providing a 'home' for an activity, such as office space occupation, and at the other end, property which forms an essential part of the end product, such as leisure provision.

It is common for operational property portfolios to be accumulated over a relatively long period of time. Often the person or team responsible for its efficient operation will have had no influence over the collection of buildings they manage. This has been identified as a hindrance in the adoption of a strategic approach to the management of property portfolios, and makes it even more important that the team makes a careful assessment of the property in the portfolio. Such an assessment must incorporate:

- the physical aspects of the buildings
- the legal obligations and rights they represent
- the value they contribute to the asset base of the operation
- the role they perform in the operation of the business.

The team responsible for the effective operational management of the property portfolio has to 'know' that portfolio on all these different levels to be able to apply effective strategic management to it.

In analysing the characteristics of the property, it is important to evaluate the property's potential and not just its current value. In this sense, the manager should be aware of any technological advances that might enable the property to be used or developed in new ways. Property routinely constitutes the second largest cost to a business organisation after labour. A reconfiguration of the space or a change in the working patterns of an organisation may create a significant increase in the capacity of a building in terms of the throughput of visitors, accommodation of workers, number of meetings or restaurant covers served. The twenty-first century manager has to think beyond the standard, expected occupation pattern of space. It is the extraordinary use of space that increases efficiency and can provide a business with a competitive edge.

The property users' characteristics

Chapter 5 explains how to identify the 'user community' involved in different types of property. The evolution of property use and management has led to a large and disparate body of stakeholders, with varying degrees of historical association and contemporary involvement with the property. For example, stakeholders of a shopping centre might include the landowner, investor, developer, occupier and the occupier's customers. A woodland's user community might involve the landowner, a shooting syndicate, local dog walkers and ramblers, the government department providing woodland grants, a mobile telephone network that has erected a mast in the woodland, and so on. It is important that we appreciate the role of institutional arrangements, which enable users to exchange information and aid decision making concerning the property.

Similarly, it is important to understand the specific attributes of the user community that must be analysed when working with the property. The importance of the user community has become increasingly clear in urban regeneration development schemes. The long-term success of a scheme has come to be associated with a clear identification of the user community and its needs, at the outset of a scheme. The provision of access to river front walks, for example, for residents and visitors increases the user community of a development and, in so doing, facilitates the acceptance and adoption of a new development by an existing community. Reducing the user community by excluding such provision has the opposite effect and ultimately undermines such a development's potential for success.

Example 2.1 The user community

A public sector building
If a building forms an access point for local authority services, the user community will be a large proportion of the local electorate. This is an important group to the local authority and the people who pay for the space. The way in which the building responds to this user group's needs will influence their opinion and relationship with the local authority. Important questions that should be asked include:

- Is the building accessible?
- Is it welcoming?
- Are services clearly identified?
- Does it suggest profligacy on the part of the local authority?
- If queuing is routine, is it well organised?
- Are there enough chairs?
- Are refreshments available?

The next time you visit a local authority building, ask yourself these questions and consider whether the building is likely to improve or worsen the Local authority's relationship with its user group.

This identification of the user community and its requirements is important for any building, not just large development schemes. Without it, no clear assessment can be made of the roles and functions a building needs to support. For an office building, the user community will include not only the workers it accommodates but also any customers or clients that visit. For a retailer, the needs and desires of the user community are essential to the success of the business. The staff are a key user group. The building needs to support them in providing space to display goods, accessible demonstration space, space to discuss a prospective purchase with a client, and so on. It also needs to be a comfortable and inspiring environment for the staff themselves.

The customers are, arguably, the most important user group in a retail space. Their needs have to be anticipated and provided for if a retailer is to keep up with the competition, let alone gain a competitive advantage. For some retailers this may amount to making the aisles easy to navigate, providing sufficient checkouts and a café to collapse in after making the weekly supermarket run. For others it may require an appointment system where a prospective bride can book the whole showroom to try on dresses with expert advice and no fear of interruption; and, of course, no obligation to buy. It is no coincidence that the fitting out costs of retail space can be high.

Organisational objectives in relation to property

Once the user characteristics and property characteristics are known, management of the operational portfolio becomes clearer. However, to manage the portfolio in such a way that it actively supports and enhances the business requires rather more. An understanding of the organisational objectives of the business, i.e. the overarching business strategy, is essential if a full interpretation of the way in which the property portfolio can support it is to be made. That is, you have to know where you are going if you are to pack the right things for the journey.

Chapter 6 explores some of the more popular strategic management theory and links it to property. It examines ways in which the operational property portfolio of an organisation can actively support the different competitive strategies available to businesses. This allows us to make clear the fundamental role property has in the successful management of a business. Where the business strategy is made sufficiently explicit to the real estate team, and that team is actively engaged in the development of the business strategy, the property portfolio can actively support the underlying business initiative. Where the real estate management team is not given a voice or even the ear of the senior management team, the best it can do is react to the business strategy laid before it. In many cases this will ultimately undermine the performance of the business as a whole.

Chapter 6 uses some of Porter's (1998) theory of competitive advantage to examine how the real estate portfolio might be used to support a particular business strategy. This does not provide a recommended real estate strategy for each type of business organisation, but identifies the ways in which property can be aligned with three generic business strategies. This then provides a framework through which the reader can relate the real estate of any organisation to its basic business strategy.

Institutional arrangement of the property market

Chapter 7 explains the relevance of institutional analysis to the study of property. It explains that 'institutions' refer to the 'rules of the game' (formal and informal) that govern the way in which we can use property. The 'institutional arrangements' are complex networks of rules that frame the choices we can make. In particular, the chapter examines how institutional arrangements affect the property market by creating a structure of rules which can be effectively enforced, thereby reducing the uncertainty surrounding the use of property by the individuals and organisations involved, and so contributing to long-term stability. The institutional arrangements may be formal, written down and detailed, or informal.

Analysis suggests that the institutional arrangements governing the control and management of property must be flexible enough to adapt to the changing demands of different property users. Chapter 7 explains that institutional analysis should be conducted at three different levels: *constitutional*, *organisational* and *operational*. The use and ownership of property, as well as being one of the oldest recognised rights, is perhaps the most regulated. The institutions regulating the use and ownership of property can be divided into *administrative*, *financial* and *legal*. The administrative institutions govern, for example, where we can develop a building, what we can do with one and whether we can take one down. The institutions relating to finance (not to be confused in this context with financial institutions such as banks and building societies) form the rules governing the use of property as a financial asset. The legal institutions regulate ownership and use through a complex set of rules governing the granting, holding and transfer of rights in and over property.

It is the robustness of each of these sets of institutional arrangements which provides the context for the efficient operation of the property markets. In countries and economies where such institutions are not robust or have been allowed to break down, the successful operation of the property market is undermined and with it the investment and trade which form the lifeblood of economic activity. Chapter 8 examines the legal and financial institutions and explores how they manifest themselves at each of the three levels identified in Chapter 7.

Consider Afghanistan, some of the Baltic States and some of the former Soviet Union states. In many of these countries the institutional arrangements that once supported economic activity have either been dismantled or have withered as new governments have lacked the power and resources to enforce them. Without effective institutions being reintroduced, regulated effective economic activity can not resume. It is interesting to see how quickly business activity began to thrive in Kabul once some level of regulated law enforcement returned and people began to feel sufficiently confident to carry out business transactions.

Knowledge and understanding of the complex institutional arrangements that govern the operation of the property markets is essential to the effective management of property as a resource. Strategic property management requires knowledge of these institutions in relation to a specific portfolio and the impact they will have on decision making. One can only anticipate the stumbling blocks to a strategy if one knows where they might crop up.

What is also clear is the importance of awareness of change in the institutions and their institutional arrangements. A good example is the Disability Discrimination Act 1995. This Act relates specifically to real estate through measures to ensure disabled people have access to goods, facilities and services and are not discriminated against in the buying or renting of land or property. This requires (amongst other things) providers of services to:

- make reasonable adjustments to ensure disabled people can have access to those services, (in force from October 1999), and
- to consider making permanent physical alterations to buildings to ensure accessibility for disabled people, (in force from October 2004).

For some users, in particular care homes for the elderly, these requirements have made their continued use of the property uneconomic. Notwithstanding the social or political implications this may have, the property market response is to find an alternative use that is more economically viable. Interestingly, this is resulting in many care homes that were originally large family houses, being turned back into private residential dwellings. The value of residential property and the cost of running care homes has effectively created a complete 'U' turn in this particular market.

The 'external world'

Chapters 8 and 9 explain the relevance of the political–economic context within which property is managed and identify a series of contextual factors for examination in different property scenarios (Edwards and Steins, 1998). It is important to recognise that the range of products and services supported or provided by the property are determined by the political economy of the situation.

This can be seen in the pattern of obsolescence that has effected real estate in the UK over the twentieth century. As the political–economic context changed, the primary extractive industries became less cost effective and the vast tracts of land devoted to the extraction, processing, storage and hauling of coal became redundant. To continue making an appropriate contribution to the economy this land had to find a new use. The large manufacturing plants reminiscent of the 'Fordist' era of economic development became redundant as new manufacturing processes such as team working, lean production systems and new technologies took over. These are the results of the external world impacting upon the function and operation of built space.

Two more recent examples of changes in the external world, or political–

Example 2.2 Institutional arrangements influence the decisions we can make

Consider a building that is surplus to requirements. The decisions that are made about it will be defined by the institutional arrangement within which we operate. Certain questions will be asked and the answers will be determined by administrative, financial and legal institutions.

Question	Determining institutions		
	Administrative	Financial	Legal
Can the building's use be changed?	✓		✓
Can it be transferred to another occupier			✓
Can it be demolished and replaced with something more useful to the company?	✓		✓
Can it be sold to release capital?		✓	✓
Can it be developed?	✓	✓	✓

Consider the building you are in now. If it was surplus to requirements for the existing user:

- What could be done with it?
- What impact would the institutional arrangement have on what happened to it?

economic context, impacting on the function and operation of space are technological changes leading to more home-working and increased use of the internet for shopping. Initial research suggested the increased use of home-working would have a major impact on the demand for office space, as we no longer travelled to a gathering point to carry out our work. The reality has been rather different. There is undoubtedly wide spread use of home-working and other more flexible patterns of work. However, a central workplace still provides an essential function; it simply has to have more sophisticated technological provision, perhaps more flexible space and space that is configured differently.

Likewise, in many early studies the internet retailing revolution was expected to change patterns of shopping quite dramatically, leading to a significant reduction in demand for retail space. The reality again is rather different. The use of the internet for shopping has undoubtedly increased but this seems to have gone hand-in-hand with an increase in retailing in traditional locations. Interestingly, however, customers seem more widely informed about prices and choices. This can lead to strategic purchases and better negotiation over price, terms and conditions and, ultimately slower price increases in spite of the volume of sales. Perhaps the internet is being used more as a shopping research tool than for actually making purchases.

The result for the retailer is narrower margins but higher sales volume. In order to keep the customers coming into the store, the environment must provide key features not available to the home-shopper: expert advice, excellent demonstration and display facilities, the opportunity to negotiate, the reassurance and confidence that comes with a face-to-face transaction.

Example 2.3 Internet grocery shopping

One of the major growth areas of internet retailing has been in grocery shopping. Tesco, Sainsburys, Safeway and Asda all identified this as a potential future market and responded in different ways. The two main strategies for making this operational were:

(1) to acquire dedicated warehouses in hub locations from which internet orders could be filled and dispatched
(2) to introduce pickers at existing stores who would fill the internet orders, put them through the till and prepare them for dispatch.

The first option required considerable investment in real estate and personnel, but provided dedicated sites in, it was hoped, appropriate locations. The second required no extra investment in real estate, just personnel, but would provide less capacity.

While being relatively low-tech, the second strategy proved the more successful. The property costs of the first strategy made it financially unviable on the basis of the volume of internet grocery orders placed. The last of the warehouses opened by Safeway was closed again in late 2001.

What can we learn from these examples? Strategic management requires awareness of changes in the political economic context and, more specifically, an understanding of the impact it will have on the operation of the business and how the property portfolio can provide support. This may demand a change of location, a change in the configuration of space, upgrading of technological capability or any number of other possible combinations of options. It may require doing nothing, but that has to be an informed, strategic decision, not a passive response.

Formulating strategies for property management

Chapter 10 begins to reassemble the jigsaw of strategic property management that is dissected and examined in the preceding nine chapters. It provides information on the different types of management strategies employed in the property market and explores the link (or lack of one in many instances) between management theory and property management.

Developments in management theory have been rapid over the twentieth and early twenty-first centuries. Property managers have largely been guilty of making very limited use of these theories to improve the efficiency with which they manage real estate, particularly operational real estate. We will explore a number of factors that have contributed to this approach. It is interesting to note that the importance of the real estate management function to the corporate executive increases substantially during periods of economic downturn, but tends to return to previous levels of insignificance in periods of economic boom (Bon and Luck, 1999). Historically this has largely been driven by the view of operational real estate as a given (i.e. capable of limited, if any) change, and the expectation that it will increase in value over time anyway. This approach at best seems to confuse the operational and asset functions of property and at worst seriously underestimates the financial hardship a business can suffer as a result of poor property decision making.

Awareness of the significance of property to the operational effectiveness of a business has been forced into the spotlight. Bootle and Kalyan (2002) estimate that a potential saving of £18 billion a year could be made by UK businesses through more efficient use of property. Their research estimated the value of commercial property to private sector business in the UK to be approximately £400 billion: 34% of total business assets. Businesses that fail to manage this level of assets effectively will simply not be operating at optimum capacity. At best profits will be undermined and capital will eventually locate elsewhere, at worst such a business will be taken over by another business which does recognise the value of the property.

All these issues have to be explored in the formulation of strategies and are addressed in Chapter 10. The importance of understanding the property, the users, the business objectives of the organisation, the institutional framework, the political–economic context are all explored and restated.

Selection of strategies and implementation

The selection of strategies and their implementation is the point at which the first six boxes in the framework are brought together and applied to a portfolio. This makes a chapter dedicated to strategy selection somewhat redundant, as each factor will have been addressed in a previous chapter. The issues surrounding strategy selection and implementation are therefore addressed through the case studies that form the second section of the book. Each one applies the first six boxes of the framework to a particular operational property portfolio, allowing the process of strategy selection and implementation to be explored through practical examples and real situations. In this way it is possible to begin to see the rich variety of decisions and influencing factors that face anyone responsible for the management of an operational portfolio. This in turn clearly demonstrates the importance of the strategic approach.

Use of the framework

We believe that our framework will be useful in the analysis of relatively simple and small-scale property portfolios and in much larger, more complex portfolios. However, in developing the framework and applying it to our case studies, we were able to identify potential problems with its application. A first problem concerns preferred outcomes for the use of property. The framework developed in this book is generic in that it is relevant for the analysis of property for an array of different outcome measures. We prefer to allow the manager to determine the appropriate outcome measures, rather than to prescribe specific criteria. While we acknowledge that the economist's criterion of economic efficiency in measuring the performance of property might be useful, we believe that the criterion must be developed by the users of the property, in the widest sense.

A second problem of using the framework, and frameworks in general, lies in the temptation to employ it as a blueprint rather than a heuristic tool. Frameworks should be used to order information and to facilitate understanding of property problems. Real estate management is a complex, dynamic, social process; it is the outcome of the intermingling of the management system and the political economy of a situation. As such, isolated examination of the interactions between the component parts will not provide a blueprint for design of property management systems. It is vital, therefore, that the framework is used to assist in the diagnosis of problems. In this role, we have found it invaluable, by providing a means of ordering analysis of different uses and different users and evaluating their dynamic interaction.

References

Bon, R. & Luck, R. (1999) Annual CREMRU-JCI survey of corporate real estate practices in Europe and North America: 1993–1998. *Facilities*, **17** (5/6) 167–176.

Bootle, R. & Kalyan, S. (2002) *Property in Business: A waste of space?* RICS Books, London.

Bromley, D.W. (1985) Resources and economic development: an institutionalist perspective. *Journal of Economic Issues*, **19**(3), 779–796.

Bromley, D.W. (1989) *Economic Interests and Justifications: The conceptual foundations of public policy*. Blackwell, Oxford.

Disability Discrimination Act (1995) (c.50) The Stationery Office, London.

Edwards, V.M. & Steins, N.A. (1998) Developing an analytical framework for multiple-use commons. *Journal of Theoretical Politics*, **10**(3) 347–383.

Edwards, V.M. & Steins, N.A. (1999) A framework for analysing contextual factors in common pool resource research. *Journal of Environmental Policy and Planning*, **1**(3) 205–221.

Kiser, L.L. & Ostrom, E. (1982) The Three Worlds of Action: A Metatheoretical Synthesis of Institutional Approaches. In: *Strategies of Political Inquiry* (ed. E. Ostrom). Sage, Beverly Hills, CA.

Oakerson, R.J. (1986) A Model for the Analysis of Common Property Problems. In: *Proceedings of the Conference on Common Property Resource Management*, National Research Council, pp. 13–30. National Academy Press, Washington, DC.

Oakerson, R.J. (1992) Analyzing the Commons: A Framework. In: *Making the Commons Work: Theory, Practice and Policy* (ed. D.W. Bromley) pp. 41–59. Institute for Contemporary Studies Press, San Francisco.

Ostrom, E. (1986) An agenda for the study of institutions. *Public Choice*, **48** 3–25.

Ostrom, V. (1976) John R. Common's foundations for policy analysis. *Journal of Economic Issues*, **10** (4) 839–57.

Porter, M. (1998) *Competitive Strategy: techniques for analysing industries and competitors.* Free Press, New York.

Endnote

[1] Metatheoretical refers to a theory focusing on problems or issues beyond the immediate, i.e. those that might underlie the immediate.

Chapter 3
Property Performance Evaluation

Introduction

Property performance evaluation has traditionally been accepted as referring to the performance of an investment asset. In the more strategic approach we are taking to corporate property management it is inevitably too simplistic to take such a narrow view. This chapter therefore separates the evaluation of property performance as an investment asset from its performance as a corporate asset. The variety of means that might be available for property performance measurement are discussed alongside how these methods are useful in identifying ways of adding value to property as a means of improving performance, rather than simply measuring it.

It is important to note, however, that corporate property, not investment property, forms the focus for this book. Furthermore, there are a variety of comprehensive texts devoted to the subject of property investment analysis.[1] The discussion of property investment analysis here is therefore introductory in nature. It does, however, provide useful context for the corporate property evaluation that follows.

Data issues

Links between the two types of evaluation, investment and corporate, arise within the strategic management issues they raise and the data that are required. Data required for the assessment of both operational and investment performance include:

- estimated rental value
- rent passing
- capital value
- physical characteristics
- management costs
- tenure
- yields.

Evaluative questions that need to be asked include the following.

- Is the property being used in a way which maximises revenue, either investment return or business profit?
- Are there identifiable ways of improving the performance of the property?
- Is the property appropriate within the overall portfolio?

There has been a tendency to underinvest in the collection and monitoring of data specific to property performance, particularly where property is an operational asset (Then, 1997). Strategic decisions are often made with scant information on the cost or management implications for the real estate portfolio. This is slowly changing as corporate occupiers have begun to understand the importance of real estate to the business function (Bootle and Kalyan, 2002).

Research has suggested that business organisations that use their property strategy explicitly to underpin and support their corporate strategy reap benefits (see for example: Manning, 1986; Nourse, 1986; Veale, 1989; Duckworth, 1993; Joroff *et al.*, 1993; Nourse and Roulac 1993; Bon *et al.*, 1994; Nourse, 1994; Lyne, 1995; Manning and Roulac 1996; O'Mara, 1997; and Carn *et al.* 1999). Within these businesses attention has been paid to the efficient data collection necessary to make this possible. However, surprisingly few businesses have so far recognised the utility of this approach (Bon and Luck, 1999; Bootle and Kalyan, 2002).

The role of property within business

The issues being examined for the purposes of evaluation can be linked to the three roles that property plays within any business: *asset base*, *cost base* and *trading base*. Each role has to be considered in the evaluation of the performance of a property, either for investment or operational purposes.

Evaluation comes at the end of the analytical framework we have developed but is perhaps more accurately seen as part of a continuous loop. Once the initial data have been gathered and issues within the first three stages of the framework have been addressed, evaluation and review are required in order to formulate strategies for more effective management. Thus performance evaluation has to be monitored continuously and systematically for the portfolio to operate at optimum efficiency.

Performance evaluation: property held as an investment asset

Evaluating investment property is common territory within the field of real estate and related texts. Given the importance of investment as a primary motivator behind property ownership, the objectives of investment and means of evaluating the performance of property as an asset have been well rehearsed and a wide range of data is available for measuring the performance of a particular property as an asset.

This has not always been the case. While investment objectives have routinely been acknowledged, the performance of property as an investment was not widely monitored and recorded until the late 1980s and early 1990s.

The property market crashes of 1974 and 1990 were significant drivers behind this increase in the availability and quality of data, as it became clear that the property markets were increasingly volatile and invested with capital sums so substantial that poor decisions could have an impact on the whole economy. Extensive analysis would be required if investors, banks and property companies were to develop any thorough understanding of how and why they had become so overexposed to the market at a period of high risk.

The major property companies increased their research output and publication of consistently collected and analysed market data. Jones Lang La Salle, Healey and Baker, Hillier Parker, Knight Frank, DTZ, King Sturge and Co. and Investment Property Databank all produce regular updates on the markets, focusing on rental levels, yields, capital values, available space, etc., most of them specialise in one particular market, for example, Knight Frank on residential and King Sturge and Co. on industrial.

For investors, the overall objective of investing is to maximise returns whilst minimising risk, or at least keeping it at a level appropriate to the investor. If we look back to the three roles property plays within the achievement of business objectives generally, the performance of property within the investment portfolio must be assessed in the same way: as a cost base, an asset base and as a trading base. Each is addressed in turn.

Cost base

While one expects an investment property to produce a return, it will inevitably have costs associated with it as well. These will be incurred in a variety of ways.

- Negotiations with existing tenants. These can be very time consuming if a property is multi-tenanted, and are required for:
  - rent reviews
  - lease renewals
  - surrenders
  - enforcement of insurance/repairing obligations
  - dilapidations
  - break clauses
- Collection of rents/service charges
- Legal pursuit of guarantors
- Marketing and re-letting.

Some prime investment property will have quite limited management costs, being blessed with occupiers of impeccable covenant, 25-year leases with 5-yearly, upwards-only rent reviews and no landlord repairing obligations.

Beyond ensuring that the building is insured, the management of the investment should be little more than the issuing of the correct notices at rent review and the negotiation and collection of rent.

However, it might be that such properties and such tenants are in short supply. It might also be that your investment portfolio is not so large as to be able to afford to purchase this type of investment. It might be that as a dynamic strategic property manager you can see greater opportunity to increase the investor's return on assets that are less straightforward. A multi-tenanted property in a secondary pitch location of an unfashionable but prosperous town may actually reap quite substantial rewards as an investment and will require outlay of much less initial capital. It will have higher management costs associated with it but, if these are measured as a proportion of the yield, good active management can pay substantial dividends.

This is particularly the case if good management systems are in place, for instance:

- data requirements are identified and collated
- familiarity is developed with the location, local development control, local authority policies and the tenants themselves
- opportunities to increase the rental return through surrender and renewal of poorly structured leases are identified
- the tenants' business objectives and possible opportunities are understood
- a forward thinking approach is taken to possible development opportunities.

Active management can increase the performance of even relatively weak investment portfolios and will be crucial to ensuring satisfactory performance of portfolios dominated by non-prime property. The strategy has to be to strive to reduce costs as a proportion of revenue while maximising revenue as a proportion of capital invested. The management costs have to be regularly monitored against improved investment performance if good returns are to be maintained.

Exercise 3.1

Consider a property with which you are familiar; it may be where you work, where you shop, where you go out at night.

- Would it be classed as a prime or secondary property investment opportunity within its area?
- Would it be onerous to manage?
- Can you identify any opportunities that might increase or improve it as an investment?

One of the reasons why residential property has for so long been the province of the smaller investor and eschewed by the investment institutions has been the high management costs involved. However, the strong rental and capital growth that can be made from residential property and the more attractive tenure options that are now available are beginning to change this situation. In terms of investment return, residential property tracks personal income levels much more closely than commercial property, and with less volatility. Given that the obligations of pension funds are directly related to personal income, residential property is becoming more attractive as an investment medium in spite of the management costs involved. However, these types of portfolio need very efficient management to be cost effective.

Asset base

Rental data

To evaluate the performance of property as an asset, basic information regarding actual and potential income must be collected. Rent passing will be relatively straightforward to determine, but must be placed in context. Has this rent been recently set or is it historic? What were the market conditions when the rent was set? If it was set during a period of very high demand and low supply, and the current market reflects the opposite conditions, an upcoming rent review may not result in any increase in rent. Assuming a standard lease with an upwards-only rent review clause, the rent will not go down, but there are no guarantees of an uplift.

It is particularly important to be aware of the context provided by the external world when looking at rents. It might be that a property has moved from being prime to secondary. This may be for a number of reasons, for example:

- functional obsolescence
- locational obsolescence
- demographic change
- fashion
- economic change.

It is equally possible that a property can move from being secondary to prime. Any external factors, such as an urban regeneration initiative, the relocation or development of a road, rail or other transport link will affect the rental value of a property.

Terms of occupation

In terms of occupation, it could it be that your tenant does not want to renew on the lease terms you are offering because shorter terms are available elsewhere. The current rent the property is producing is a direct product of the terms under which it is occupied, so this information is also required. The standard commercial lease is taken to be for a period of 25 years with 5-yearly upwards only rent reviews. This may not, however, be the standard for the foreseeable future. Lease patterns ultimately have to reflect not just the requirements of the investor but also the needs of the occupier, and research has shown that the average length of a lease has fallen and is now nearer 15 years than 25 (RICS, 1997; 2001).

This is an important area where strategic management has long been absent, mainly because of a reluctance on the part of both surveyors in general and investors in particular to divert from normal practice. However, opportunities are increasingly arising where a better return can be obtained from a property, in terms of rent, if more flexible lease terms are offered to tenants. While this may be offset in terms of capital value by a higher initial yield, if the investment is less attractive, this does not need to be the case.

Increasingly the small and medium-sized enterprises (SMEs) within the business sector are the major drivers behind economic development. These are companies with changing space requirements, and perhaps smaller space requirements than large multinationals, but which are no more risky in terms of their ability to pay the rent. If a property can be made attractive to this type of occupier, the owner/investor will immediately increase the number of potential tenants and be able to demand a higher rent in return for more flexible lease terms, with perhaps a shorter term or break clauses. There is a possibility that the yield will rise but this may not necessarily be the case.

The extreme of this situation is the provision of totally serviced commercial space (normally offices) for as long or short a term as the tenant requires, starting at the most flexible end of the market with hourly rates. For companies with short-term projects, this enables rapid access to appropriate space with perhaps relatively high overall charges when compared to rental levels of similar space, but which when compared to the overall cost of occupation, including rates, maintenance and transaction costs, look much more attractive.

From the investor's point of view, this may seem less attractive, being high maintenance, but given the ability to charge a premium rent, plus the spreading of risk in terms of tenants defaulting, the opportunity begins to look more attractive. It should be noted, however, that the higher level of management required might make such a strategy unattractive to some investors. As with any investment, it has to align with the objectives and characteristics of the organisation.

Yield

The risk/return ratio is the basis of portfolio performance and cannot be adequately evaluated without careful attention to the requirements of the investor. A large institutional investor, for example a pension fund, has a great deal of money to spend but also has specific obligations to meet.[2] The portfolio has to provide sufficient returns to grow at least as fast as the level of incomes, otherwise the assets will be insufficient to pay the pensions people are due. This means the funds want relatively high returns but need to spread risk across a range of portfolio options, usually property, equities, gilts and cash. Within the property portfolio, investments will be spread across the available categories with an increasing interest in residential property, although this remains minimal in relative terms at present.

The return on capital invested required by the investor has to be established. It is difficult to generalise on this point, which has to be discussed in detail with the investor in question for a suitable target rate to be established. However the target rate will reflect:

- the return available on risk-free investments such as gilts
- the potential for income growth
- depreciation
- the return required for risk.

Once the target rate is established the yield produced by assets within the client portfolio can be evaluated. It is important that all costs associated with the property are allowed for when calculating the yield in order for the value of the asset not to be overstated.[3]

The yield will rise as the net rental income rises. It is important therefore, to look for ways of improving the rental income of the property in order to maximise the return it is producing. This may be something as straightforward as ensuring rent review notices are served correctly, or it may require more imagination (see discussion of cost base on p. 32 above).

It is also important to accept that the return the asset is actually producing should be based on its current capital value.[4] Unless this is understood it is impossible to make an informed decision as to whether the asset should be retained or sold. Only by knowing the value in today's market is it possible to realise the opportunity cost of the capital invested in the property. This is not simply the initial sum invested. Whatever the property is worth today is capital that could be invested elsewhere. If the future rental growth prospects look poor it may be worth selling the property now and investing that capital in another sector. (For further discussion of this subject see Dubben and Sayce (1991).)

Trading base

This brings us neatly to a consideration of investment property as a trading base. This is sometimes more obvious as an area of evaluation for an operational asset, but it is equally valid from an investment perspective. If the business is investment then the property must be assessed in terms of whether it should be traded in for something else. There is continual trade in such investment assets and each property within a portfolio has to be evaluated in terms of:

- existing investment return
- potential return

- open market value
- portfolio size
- portfolio spread
- geographical spread
- returns available on alternative investment media.

This enables informed decisions to be made regarding trading of the investment.

The demand and supply side of the property investment market inevitably reflects the performance of other investment assets. When equities markets are performing poorly, property might become more attractive with strong demand pushing capital values up and yields down. When demand is particularly strong, it can be difficult for investors to find enough real estate for their funds. In particular, the smaller investment funds and private investors will routinely be outbid by major financial organisations in these kinds of market conditions.

Example 3.1

An investment portfolio contains an industrial property occupying a site with development potential but limited access via a rear entrance that is shared with the neighbouring occupier. The boundary to the front of the property faces on to a busy road from which the local authority will not allow access directly into the site. The limited access is the stumbling block to the further development of the site (Fig. 3.1).

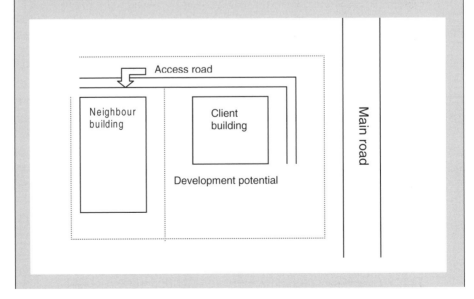

Applying the analytical framework
Property characteristics   This industrial site was underperforming as an investment asset and as an operational asset.
Property user characteristics   The industrial occupier was being hampered by poor access.
Organisational objectives   To improve the performance of the property for the occupier, thereby improving operational conditions for the occupier, rental performance and realising development potential.
Institutional arrangement of the property market   The property was occupied on a lease, therefore improved rental return could be relatively easily achieved and the site had development potential free for exploitation by the investor.
External world   The local authority was limiting current use of the site. Complete re-routing of the traffic was uneconomic, given the value of the site.
Strategy   In this case the manager of the portfolio simply rang the owner of the adjacent property. He proposed that an improved site access would be beneficial to both parties and suggested they negotiate a deal over paying for it.
Performance evaluation   The end result was a better rental value for the property as access was improved, and the realisation of development potential for the rest of the site, whilst paying less than half the cost of the access improvements. In this case both the investment and operational performance of the property were improved through the application of strategic management to the asset.
Investment performance indicators   Rental level, capital value, return on new cost of new property.
Operational performance indicators   Occupier satisfaction, rental level, continued occupation of the property.

Performance evaluation: property held as an operational asset

This area is much less well covered in the property literature than investment performance but has recently begun to influence decisions made about the management of an operational portfolio. Research has shown that property is becoming more expensive over time, relative to other factors of production, and more significant within the development of the economy (Ball, 1988).

This became very clear in the early 1990s when many operational portfolios were found to contain property that was expensive relative to market rents, but occupied on lease structures that tied occupiers in to long tenancies and forbade reductions in rent. Research carried out by Debenham Tewson Chinnock (now DTZ) (Debenham Tewson Chinnock, 1992) reported that out of the 29 trading organisations owning the largest amount of real estate by value, 21 did not consider property investment as a primary activity. Companies such as Marks and Spencer, Trust House Forte and the high street banks were major holders of property as an operational asset but 'not in the real estate business'.

Research conducted by Teoh (1993) on corporate real estate in New Zealand found that over 80% of respondents did not perform financial analysis that would allow comparisons of real estate and overall corporate returns to be conducted.

'They simply treat real estate as a cost expense item and do not specifically evaluate its returns as they would do with a profitable asset.'

Teoh, 1993, p. 616

The technological advances of the late twentieth century which could have led to lower space costs as fewer employees were required and decentralisation was an option, had not been exploited, mainly because management strategy had focused on more direct drivers of business performance and ignored the impact of the companies' property holdings. The recurring phrase 'we are not in the real estate business' from executives and managers of business organisations with large real estate holdings, was demonstrably untrue. Any business organisation that occupies property is, to some degree, in the real estate business.

The opposite situation began to occur in some sectors in the 1990s. Having experienced the deep property recession of the early 1990s, some businesses began to look at releasing large portions of their portfolios, in some instances with scant regard for other areas of the business. This became particularly obvious within the retail banking sector when a round of branch closures began to take place, causing great customer dissatisfaction. A real estate strategy that fails to reflect the requirements of the business organisation is no better than no real estate strategy at all. Some of these strategies have since been reversed.

Following the property crash of the early 1990s more attention has been paid to the property portfolio in terms of organisational objectives and this has led to more attention to the performance of property as an operational asset. The setting up of the Corporate Occupiers Group within the RICS Royal Institution of Chartered Surveyors, the establishment of NACORE National Association of Corporate Real Estate Network International and the Corporate Real Estate Management Research Unit at Reading University reflect an increasing awareness within the property professions of the impact a property strategy can have on business performance. The Corporate Real Estate Management Research Unit carries out an annual survey of corporate real estate practices, the findings of which provide valuable information on issues affecting corporate occupiers and the approaches they are adopting to manage their real estate.

It is important to establish basic facts about the real estate holdings of a business in order to make an effective assessment of its performance. Weatherhead (1997) provides the following list of data requirements she considers vital to a true understanding of the role of real estate within a business:

- total value of the portfolio
- total annual expenditure on the portfolio
- time scale of existing commitments (i.e. lease terms, rent reviews, etc.)

- extent of future liabilities – (particularly in relation to repairs)
- real estate costs as percentage of total costs
- value of real estate as a percentage of total assets
- return on real estate investments compared with business overall.

In addition to these basic data requirements, performance indicators that reflect the activities of the organisation itself should also be considered. For example, British Airways use costs per passenger kilometre and costs per tonne kilometre as measures of performance, for both passenger and cargo transport. It would be logical therefore to adapt such a measure for assessing the performance of the property portfolio by establishing property costs per passenger kilometre and property costs per tonne kilometre (Bon *et al.*, 1994).

It is also important to consider whether a particular property within a portfolio has special significance for an organisation, perhaps in terms of corporate image. Many international companies seek to establish their identity within a local community through the property they occupy. Alternatively a property may have become internationally recognised as a symbol of a particular organisation: Harrods or the Sears Tower for example. Even if the cost per customer of occupying the Harrods building is relatively high compared to competing retailers, it would probably not make sense for the business as a whole to vacate.

Having established the data requirements we can return to the three roles of property within the business, trading base, asset base and operational base, and look at evaluation from the point of view of each.

Evaluation as a trading base

As an operational asset, the performance of a property in its role as the trading base of the company can be seen as the most crucial of the three roles. Furthermore, performance in this criterion has to be measured in terms of the objectives of the occupier, so these have to be established as the first phase of any evaluation. Consider the different property requirements of a hospital with those of an internet business. The performance of each could hardly be evaluated on the same basis.

It is also crucial to understand the stage the business has reached in terms of its own development. A new business which is rapidly expanding will be more concerned with having sufficient space to allow for that expansion than with reducing cost overheads through space saving. Many businesses have suffered setbacks in their strategies for business expansion through lack of available space. Having learned from this experience, some organisations that expect rapid expansion purchase land adjacent to and around their initial operating site in order to safeguard future plans.

Businesses that grow rapidly and are ultimately successful can suffer from the increased land prices that result from success. A successful business can so improve the economic status of a location as to lead to markedly increased rental and land values, in some cases pricing them out of the market. When Walt Disney developed the first Disney Land in the USA he failed to foresee the impact his investment would have on surrounding land values. As he made plans to expand he quickly realised it was going to be enormously expensive, due to the increase in land values he himself had created. When the Disney corporation developed the second Disney theme park in the US, it bought sufficient land surrounding the initial development site to be able to expand when necessary, or sell surplus land once it had appreciated in value, allowing it to recoup some of its own investment. This was simply good strategic corporate property management.

By contrast, a well established business with a relatively low profit margin will have to ensure space costs are as low as possible in relation to overall business costs in order to remain competitive. Such a business may well consider the greater exploitation of communications systems to open the possibility of decentralisation, or more dynamic use of space through hot-desking or teleworking, for example. Alternatively, the properties that make up the portfolio may be essential to the operation of the business, a hotel chain for example. Limited benefit will be gained from reducing the amount of space, unless that particular unit is unprofitable. Great benefit could be had, however, from more intensive use of the space.

Data requirements

Information is required in the following areas for trading base evaluation:

- primary focus of the business
- primary revenue generators
- primary cost centres.

Given that demand for property is derived from demand for the goods produced within them, it may seem obvious that the function of real estate is to provide space in which to carry on business operations. However, it is important to consider the importance of retail space to a manufacturer, the use of warehouse or storage space to a retailer, the use of an office building in a central location to a call centre. If the primary focus of the business has a requirement for a specific type of space, holdings of any other type of space must be carefully examined.

Occupiers of different types of space will use different measures to interpret property performance as an operational asset. Where data are being collected it is therefore important that they reflect the primary business objective. For example, if the business is retail, the level of sales in each store or per square foot will be more informative than the cost per square metre alone. Retail occupiers will use:

- turnover per square foot or square metre
- turnover per department

- turnover per store
- market share within a shopping centre
- ratio of occupancy costs to sales
- market value of property.

Office occupiers will use:

- cost per square metre
- cost per square metre per employee
- total square meterage
- percentage of space occupied
- income generated per square metre
- ratio of square metres to revenue
- occupier satisfaction.

Nourse (1994) identified a link in his research between the number of measures monitored by an occupier and tighter links between their business strategy and real estate operations.

Performance measures used by industrial occupiers will depend on the activity but will also reflect productivity per square metre and cost per square metre, cost per employee and cost as a proportion of productivity, for example. Where the property houses a bespoke manufacturing process, the performance of the building in supporting that process should also be monitored, through observation, employee feedback and so on.

Sainsbury's, the supermarket chain have made extensive use of just-in-time delivery systems to reduce the amount of storage space they require at each retail outlet. The retail space is the major revenue generator and a major cost centre, so their strategy is to use an efficient delivery network in order to maximise the amount of space devoted to retail at each outlet. The storage function is performed by cheaper warehouse space located at strategic road network points.

Improved communications have increased the options available for business location in a variety of ways. We have moved from being a manufacturing economy with location dictated by the presence of raw materials, to a high-tech/service sector dominated economy with extreme flexibility in locational requirements of space. In Chapter 1 we developed a simple locational flexibility continuum with, at one end, location non-specific operations such as call centres, and, at the other, location-specific operations such as site-specific leisure attractions. Factors such as the importance of local market knowledge, proximity to a customer base or supplier, proximity to export routes or motorway networks and proximity to other similar businesses will all affect the position of each type of business within that locational flexibility spectrum. Once you have established the importance of location you can begin to consider whether the performance of the portfolio can be improved by changing its location.

Exercise 3.2

- Find out what performance measures are used to assess the property in which you currently work or study. The information should be available from the property services or management team.
- Consider what additional performance measures might improve the performance measurement process, given the business function of the occupying organisation.

It is important not to dismiss location as a factor in the effective performance of real estate as a trading base. While communication improvements have undoubtedly given us greater flexibility, it remains important for some businesses to be correctly located. This is most obvious with retail businesses. Any retail business planning to expand will research both possible areas and sites within those areas with great care.

Cost base

The real estate occupied by any business will contribute substantially to the costs of the organisation, and so reducing occupancy costs is a priority in seeking to improve the performance of a real estate portfolio. This is reason enough to analyse performance.

Such an analysis needs to address the following:

- the number of employees a property contains
- whether this can be improved through layout changes
- the revenue generated by those employees and how this compares with other properties within the portfolio
- whether changing the building would increase or decrease that revenue.

This will require the following data:

- occupier costs
  - rent (notional space charges if freehold)
  - management costs
  - rates
  - energy costs
  - maintenance costs
  - repair costs
  - insurance costs
  - total costs per square metre, per employee
  - total costs as a proportion of overall business costs
  - total costs as a proportion of business revenue

- occupier terms
  - ○ lease terms
  - ○ rent review patterns
- occupied space (square metres)
- revenue.

Once this information is collected it can be analysed to identify the main drivers of cost within the portfolio. If a large proportion of the estate is occupied on short-term leases, but will be required by the business on an ongoing basis, it may be beneficial to renegotiate those leases on longer terms. This may also afford the opportunity to obtain more favourable rental levels in return for being willing to take a longer term. If a high proportion of the real estate is in small units, spread out on a regional basis, it may be more sensible to consolidate into larger regional offices. If this does not support the business strategy, which may require a local presence, it will be imperative to encourage maximum efficiency in the use of space.

Consider also the quantity of space held. Could this be reduced without compromising the operation of the organisation? The more efficient operators will monitor lease renewal dates and break clauses and contact business managers as much as two years in advance of these dates to discuss the continued space needs of the business in question. This then presents the possibility of improving the performance of the business through restructuring its corporate space with sufficient time to incorporate change into a business plan or strategy.

Collecting this information and analysing the performance of real estate on this basis is useful and should be an ongoing process. It should be noted, however, that while costs must be contained, this has to be at a level appropriate to the business occupier. A retailer moving to a new retail location where the rent is lower but there is less passing trade, will reduce costs but revenue as well.

Exercise 3.3

Consider the business benefits that accrue to the companies that occupy the most expensive real estate in a central business district (CBD), such as the City of London.

What aspect of their businesses would be affected by moving to a less prominent location?

What strategy would you suggest to enable them to make cost savings while maintaining a presence in the CBD?

Performance measurement can be made even more effective if there is opportunity to compare the performance of the organisation's real estate as a cost base and as an operating base with other occupiers in a similar business. The recognition of the value of this type of comparison has led to the development of 'benchmarking' as a growing activity within corporate real estate management.

Benchmarking

Whereas basic comparisons can be made across portfolios to assess the performance of a particular property it can be helpful to make comparisons outside the business, particularly where the operation of one aspect of the business is causing concern. For example, if communication is failing within an organisation it may be that a study of an organisation that performs well in this area is of value. This has come to be known as *benchmarking*. It is more complex than the comparisons of data we looked at earlier and requires full cooperation by both organisations, but can reveal useful opportunities to improve performance.

To this end, benchmark clubs have been set up to share and benefit from information. The members of such clubs may not be within the same industry but may have similar working patterns; for example, firms within different professions. Where one firm may have made good use of IT to successfully encourage home working or hot-desking, another firm, possibly within a different profession, may study how this has been implemented. Information ranging from the equipment required, to the staff most successfully involved, would be useful in attempting to make effective use of a similar approach. This is an area of strategic management that is likely to become more prevalent as corporate strategy begins to take a more sophisticated approach to the long-term use of space in the drive to maintain a competitive edge.

There are four stages to the benchmarking process (Noha, 1993):

(1) understand real estate assets and business objectives
(2) identify opportunities by comparing key real estate measures against competitors and best in class
(3) identify solutions by assessing critical drivers
(4) implement and revise solutions consistent with changing business objectives.

Embarking on a benchmarking exercise requires considerable commitment of both time and resources from an organisation, and a willingness to share information. However, research suggests that those organisations in a position to implement the process find the resulting efficiency gains justify the investments.

Noha's research (Noha, 1993) focused on nine benchmarking studies carried out with over 60 companies in the USA. Where they looked at occupancy costs, one study revealed a maximum difference of 75% in the occupancy costs per employee incurred by the six different companies involved. By analysing location, quality of space, the size of each facility, the length of lease terms, the decision-making and approval process and the use of external resources, it was possible to identify the key factors driving the high occupancy costs of the organisation incurring 75% extra expenditure.

Cost centre v. profit centre

It is quite possible for the real estate portfolio within an organisation to be run as a separate business that is expected to show a profit. This turns a cost centre within the organisation into a profit centre which can be formed as a separate business entity (Behrens, 1982). Each business unit 'rents' space from the real estate management unit, providing a revenue stream and an incentive for the business unit to use its space efficiently. The real estate management unit is able to make strategic decisions regarding the expansion, development and transfer of holdings within the portfolio with the advantage of an overview of the operation. The management strategy must reflect and support the objectives of the organisation.

Such a system has the added benefit of making business units which are being subsidised in terms of space costs by other parts of the organisation apparent, allowing strategic management decisions to be taken about such business units in a more informed way. However, they tend to work best in larger organisations and will only be truly effective if the real estate management unit has representation at board level. A surprising number of businesses still leave the real estate function out at this crucial decision-making level, seeing it as a service to be consulted later, following decision making or strategy development. The results of such a management system are usually less than optimal.

Research in the USA has found that employee satisfaction with a work environment is also identified as an important criterion when assessing the performance of a property. This is less common within the UK but becoming increasingly important due to two overriding factors:

- the short supply of skilled workers
- the reduced profit margins on which many businesses operate.

Businesses can find that employee productivity increases with an improved working environment. This is not just about the psychological benefits of a pleasant environment but more importantly, it is about the suitability of the property for the functions of the occupier. For example:

- where communication is a fundamental aspect of the business, a building layout with no space set aside for meeting rooms or informal discussion will severely hamper productivity

- where buildings are operating 24 hours a day, poor lighting systems will increase tiredness and reduce productivity levels during darkness
- poor air conditioning systems are renowned for increasing the incidence of poor health amongst staff, inevitably reducing productivity.

Bon *et al.* (1994) identified a bank which used help-desk calls as a measure of employee satisfaction with a property. By analysing the number of calls received by a property services help-desk, this organisation was able to pin-point a problem building within the portfolio. Requests received across a range of issues from health and safety to space planning and furniture were analysed per square foot for each property. A system which uses real data like this can be more effective than a system that tries to establish employee satisfaction through survey, for example, which is inevitably subjective and difficult to monitor. Of course, it requires an effective help-desk system and reporting procedure but can highlight problem buildings or problems within a property relatively quickly, helping to reduce costs.

Asset base

It is clearly important to understand the current open market value of property as an asset within the business, even if investment is not the primary activity.[5] There are plenty of examples of businesses that have undervalued their property portfolio, having bought relatively cheaply and the assets having been broken up, or the sites redeveloped. It is crucial that an accurate record of the value of each property is maintained. This requires knowledge of:

- rental values
- open market value
- market yields
- property assets as proportion of total assets
- return on capital invested in the business
- redevelopment potential.

One of the most important decisions facing any business with substantial property holdings will be whether to retain the freeholds or sell them to an investor and lease them back: the *own* v. *lease* decision. At a business efficiency level, Bootle and Kalyan (2002) identified rental occupiers as making much more effective use of their corporate real estate than owner occupiers, supporting the findings of Nourse (1994).

If real estate is leased it does not appear on the balance sheet, making the business return a truer reflection of the primary activities of the organisation. The capital realised from the sale and leaseback can be used for investment in other areas of the business. A business within a high growth sector is likely to achieve a much higher return on capital invested in core activity than it will on capital invested in real estate.

Some public sector organisations with large property holdings have begun to explore the potential cost savings and risk reduction of selling all their operational property assets to a property company who will manage the estate in line with the organisation's strategic requirements in return for rent (Gibson, 1994; Gibson and French, 2002). This form of outsourcing can realise substantial cost savings and efficiency of the portfolio in both operational and investment terms can be improved whilst relieving the organisation of the direct responsibility of holding and managing the property asset base.

Manning *et al.* (1997) point out that there are disadvantages as well as advantages to outsourcing of the real estate function. Cost savings may be available, particularly if the contractor is a specialist with a number of clients. More effective management and reporting systems may be introduced for the portfolio. However, these benefits need to be weighed against the loss of control over the real estate function. If the contractor is not party to the business strategy and does not have a detailed understanding of the client's business function, the real estate will not be managed in accordance with it and this is likely to be expensive in the long run. For outsourcing to be really effective, a strong relationship needs to be developed between contractor and client.

Conclusion

Property performance measurement is becoming standard practice amongst business organisations seeking efficiency within their operation. Given the scarcity of land as a resource and the high proportion it represents of a business's operating costs, it is important in terms of economic and environmental efficiency that organisations seek optimum performance from their real estate holdings. It is no longer possible for any business with a property interest to claim not to be in the real estate business. It is certainly not possible to manage corporate (or any other) real estate efficiently let alone strategically, without a comprehensive set of data and systematic performance evaluation.

References

Ball, M. (1988) *Rebuilding Construction: economic change and the British construction industry.* Routledge, London.

Baum, A. and Crosby, N. (1995) *Property Investment Appraisal* (2nd edition) Routledge, London.

Behrens, A. (1982) Managing corporate real estate as a profit centre. *Industrial Development*, July/August, 4–8.

Bon, R., McMahan, J. & Carder, P. (1994) Property performance measurement: from theory to management practice. *Facilities*, **12** (12) 18–24.

Bon, R. & Luck, R. (1999) Annual CREMRU-JCI survey of corporate real estate practices in Europe and North America: 1993–1998. *Facilities*, **17** (5/6) 167–176.

Bootle, R. & Kalyan, S. (2002) *Property in Business: A waste of space?* RICS, London.

Carn, N., Black, R. and Rabianski, J. (1999) Operational and organisational issues facing corporate real estate executives and managers. *Journal of Real Estate Research*, **17**(3) 281–99.

Debenham Tewson Chinnock (1992) *The Role of Property: managing cost and releasing value.* Debenham Tewson Chinnock, London.

Dubben, N. & Sayce, S. (1991) *Property Portfolio Management.* Routledge, London.

Duckworth, S.L. (1993) Realizing the strategic dimension of corporate real property through improved planning and control systems. *Journal of Real Estate Research*, **4**, 495–509.

Gibson, V. (1994) Strategic property management: how can local authorities develop a property strategy? *Property Management*, **12** (3) 9–14.

Gibson, V., & French, N. (2002) *Whose property is it anyway?* RICS, London.

Hoesli, M. (2000) *Property Investment: Principles and Practice of Portfolio Management.* Longman, Harlow.

Isaac, D. (1998) *Property Investment.* Macmillan, Basingstoke.

Joroff, M., Louargand, M., Lambert, S. & Becker, F. (1993) *Strategic management of the fifth resource: corporate real estate.* Industrial Development Research Foundation, Atlanta.

Lyne, J. (1995) IDRC'S real estate revolution: occupancy costs plummet, productivity crests. *Site Selection*, April, 198–212.

Manning, C.A. (1986) The economics of real estate decisions. *Harvard Business Review* **86**(6) 12–22.

Mannning, C. & Roulac, S. (1996) Structuring the corporate real property function for greater bottom line impact. *Journal of Real Estate Research* **12** (3) 383–396.

Manning, C., Rodriguez, M. & Roulac, S. (1997) Which corporate real estate functions should be outsourced? *Journal of Real Estate Research* **14** (3) 259–274.

Noha, E. (1993) Benchmarking: the search for best practices in corporate real estate. *Journal of Real Estate Research* **8** (4) 511–523.

Nourse, H.O. (1986) Using real estate asset management to improve strategic performance. *Industrial Development*, June/July 1–7.

Nourse, H.O. (1992) Real estate flexibility must complement business strategy. *Real Estate Review.* **4**, 25–29.

Nourse, H.O & Roulac, S.E. (1993) Linking real estate decisions to corporate strategy. *Journal of Real Estate Research* **8** (4) 475–494.

Nourse, H.O. (1994) Measuring business real property performance. *Journal of Real Estate Research* **9** (4), 431–444.

O'Mara, M.A. (1997) Corporate real estate strategy: uncertainty, values and decision making. *Journal of Applied Real Property Analysis* **1**(1) 15–28.

Prudential Property Investment Managers (2002) *Environmental and Social Report 2002.* Prudential, London.

RICS (1995) *Valuation and Appraisal Manual.* RICS Business Services, London.

RICS (1997) *Right Space Right Price; A study of the impact of changes in business patterns on the property market.* RICS, London.

RICS (2001) *Lease Structures, Terms and Lengths: does the UK lease meet current business requirements?* RICS, London.

Teoh, W.K. (1993) Corporate real estate asset management: the New Zealand evidence. *Journal of Real Estate Research* **8**(4) 607–23.

Then, S.S. (1997) A model for considering operational property as an enabling resource to business. Paper presented to the RICS COBRA Conference, 3–5 September, University of Portsmouth.

Veale, P.R. (1989) Managing corporate real estate assets: current executive attitudes and prospects for an emergent management discipline. *Journal of Real Estate Research*, **4** (3) 1–22.

Weatherhead, M. (1997) *Real Estate in Corporate Strategy*. Macmillan: Basingstoke.

Further reading

Hiang, L.W., Leong, J., Ebrahim, M. & Brown, G. (2001) Performance measurements in corporate real estate: issues, evidence and research agenda. *Journal of Financial Management of Property and Construction*, **6** (2) 71–79.

Pavan, M. (1996) Marketing benchmarking in professional firms. *Professional Practice Management*, **14** (4) 50–52.

Endnotes

[1] See for example: Baum and Crosby (1995); Isaac (1998); Hoeseli (2000).

[2] Prudential, for example, has approximately £11 billion invested in the UK property markets (Prudential Property Investment Managers, 2002). A company like Standard Life may have upwards of £50 million to invest *each month*.

[3] It is usual for investment yields to be quoted gross of tax.

[4] See the *RICS Valuation and Appraisal Manual* regarding valuation of business assets (RICS, 1995).

[5] See the *RICS Valuation and Appraisal Manual* with regard to asset valuation and regular re-valuation requirements (RICS, 1995).

Chapter 4
Understanding Property
Characteristics – Information
Requirements

Introduction

Information is a crucial resource for property managers. In pursuit of their aim, property managers must manage a vast flow of diverse information through interrelated stages of analysis. This chapter explains the different information requirements of the property manager. It presents a taxonomy of property characteristics that must be identified for each sector of property, including physical, legal, and financial characteristics. The chapter explains how information obtained and analysed must come from both the past and the present, and should include some element of forecasting.

When discussing strategic property management, one question we often ask our students is, 'if you were appointed the property manager for the University estate, what is the first task you would undertake?' Answers always vary according to each individual's perceptions and aspirations. Of course, we have the usual collection of humorous remarks, such as 'ask where my office is', 'award myself a pay rise', etc., but most students recognise that fundamental to undertaking a new role in an organisation is to ask 'what properties am I responsible for'? Indeed, in a series of case studies on strategic property management commissioned by the RICS, the authors summarise the process of successful strategic property management under thirteen headings: at the top of the list is 'Know your estate' (Evans and Weatherhead, 1999).[1]

Good record keeping

No property management can succeed without a rudimentary inventory of the total property base and compilation of some sort of register. However, surveys conducted in the late 1980s and early 1990s revealed an alarming lack of such property registers and inventories. Avis *et al.* (1989) reported that only 75% of private organisations and 68% of public organisations had a full property inventory (20% and 29%, respectively, held a partial inventory) and 3% of both private and public organisations had no inventory at all. The Chartered Insti-

51

tute of Public Finance and Accountancy conducted similar surveys of local authorities and found that while some local authorities held a comprehensive record of their property, many did not know the extent of their ownership (CIPFA, 1992). Discrepancies also existed *within* authorities in that '... not all properties are insured, sold properties were still insured and water bills are being paid in respect of demolished properties...' (CIPFA, 1992).

The most common problem seemed to be that although organisations, public and private, have all the necessary information about their properties, it was seldom collected in one place. If computer-based solutions were sought, it was largely as a result of the IT capabilities of the person directly responsible for the task (Erdman, 1992). Strutt and Parker report on how they were asked by a company with around 50 properties to create an occupational property database. They were told that they would be given access to all the information needed. However, 'after a day of ploughing through dirty files and leases we had hardly unearthed a single current lease. Assembling all the relevant information from a variety of sources took months' (Elphick and Wright, 2002).

A review of published research reports and surveys conducted in the public and private sectors prior to 1997 revealed inadequate data for informed decision making as one of the main weaknesses in organisations' management of operational property assets (Then, 1997).[2] As a consequence, a recent set of guidelines for property management in local government highlights the need to ensure comparability of information and use of property (DETR, 2000).

Basic property data

The traditional term for the set of records held for an estate is the *estate terrier*. The word 'terrier' is derived from a combination of the medieval Latin words *terrarius* (earth) and *liber* (book); thus, the estate terrier was simply a book containing detail about the land. Terms such as *estate inventory*, *register* or *terrier* are commonly used nowadays and imply a list of properties owned or leased by an organisation. In its most basic form, the set of records should consist of the following information:

- boundaries, plans and maps, showing sites and size of holdings
- addresses
- tenure, including abstracts of title and leases
- details of easements and other rights and obligations affecting the estate.

Before computerisation, such inventories were undoubtedly held in filing cabinets, and updated with newly typed hard copy. Most organisations now hold such records in an information database. This allows them to keep more detailed information in a single record system, which might include not only a record of the estate land and buildings, but also those of rents, insurance details, repairs and improvements.

The degree of sophistication of such records will depend on the size of the organisation, the size of its property holding and its tendency towards more modern methods of working. The Forestry Commission, Britain's largest landowner, holds all of its property on database with its own tailor made geographical information system (GIS) application, *Forester*. The *Forester* GIS system allows the Forestry Commission to call up any piece of land it owns, however small, and produce:

- maps of the land
- detailed information on the property rights attached to the land
- land use status (i.e. the habitat type)
- any recent operations – for example, the last planting or felling date, stocking density, etc.

The latest system also enables forest managers to analyse geographic imagery in forestry applications, including:

- realistic three-dimensional woodland visualisation
- the impacts of felling regimes on surrounding landscapes
- likely future planning impacts on the environment
- determinations of woodland maturity from imagery.

Forestry Commission, 2001

A property information system can be as simple or comprehensive as the organisation requires. Many organisations are beginning to see the benefit of developing a system that can hold a wide range of information about their property and are expanding systems that were once designed to cope with only specific tasks, such as budgeting, rent collection, or maintenance. One of the major challenges in constructing a truly comprehensive property database is keeping it up to date and relevant, especially during periods of rapid and/or extensive change. Such change is likely to occur in the private sector when one organisation merges with or is taken over by another, and in the public sector when property passes from one organisation to another through boundary or administrative changes. In such instances, data are often incompatible in the way in which they have been collected, collated or stored and insufficient resources are allocated to rationalising databases.

In the rest of this chapter, we will look at the type of information that ought to be collected for property and its various 'characteristics'.

Physical appraisal of the property

The physical structure of the estate and its location will be the principal factors in determining the scope for strategic planning. For most property managers, undertaking a physical inventory of their estate would seem a natural first task.

Assuming that a full list of properties, with accompanying maps, can be provided, the property manager will first need to provide detailed descriptive accounts of the physical state of each property. If deemed necessary, this might also include full structural surveys of the properties, if not already conducted. However, we would suggest that such detailed survey work would be more appropriately commissioned as part of a review of strategic options and, in the first instance, a basic physical inventory would suffice.

Such an inventory might include recording the location, size, design and year of construction of the buildings (including any additions or alterations). In addition, the basic state of repair of buildings should be recorded, together with any fixtures and fittings. A similar approach can be adopted for land, whereby the size, location and topography of the land can be recorded, together with existing habitat, special features, etc.

Proprietary features

Just as important as the physical characteristics of the structures and land in the estate is an account of the different *proprietary* features. These are the numerous property rights that could be attached to any property. For example, you might own the freehold interest in a building which has been leased to a tenant for 21 years. Similarly, you might lease 1000 hectares of agricultural land from a pension fund that owns the freehold. Over the same land, an electricity company might have a wayleave for some pylons and overhead cables.

At this stage we would like you to envisage any property as a bundle of sticks. Each stick within that bundle represents a different property right that can be separated and traded from the bundle. So, for example, a lease might represent one stick, a covenant another, a wayleave another. Our ability to separate the sticks in the bundle is what gives property its inherent value and is an extremely important tool for strategic property management. So, instead of having to trade properties in their entirety, the proprietary rights and the legal system that supports them enable us to trade *rights* in any property. This affords property a degree of flexibility that defies its initial appearance as a substantial, but largely rigid asset. It enables a property manager to maximise the value of any one property or piece of land by exploiting all its potential uses to different customers concurrently; making sure that each is traded the property right appropriate for his particular use.

For example, if you are managing a shopping centre as part of an investment portfolio, a likely scenario is that a local authority or city council will own the freehold interest. The investment might comprise a long lease on the land (say 999 years). Clearly, you will have tenants on a collection of long and short fixed term leases, ranging from 25 years for some retail tenants to maybe only 5 years for newer, smaller businesses. You might also have issued licences to food court operators or businesses selling from mobile stands within the centre, such as a barrow selling sunglasses. On top of the centre, you might have secured a contract from a mobile phone operator for the use of some of the roof space for one of its masts. Thus, by combining the physical potential of the property with its proprietary potential, we are able to fully exploit its value by creating a number of separate income streams delivered to the investor.

A good property database will contain comprehensive information about the property rights attached to the estate. In terms of leases held or granted, this might include, for example, the following:

- length and term of any leases
- level of rents paid
- regularity of rent reviews
- incidence and length of any rent free periods
- provisions and restrictions as to assignment or subletting
- payment of any premiums
- responsibility for maintenance, repair and insurance
- provisions in respect of proposed alterations and/or improvements
- inclusion of break clauses for either party
- availability and responsibility for services
- level, payment and adjustments for service charges
- works to be carried out by the tenant
- restrictions as to the type and duration of use
- control of advertisements and decoration
- payment of legal costs
- forfeiture and re-entry

Ratcliffe, 1978, p. 292

Such information must be held whether the client is lessor or lessee of the particular property. In addition, information about the history of property ownership can be very useful when reviewing estate strategies. For example, when was the freehold or leasehold bought? How much was paid? This leads us to our next category of information on the estate: financial information.

Financial appraisal

Information about freehold or leasehold purchase prices, along with current running costs, might well help the property manager assess the current 'worth' of the property. As we shall see later, such information helps the property manager make informed decisions about the future of the property and its role in her organisation's portfolio. For each property in the estate or portfolio, she needs to compile information on historic costs, current costs and anticipated future costs. Historic costs might be amongst the most difficult to identify if good records have not been kept. They should include details not only of prices paid for freehold and leasehold purchases, but also details of any capital costs of improving properties, refurbishment costs, leaseback deals, etc. Current costs can be ascertained from current records, lease agreements and accounts. They should include information on:

- rents payable
- rates

- service charges
- repair and maintenance costs
- utilities (water, sewage, electricity, etc.).

Anticipated future costs can be forecast by using a mixture of historic costs and benchmarks from other properties. Use real data wherever possible as this will produce a more accurate forecast than estimates.

Evaluation

Once a basic description of the estate has been logged, the manager can set about evaluating the property against certain criteria. If the property is held as an operational asset, the manager must first question the property's current function and its fitness.

For example, our own department at the University of Portsmouth was, for many years, housed in a linked series of large but temporary single storey buildings. This was somewhat grandly named the Cambridge Building, not because of its likeness to an ivy-clad-college court, but because of its location on Cambridge Road in Portsmouth. The Cambridge Building housed three property courses, which involved between 300 and 400 undergraduate and postgraduate students and 20 to 30 full time and part time staff. The property comprised individual offices, teaching space, an IT suite, a research suite, library and staff room.

In physical terms, the property was old, shabby, often too cold in the winter and too hot in summer and lacked any prestigious qualities to help attract good students and staff when visiting for interviews. Nevertheless, it was functional.

In Table 4.1 we have conducted a basic evaluation of the building, to show how different criteria might be applied in assessing the 'worth' of the property to the current occupier. However, in assessing the overall worth of the property, the University needed to consider the *opportunity cost* of maintaining the Cambridge Building for its property school. The opportunity cost of a property is 'the return or other benefit foregone in pursuing one particular investment opportunity rather than another. This enables a comparative judgement to be made with knowledge of their relative advantages or disadvantages'. In essence, the University had to decide whether it could make better use of the Cambridge Building or site. In 1996, the Property Department moved to the Portland Building, on another site, making way for the demolition of the Cambridge Building and redevelopment of the site into the new Students' Union. The decision was taken not solely on the basis of the fitness of the Cambridge Building for the property school, but on the overall worth of the property and its site to the strategy of development of the university estate.

In evaluating properties in an estate, each property manager needs to set criteria that suits his organisation's needs. If an estate is held for operational asset purposes, criteria will be inextricably linked to the extent to which the

Table 4.1   Evaluation of Cambridge Building for University of Portsmouth Property School

Physical state	Advantages	Disadvantages	Functionally effective/efficient? X = poor ✓ = good
Old building, low quality finish	Low cleaning costs	High annual repair costs	✓ X
Poor insulation		High energy costs	X
		Low heat retention – often cold	X
Poor ventilation		Overheats in summer	X
Temporary buildings	Low demolition costs	Lack of prestige and sense of stability for school	✓ X
Single storey	Affords disabled access easily Enables good communication	Inefficient use of prime site Susceptible to break-in	✓ ✓ X X
Simple partitioned structure	Provides flexible workspace which is easily adaptable	Poor soundproofing	✓ X

property contributes to delivering the organisation's objectives. For example, in a university this might include questions such as the following.

- Does the property provide space conducive to learning? Does it have the following attributes:
  - warm
  - rain proof
  - well ventilated
  - sound proof
  - good acoustics
  - favourable shape for lecture delivery
  - smaller rooms for small group/one-to-one teaching
  - sufficient meeting space
  - allow informal as well as formal meetings between and amongst students and staff.

- Does it suit all students' needs? Does it have:
  - disabled access and audio/visual facilities
  - the best mixture of large and small teaching space
  - individual study areas
  - adequate library facilities
  - adequate personal facilities for students such as toilets, cloakrooms and lockers
  - flexible hours of access.

- Is it prestigious, helping to attract the best students and staff? Is it:
  - aesthetically pleasing
  - accessible by car or public transport
  - provided with adequate car parking
  - provided with individual office space
  - in good repair
  - prominent in the University
  - a comfortable working environment?

- Can it incorporate new and changing technology? Has it got:
  - the ability to house computer technology, with the additional heat and wiring that accompanies it
  - good audio visual facilities
  - a library and teaching rooms that can be linked to the university computer system
  - a library that can be accessed off campus?

- Is it used efficiently? Is it:
  - used for a high proportion of the day/week/year
  - suitable for alternative uses to provide additional income sources, such as acting as a conference facility during evenings, weekends, or vacations
  - possible to reconfigure rooms to suit changing needs, by dividing larger into smaller teaching rooms with partitions?

When assessing a property that is held as an investment, the questions asked might differ in that they are likely to focus on:

- the income streams that the property is capable of producing
- capital growth in the value of the property.

However, from the list below, it will be apparent that the basic principles of assessing the property's worth remain the same as for properties held for operational purposes and identical questions are asked. For example, if an investment manager were reviewing a portfolio of retail properties, the following questions might be asked of one particular property when assessing its worth:

- Does the property provide space conducive to attracting good rents:
  - a prime retail location
  - secure, attractive selling space, with good display facilities
  - adequate storage
  - good delivery access.

- Does it suit *all* tenants' needs:
  - flexible sales floor area
  - scope for fitting out in different ways to suit different retailers

- ○ adequate personal facilities for tenants such as toilets, cloakrooms, office space.

- Is it prestigious, helping to attract the best tenants, staff and customers:
  - ○ aesthetically pleasing
  - ○ adequate car parking
  - ○ good repair
  - ○ prominence in the retail area
  - ○ a comfortable working environment.

- Can it incorporate new and changing technology:
  - ○ is there scope to house computer technology, with the additional heat and wiring that accompanies it?

- Is it used efficiently:
  - ○ are all potential income streams exploited – for example, is there scope for contracting for advertising hoardings on the side of the property, telecommunications masts on the roof, etc. – assuming this will not reduce the overall value of the property
  - ○ can the configuration of space be altered to suit changing needs, by separating the space into smaller units, for example.

Conclusion

This chapter has set out what information is required regarding individual properties within the overall estate or portfolio for management to function effectively. It has also presented a simple system that might be applied to the evaluation of a property's functional value to the estate.

The role of the property manager in gathering and maintaining data on the estate requires a delicate balancing act. She must provide sufficient information about past, present and future management to allow well informed decisions to be made on the property's place in furthering the organisation's objectives, but allow the database to remain simple enough to facilitate regular revision, even during periods of considerable change – the most sophisticated property data management system is rendered useless if the information contained within it is inaccurate or out of date.

We reviewed property performance in detail in Chapter 3. However, this chapter has also shown how in compiling the property data management system, the property manager can begin to assess the 'worth' of individual properties within the estate or portfolio. In this sense, the data management system must be part of the whole reiterative process. That is, a certain amount of basic property information is needed as foundation to any strategic property management. However, as the property manager begins to assess the performance of individual properties and to identify different possible uses for them, she will require additional information. Such information might be historical (such as why certain improvements were executed in the past), might be current (such as the development potential of a particular property) or might involve foreseeable changes in and around individual properties (such as the development of nearby properties). It will all help to inform the formulation, selection and implementation of 'test' strategies, which might, in turn, lead to new information requirements. Essentially, therefore, the property manager must maintain an information system which proves a flexible working tool and meets changing information requirements about the characteristics of the properties in her charge.

Exercise 4.1

Does the building you are currently working in effectively support the business function it houses? Consider the following aspects.

- What is the business function?
- What activities does it require?
- Is the building configured to support this?
- Could it be configured differently?
- Do you find the building a pleasant environment to work in?
- What, if any, changes would you make to the building or its operation to align it more accurately with the business function?

References

Avis, M., Gibson, V. & Watts, J. (1989) *Managing Operational Property Assets*. Research Report, Department of Land Management and Development, University of Reading, Reading.

CIPFA (1992) *Capital Accounting by Local Authorities – Report of the Implementation Studies*. Chartered Institute of Public Finance and Accountancy, London.

DETR (2000) *Draft Good Practice Guidelines for Property Management in Local Government*. Department of Education, Transport and the Regions, London.

Edward Erdman (1992) *Property Asset Registers – A National Survey of the Local Authority Response to Implementation*. Edward Erdman, London.

Elphick, R. & Wright, J. (2002) Assets that are leaking money. *Estates Gazette*, 2nd February 2002.

Evans, M. & Weatherhead, M. (1999) *Think Profit, Act Property*. RICS Corporate Occupiers Group, London.

Forestry Commission (2001) *New software brings the future on screen*. Press release no 3748, 14 March.

Ratcliffe, J. (1978) *An Introduction to Urban Land Administration*. Estates Gazette, London.

Then, S.S.D. (1997) *A Model for Considering Operational Property as an Enabling Resource to Business*. RICS COBRA, Conference, 3–5 September University of Portsmouth.

Endnotes

[1] The rest of the list reads: Have vision; Meet your business needs; Exceed shareholder expectations; Be flexible; Find your route map; Achieve the right solution; Provide senior management support; Make a commitment; Develop team skills; Meet financial targets; Measure performance; Make theory reality (Evans and Weatherhead, 1999).

[2] The other weaknesses included a reactive approach to management; conflicting landlord and tenant objectives; and lack of performance monitoring. These are addressed in other chapters of this book.

Chapter 5
Understanding Property Users' Characteristics

Introduction

This chapter identifies the user communities involved in different types of property. It fully explains this component of the analytical framework and its concern with the social characteristics of the user community and their patterns of interaction.

The chapter explains how the evolution of property and property use has led to a large and disparate body of stakeholders, with varying degrees of historical association and contemporary involvement with property. For example, a single property might number amongst its stakeholders a landowner, investor, shareholders, developer, occupier, occupier's customers, local community neighbours, city council, police and a whole host of other community interests.

The chapter ends by discussing the role of forums for users to exchange information and aid decision making concerning the property. Using case study examples, the chapter explains the attributes of the user community that must be understood and analysed when working with property.

Who do we mean by 'property users'?

As shown in other chapters, the function of the property manager is to plan strategically, take decisions, implement those decisions and then take responsibility for the consequences, whether or not those consequences are intended. As such, the property manager is not only responsible for the management of the estate but is also accountable. In making decisions, the property manager has to decide on the appropriate mix and use of available resources:

- land or property
- labour (including her own skills)
- capital
- technology and information.

However, in a modern property society, an important issue is how autonomous should the property manager be? Generally a more *pluralistic* attitude to management prevails nowadays. By that, we mean a system that recognises that the property manager has more than one ultimate principal. No longer can the agent recognise only the interests of the organisation that employs her, other individuals and groups have interests in the way in which the property is managed and these 'stakes' must also be recognised.

For example, the property manager of a large shopping centre is accountable not only to the investment company that owns the shopping centre and pays her salary, but, arguably, also to:

- the retail tenants in the centre
- the centre staff, including contractors, such as cleaners, security and maintenance
- the shoppers and visitors, some of whom might be from overseas
- the city council
- the local police
- local schools/youth groups
- interest groups who might use the centre, for example, for displays
- local charities that hold fund raising and collection days in the centre
- neighbouring property owners and occupiers.

An effective shopping centre manager must recognise and integrate the needs of all these users, and more, to carry out the role properly.

Some of the stakeholders listed above will hold formal property rights to the shopping centre. For example, the city council might own the freehold of the land on which the centre is built, having acquired it by compulsory purchase in order to facilitate the centre's development. In such a scenario, they are likely to lease the land on a ground rent to the shopping centre owner.

Exercise 5.1

Construct a list of all the possible stakeholders who might have an interest in the property in which you are currently sitting. This might be a library, university building, office, or your home.

In many studies of property management, the *user community* is narrowly defined as the landlord and tenant; little attention is paid to other individuals situated around the property who may affect or be affected by its use and management. By introducing the concept of other users, and other people who have an interest in how the property is managed, we extend the definition of the user community. The proposed definition of user community in a multiple-use situation reflects the importance of recognising different stakeholders: all individuals who have an influence over or are influenced by the property, either directly or indirectly.

Society and stakeholder relationships

In a complex but open society such as in the UK, stakeholders affect and are affected by others in extremely varied and inconsistent, but nevertheless reciprocal, relationships. Each stakeholder holds different values, expectations and aspirations for the property. Every society is an amalgam of numerous structures and systems, based on formal and informal rules, which we refer to as institutions (see Chapter 7). Each person is positioned within his or her own society in an inclusive way, in which the society influences the person, but conversely each person also influences the society. Thus, there are continuous and complex interactions between a person and his or her society.

Exercise 5.2

Go back to the list of stakeholders you drew up for the property in which you are currently sitting. Try to link different stakeholders if they have a relationship with each other, with a 'relationship line'. Next to each stakeholder, make a note of the type of interest that they might have – what are their aspirations for the property?

Individuals also form into identifiable groups of stakeholders, from small families through to large corporations or political parties. In a modern society, individuals invariably belong to many disparate groups, in which they usually play different social roles, which are not necessarily mutually consistent.

The nature of an individual's actions varies between different groups, since the norms and values of these groupings might be, and often are, dissimilar. An individual will, therefore, choose which type of behaviour to adopt in each circumstance. For example, a person might choose to behave differently when in his family life, at work, when participating in sport, when travelling, etc. The result, which might be a compromise or an inconsistent set of values and behaviour, will depend on what the person expects of himself, and what he thinks society expects of him and will allow in different circumstances, according to the group to which he belongs.

In turn, society shapes the choices a person can make, by providing a framework of formal and informal rules. This framework constrains the extent to which the individual can exercise her freedom to act on her own initiative and the extent to which she is expected to comply with certain types of behaviour. For instance, as a commuter group member, there are certain

Exercise 5.3

Identify the different 'titles', and thus identities, that you might already hold within society. For example, you might be a student, mother, wife, tennis player, youth leader, sister, lay preacher, neighbour, lover, committee member, commuter, etc. Consider the different rules you adhere to in each of these roles, whether formal (and sometimes legal) or informal.

specified rules that she is expected to comply with when travelling on a train. For example, she is expected to have a valid ticket and be willing to show it to the inspector when requested. She is expected not to smoke in the non-smoking carriage. There are also certain *un*specified rules, which are commonly recognised throughout society, with which she is expected to comply. For example, she is expected to give up her seat to an elderly or disabled person, not to play music so loudly that it disturbs other passengers, not to put her feet on the opposite seat, etc. Although she might get away with reneging on such informal arrangements, she will certainly be frowned upon by other passengers, who might alert her to the error of her ways.

Management relationships with stakeholders

In this section, we hope to provide some guidance on how property managers might understand the differing user requirements of the different stakeholder groups. We have chosen to discuss the key stakeholder groups of:

- occupiers
- the occupiers' customers/clients
- the local community.

Clearly, many more diverse stakeholder groups can be identified, but these generic categories will at least provide some understanding of how to gain insights into the needs of such groups.

Occupiers' requirements

Occupiers' requirements will vary with particular properties and particular occupiers. The property manager managing an operational asset on behalf of the occupier is best placed to research and fully understand his/her requirements. This does not mean, however, that the property manager of an investment property cannot approach the management of property occupied by the business in a similar way.

First, the manager must consider the general nature of the business or activity in which the occupier is engaged. Then, with increasing degree of detail, she should attempt to understand the specific characteristics and be able to place them within the context of the marketplace in which the occupier operates. For example, for retail occupiers, apart from understanding the type of products that they sell (e.g. clothing, food and drink, household goods/ interiors, pharmaceuticals, etc.,), one might differentiate between:

- independent retailers (fewer than 10 shops) and multiple chains
- specialist outlets (e.g. tie shops) or variety stores (selling a variety of goods)
- discount stores (competing on price) or customer-focused stores (competing on service)
- in-house managed chains, or shops managed on a franchise basis
- supermarkets
- charity shops.

This list is not comprehensive by any means, but such differentiation will help to provide some understanding of the nature of the retailer's business. However, further information must be sought before their property requirements are considered. For example, the property manager might consider the parent company's:

- size
- length of trading history
- recent acquisitions and mergers history
- ownership – is it family owned or a public limited company
- expansion plans
- main competitors.

Once such general information is understood, it is easier to analyse the requirements of the property user within this overall context of operation. First and foremost, the property manager must consider specific activities that will be carried out in the property. There may be a whole host of activities beyond selling on the shop floor that are required if it is a large retailer. The retailer might require:

- storage space
- office space
- staff facilities (including a canteen, changing facilities, relaxation area and crèche)
- a goods delivery area
- customer care facilities (lavatories, changing rooms, telephones, food and drink facilities, information and enquiries desks, etc.)
- display areas
- car parking.

Such lists provide the property manager with a basic understanding of the occupier's space requirements, but not necessarily the latter's specific needs in relation to that space. It is important to question how the particular property aids or hinders the occupier's business. Are there special features of the property that *directly* enhance sales, or are there impediments? Features to help increase sales might include good display areas or comfortable and clean customer care facilities. Features that might directly impede sales might include a lack of car parking or a lack of appropriate infrastructure to accept the most up to date electronic sales technology. Features that might *indirectly* impede sales might include poor staff facilities; thus hindering the chances of attracting and retaining good quality staff.

When considering the users' requirements, the manager should not only evaluate the state of the property in terms of the users' current requirements, but also consider their likely future requirements, whether that is expansion, contraction, relocation or diversification into other businesses. For example, see Case Study 1 on Borders Books to see how their real estate team has been focused on the identification of new sites.

Customers' requirements

For some property occupiers, their own requirements will be directly related to their customers' or clients' requirements for the property. Thus, in our retail example above, the retailer is concerned with the customer care facilities and the subsequent effect that will have on sales.

Similarly, surveys conducted for the brewing industry in the 1990s showed that amongst other features, such as clean lavatories and a smoke-free atmosphere, women customers preferred licensed premises to have clear window space, so that they could view the interior of the premises before choosing whether or not to enter. In an era of increased spending power for young women, such information was an important aid to the strategies of licensed premises occupiers (breweries and pub chains) who were trying to expand their customer base. Frosted pub windows were soon replaced with open, café style facades (and cleaner, more comfortable lavatories). Indeed, the public house retail chain, JD Wetherspoon, has attributed the success of its 2002 profits to its 'clean lavatories strategy': it has invested considerable capital in its property specifically to refurbish its lavatories and so continue to attract a large proportion of the female customer base.

In our case study of Clifford Chance (Case Study 2), you will see that the solicitors firm now provides a 'business lounge', where its clients can relax or work while waiting for responses or redrafts of documents.

In other types of business, the occupier's customers' requirements will not be so obvious. For example, for a manufacturing company, the client's requirements in the property might be more location related. The customers might never visit the company's premises, but might value its easy access to good transport networks (road, rail, air), which allow rapid dispatch of goods once ordered.

As we said above, the manager of an operational asset is probably best placed to keep up to date on the customer requirements of his particular organisation. However, the manager of an investment property would be advised to keep similarly informed of trends in her occupiers' marketplace, to ensure that her property continues to meet the needs of the most demanding users.

Local community requirements

Although the most important users might be seen as the occupiers and their customers or clients, increasingly, the local community in which the property is located can play a vital role in its success and development, or failure and demise. The degree to which the property manager should engage with the local community will depend largely upon the type of property being managed and its importance within that community. Similarly, the issues in which the property manager might become involved will also depend on property type and location. However, one universal factor is that cooperation and the building of long-term networks and relationships in the local community will prove far more successful than a 'head in the sand' approach, where the property manager communicates with the local community only when conflicts arise.

Property managers whose properties rely on the custom and goodwill of the local community, such as shopping centre managers, must become fully engaged with that community. Not only can this help to stem problems, but it can also reveal opportunities to further the property's success. The manager of one of the most successful shopping centres on the south coast has built up a complex network of support with which to tackle shoplifting and vandalism in the centre. The work of his own team of security guards is now augmented by local retailers *outside* the centre, the local police force, heads of local schools, youth leaders, etc.

People from the same network equally support him when it comes to promoting the centre. For example, the centre might sponsor a primary school's painting competition at Christmas, whereby all of the paintings are displayed in the forum of the shopping centre: an inexpensive but highly successful means of ensuring that children bring their parents to shop in the centre at least once at Christmas.

For managers of property more remote from residential areas, different local community networks will have to be built. For example, the manager of an out-of-town industrial park might be more concerned with the local wildlife trust, who have an interest in the birds nesting and feeding in and around the park, or badgers building their setts on the park's edge. More often than not, the coexistence of wildlife is compatible with the property's primary use and, indeed, might be very complementary. The erection of a dozen nesting boxes in the park's trees might not only satisfy good relations with the wildlife trust, but enhance the environment for the employees on the industrial park.

In essence, it is up to each property manager to seek out the relevant user groups in the local community and address their requirements. There is no short cut to building relationships with different stakeholders, but in the next section we provide some suggestions for how to facilitate better networks.

Management relationships with the wider user community

The property manager must understand the user requirements of the different stakeholders, and try to appreciate the special relationships that she might have with each of the stakeholder groups and which they, in turn, might have with each other. To assist in this understanding, we have identified four key stakeholder groups who form part of the wider user community and believe that it is worth discussing relationships amongst them.

The landlord and tenant relationship

The landlord and tenant relationship is one of the most important and interesting to observe and an examination of it is of particular interest in the context of modern strategic property management. Indeed, the history of the landlord and tenant relationship in the UK is primarily responsible for the way in which property management has been perceived, practised and taught for decades. It is the relationship that has perhaps changed most dramatically in our increasingly pluralistic society. For the change in emphasis in this relationship has acted both as a driver of a more strategic approach to management and, in some sense, is a direct consequence of this approach.

In the UK, the landlord–tenant relationship has been rooted in the notion of continuity, and the permanence of ownership has been important. This culture prevails, even with new types of landowner, where there is a presumption that stability and long-term relationships are best. The relationship with tenants might be viewed at best as one based on protectionism and mutuality, and at worst, as exploitative. Traditionally, power has been seen to lie with the landlord and in terms of tenant rights, security for the tenant has been seen as a particularly important issue.

Implications for the role of property management
The problems arising from the old landed tradition have left a legacy of:

- perceived need to simplify and restructure old systems of land holding (e.g. the Law of Property Act 1925 and the Commonhold and Leasehold Reform Act 2002)
- perceived need for government intervention to protect the position of tenants (e.g. the Rent Acts, Landlord and Tenant Acts, Code of Practice for Commercial Leases in England and Wales)

- a need for action to enable residential occupiers to gain certain rights including Enfranchisement (e.g. Leasehold Reform Act 1967, Leasehold Reform, Housing and Urban Development Act, 1993; Commonhold Act and Leasehold Reform 2002).

Within the commercial sector the emphasis of management has been on achieving an equitable division of power and rights between the landlord and tenant, while not disturbing the ultimate ownership balance and so maintaining our tradition of leasehold occupation. For most commercial property owners, the goal is achieving an acceptable balance between the risks involved in investing large capital sums in property and the returns that might be achieved. The nature of property, *per se*, is often irrelevant.

This arm's-length attitude to property has resulted in an increasing 'technicalisation' of the process of property management. Any notion of management theory in relation to property management was almost ignored. Estate or property management was seen as a *technical* exercise to be carried out on behalf of commercially minded owners with the aim of efficient management to ensure that:

- tenants paid rent
- tenants fulfilled their (seemingly increasing) liabilities
- tenants accepted the risks of occupation.

On the other side of the equation:

- landlords reserved the right to enter in case of default
- landlords reserved the right to terminate the lease for their own occupation or to redevelop.

As a rule, this technical form of property management has traditionally been undertaken by qualified surveyors either in-house, or more frequently, acting as agents. With the evolution of the role of the surveyor as property manager, the emphasis has been on:

- property maintenance
- rent collection and review
- ensuring tenant compliance
- other matters involving legal and associated work (e.g. taxation, boundary disputes, building contracts).

Emphasis has been on *control*, *regulation* and *knowledge*. The prevailing culture for landlords and tenants at the time we started teaching the 'user perspective' at Portsmouth was certainly not one of partnership, but more one of divorce. This is further evidenced in the property development field, where the literature is devoted to developing models that describe a series of 'players', most of whom are viewed as in conflict. In the USA, developers tried to respond to occupier demands. However, in the UK there was an underlying belief that the *user* of the building was not the driving force behind property development, it was the needs of the developer and investor that held sway (see for example: Healy, 1992; Scott, 1996).

There are now growing signs that the occupier is a recognisable force (see Sayce *et al.*, 2000), and recent discussions between the UK government and the British Property Federation have resulted in a voluntary Code of Practice in respect of the grant and management of leases (see Chapter 8). Nevertheless, work still needs to be done to ensure that there is a common understanding of the needs of different property users. If the landlord–tenant relationship is not capable of achieving this shared understanding, productivity will be consistently undermined in a world where the property manager is increasingly expected to build relationships with multiple stakeholders.

Implications for the efficient operation of the property markets

As we said earlier, institutional arrangements affect and are affected by relationships in society. Thus the institutions that helped to shape the landlord and tenant relationship acted to preserve this arm's-length approach in the 1970s and 1980s. The financial organisations that dominated the ownership of property (insurance companies, banks, pension funds) were powerful not only with their influence over the design of large buildings and the shape of lease arrangements, due to their purchasing power, but also in the direction of property research and publications.

As a consequence, the institutional arrangement of the commercial property market by the late 1980s was characterised by:

- leases that had evolved into the so-called *institutional leases* (McIntosh and Sykes, 1985), of 25 years, with full repairing and insuring ('FRI') obligations on the part of the tenant and 5-yearly, upwards-only rent reviews
- leases that contained covenants which passed property risks from the landlord to the tenant
- landlord and tenant relationships that were characterised by conflict
- an apparent lack of challenge to the hierarchy.

This situation is detailed in Dubben and Sayce (1991), who argued that:

- the UK lease structure was out of step with other countries
- the desire to operate a 'hands off' approach to property could lead to lack of taking of opportunities to enhance performance
- changes (including the growth of international companies) might challenge the accepted view of lease length and lease terms.

In turn, the collapse of the property markets in the early 1990s (see Fraser, 1993; Isaac, 1998) and the increasingly global nature of economies – and hence major property occupiers (see Dicken, 1998) – have led to a reappraisal of the institutional arrangement of the property market. However, despite recognition of technological, social and political change, Lizieri *et al.* (1997) argue that leases and occupiers' demands have not changed as much as had been thought, although more flexibility has been occasioned by stronger tenant power, brought about by weak demand.

We believe that this is an ongoing trend. We recognise that the investment market must be based on the stability afforded by longer leases and terms that reduce the landlord's risk at the expense of the tenant's. However, societal trends suggest that more flexible working relationships will prevail, based on a forward looking partnership approach, which acknowledges the role of *multiple* stakeholders in the management of the property. The landlord–tenant relationship will still form the lynchpin to this pluralistic approach.

Implications for future patterns of tenure

As a consequence, the institutional arrangement of the commercial property market in the early twenty-first century is more likely to be characterised by:

- shorter leases with break clauses, fewer of which will have upwards-only rent reviews
- leases that contain covenants which *share* property risks between landlord and tenant or involve shared risks and returns, through, for example, turnover rents
- landlord–tenant relationships that are characterised by partnership approaches
- a breakdown in the hierarchy of the landlord–tenant relationship, replaced by a system of much more dynamic power relationships; and
- a more 'hands on' approach to property management which seeks opportunities to enhance performance of the property – economically, socially and environmentally.

Property managers and relationship with government

When considering the relationship between the property owner and the state, or government, it is worth considering the power connotations associated with the ownership and management of land. The notion of land as power is embodied within UK law, with the technical ownership of land lying in the Crown. In theory, land belongs to the Crown and, in theory, the monarch therefore has power. In practice, neither is true.

The development of *organisational* power (such as the Church), *individual* power (the aristocracy) and *corporate* power (global corporations) is reflected by their effective control over land. In the early twentieth century, power in the UK was seen to lie with landed individuals and organisational landowners: predominantly the aristocracy and organisations such as the Church. Nevertheless, writing in the 1970s, Ratcliffe acknowledged the change that had already been brought about by the state exercising its regulatory control over land. He contended that land markets were so constrained by administrative and legislative frameworks that public policy was actually the main driver 'little influenced by any other action on the part of the owner'. (Ratcliffe, 1976).

Since then, the advent of global corporatism has shifted the power pendulum from state to corporation in many countries around the world (Hertz, 2001; Monbiot, 2001). However, citizen groups are becoming more vociferous in their attempts to redress this balance and stem the tide of globalisation. Big issues in terms of land tenure and management over the first decade of the twenty-first century are likely to involve environmental requirements and imperatives arising from closer economic and social integration. Corporate social responsibility has moved surprisingly rapidly up the corporate agenda and is already becoming a factor within property decision making.

While global corporations will undoubtedly remain powerful, in the UK there is a strong alliance between government and citizen groups to push an agenda of social inclusion and environmental improvement. Both political priorities are likely to give rise to the need for more liaison between the property manager and the state, and the property manager and local community.

The property manager's relationship with the state is increasingly based on adherence to complex sets of regulations, many stemming from Europe, but now enshrined in UK institutions. As well as being an expert on property, the property manager must now constantly update her knowledge of legislative requirements, and keep herself informed and involved in the emerging economic and social development policy of the region, county and district/borough. Property managers should become involved in local business associations and maintain regular formal and informal contact with the local authority officers.

The property manager and the public

Social systems are not only complex, but also stretch across time and space. However, although in the UK we have moved towards distributed *networks* of social organisation, hierarchies are still a feature of society in many countries. Many societal elements, such as families, corporations and government agencies continue to operate in a top-down manner. The family is generally considered to be the basic building block of any society. Social norms are built around the home, and then comprise widening circles of interactions (like ripples on a pond), with friends and neighbours, other citizens and government agencies.

The way in which society functions, is a reflection of its dynamic nature and a continually emerging process, defining social, cultural, economic and political boundaries. All property managers will find themselves in complex and uncertain situations from time to time. Based on their social experience and professional training, they have to choose between different courses of action and believe that they can judge the appropriateness of these (Long, 1989).

The way in which the property manager can interact with the local community will depend on the following.

Existing networks of social relations

For example, in a community characterised by multi-stranded relationships, with many diverse subgroups and no clear hierarchical structure, the property manager may have difficulty in interacting with the community because of its disparate nature and its lack of experience in operating collectively (see Steins, 1995). In such situations, there might be no clear path into the community, and no obvious community leaders to offer introductions and help commend the property manager to the community. This is, perhaps, the most difficult of situations in which to find oneself. Often the property manager will need to initiate liaison by advertising the need for an informal 'advisory' group, such as 'Friends of the … [property's name]'. In two of our Case Studies (4: The Youth Hostel Association and 5: Ardtornish Estate), employees of the property owning organisation live within the local community and provide an instant connection between management and the community.

Interaction between the property users and the property

The degree of interaction already taking place between the local community and the property will provide the property manager with an avenue to begin community liaison. This might be something that is initially based on potential conflict. For example, the manager of an office development might find that the attractive piazza outside the office has become a magnet for local skateboarders. Rather than try to resolve the conflict by getting security guards to deal with each individual skateboarder in turn, a more constructive long-term solution might be to encourage the skateboarders to form as a group and then support their application to the local authority for improved facilities elsewhere. The formation of individuals into groups in such situations is usually imperative before constructive liaison can take place.

The meaning the stakeholders attribute to the property

It is common for different property users to attribute quite different meanings to a property. For example, on a landed estate, the woodland that is favoured by the head forester and gamekeeper for shooting purposes might also have become a popular dog walking area for local residents. At certain times (during the rearing of the pheasants and, of course, shooting days) dog walking might be totally incompatible with the shoot.[1] Resolution in this situation must be based on shared understanding and respect. Formalising the situation might result in the dog walkers being issued annual permits to walk, with restrictions (such as dogs on leads at certain times and no access on shooting days) and responsibilities (such as a requirement for walkers to look out for poachers, etc.).

Perceptions of the wider environment in which the property is embedded

Users will react not only to their expectations of the property itself, but also to the wider environment in which it is embedded. Sometimes the property manager's attempt to resolve multiple use might need to extend beyond her own boundary. For example, the manager of a hotel in a rural community might realise that the local community has no village hall or meeting place. While the hotel is able to charge high prices for conference facilities, it might be useful to act as a low-cost venue for local groups. The place of the hotel in the community as the primary meeting hall could be vital in both securing the future of the community and of the hotel. A West Country pub, which was threatened with closure by a brewery was felt to be so important by the local community that they purchased it, and it now provides a wealth of functions for the village.

Observations and expectations of how others behave

In the evaluation of others' behaviour, users will use social experience gained from their involvement in the property, as well as experience from everyday life (Runge, 1981). Often, if users believe that other users are reneging on agreements, then they will soon refuse to adhere to their own conditions. So, in our example of the dog walkers above, regulars will be expected to put peer pressure on an influx of new dog walkers to obtain permits and comply with the conditions along with everyone else. If they do not obtain permits, the system will break down.

The property manager, faced with different stakeholder groups, must try to anticipate and work with the needs of each group. In determining their motivations, values and norms, the property manager must appreciate the effect that local influences have had on individuals' strategies, including, amongst other things: (1) knowledge of the opportunity cost of selecting certain strategies (see Galjart, 1992); and (2) past experiences.

For example, a successful collective action will have a positive influence on collective decision making. Thus, if a university has a history of working well with its neighbours, the local council, local interest groups and local businesses, then individual members of such groups will be encouraged to seek mutually satisfying solutions to new problems as they arise. If, however, there is a history of conflict and an adversarial approach, which encourages each stakeholder group to negotiate hard for its own interest, then this culture will tend to prevail and may well discourage a collective approach to future problems.

As a general rule, it is desirable to construct categories of user groups, so that some patterns of use, norms, values, etc., can be established. These in turn will help to establish separate incentive structures for different types of user groups. Such distinctions are important since they help to explain the types of pressures on property and the interests of the different groups in the evolution of institutions governing its use. It is only through the determination of varied incentive structures that we will be able to understand the relative needs of each user group. Such observations will help to predict the type and extent of demands that specific user groups might make on the property. This will help us to understand the likelihood that they will be able to: (1) act in cooperation with other users from their particular group to restrict use of the property; and (2) act in cooperation with other types of users, in the overall management of the property.[2]

For many properties, continued viability is dependent upon the continuation of combined uses (see Case Study 5). Limitation of the property to a single use is not an option and institutions must be based, therefore, on this multiple-use imperative.

Conclusion

Knowledge of the property's user community and their interests and requirements is essential to the development of an effective strategy for property, whether for corporate, community or investment purposes. This chapter has demonstrated how wide the stakeholder community can be for different types of property. Through social and cultural exploration, we have tried to broaden the reader's understanding of the 'property user group' concept by providing some historical context. However, we hope we have also provided something of a framework through which it is possible to identify different stakeholder groups and some practical ideas as to how problems might be approached and resolved. Perhaps the most important message to take from this chapter is the positive impact dialogue with key property users can have for strategic development and implementation.

References

Dicken, P. (1998) *Global Shift: transforming the world economy*. Paul Chapman Ltd, London.

Dubben, N. & Sayce, S. (1991) *Property Portfolio Management: an introduction*. Routledge, London.

Fraser, W.D. (1993) *Principles of Property Investment and Pricing*. Macmillan, Basingstoke.

Galjart, B. (1992) Cooperation as pooling: a rational choice perspective. *Sociologia Ruralis*, **XXXII** 389–407.

Healy, P. (1992) An institutional model of the development process. *Journal of Property Research*, **9** (1) 33–46.

Hertz, N. (2001) *The Silent Takeover: Global Capitalism and the Death of Democracy*. Heinemann, London.

Isaac, D. (1998) *Property Investment*. Macmillan, Basingstoke.

Kiser, L.L. & Ostrom, E. (1982) The three worlds of action: a metatheoretical synthesis of institutional approaches. In *Strategies of Political Inquiry* (ed. E. Ostrom). Sage, Beverly Hills.

Lizieri, C., Crosby, N., Gibson, V., Murdoch, S. & Ward, C. (1997) *Right Space, Right Place? A study of the impact of changing business practices on the property market.* RICS Books, London.

Long, N. (1989). *Encounters at the Interface: A Perspective on Social Discontinuities in Rural Development.* Wageningen Sociological Studies No. 27, Wageningen Agricultural University, Wageningen, Netherlands.

McIntosh, A.P.J. & Sykes, S. (1985) *A Guide to Institutional Property Investment.* Macmillan, London.

Monbiot, G. (2001) *Captive State: the corporate takeover of Britain.* Pan, London.

Porter, M. (1998) *Competitive Strategy: techniques for analysing industries and competitors.* Free Press, New York.

Ratcliffe, J. (1976) *Land Policy: an explanation of the nature of land in society.* Hutchinson, London.

Runge, C.F. (1981) Common property externalities: isolation, assurance, and resource depletion in a traditional grazing context, *American Journal of Agricultural Economics*, **63** 595–607.

Sayce, S., Cuthbert, M., Iball, H. & Parnell, P. (2000) The business case for sustainable property: initial findings of the research team. Presentation to *The Sustainable Construction Conference*, London, 12 July.

Scott, P. (1996) *The Property Masters: a history of the British commercial property sector.* E.&F.N. Spon, London.

Steins, N.A. (1995) Securing access to the sea: the creation of an artificial common property resource. Paper presented at the *5th International Conference of the International Association for the Study of Common Property*, 24–28 May, Bodoe, Norway.

Sugden, R. (1984) Reciprocity: the supply of public goods through voluntary contribution. *Economic Journal*, **94** 772–787.

Further reading

Callon, M. & Law, J. (1995) Agency and the hybrid collectif. *South Atlantic Quarterly*, **94** 481–507.

Endnotes

[1] The local dog walkers might have no rights to the woods at all if there are no defined footpaths through them, nevertheless, their long-term presence and attitude might be a force to be reckoned with!

[2] Kiser and Ostrom (1982) identify three characteristics of the community which are relevant to such institutional analysis: (1) the level of common understanding; (2) the similarity in individuals' preferences; and (3) the distribution of resources among those affected by a decision to be made. Sugden (1984) argues that the more heterogeneous a community, the more difficult coordination becomes. Ostrom (1990, p. 36) explains that the type and extent of shared norms amongst the user group will have an important impact on the degree of opportunistic behaviour employed by individuals.

Chapter 6
Organisational Objectives in Relation to Corporate Property

Introduction

Whatever industry a firm is part of, and whatever its organisational objectives, it will rely on property to support its business function. Most often this will be through its role as an occupier, but also frequently as an investor, wherever corporate property is held freehold and particularly where the portfolio is used to raise funds, and as a developer where the existing estate needs to undergo physical change. Property is thus a vital component of business, just as human resources, customers and capital are.

As firms have become more aware of the value of their real estate portfolio, both as a capital and operational asset, it has become more common (although not commonplace) and increasingly necessary for business executives to consider the support that the corporate property can offer to the overall corporate strategy. Research suggests firms that tie their property strategy to their corporate strategy and management system enjoy an improved competitive position as a result. Furthermore, the review carried out by Rodriguez and Sirmans (1996) suggests that 'decisions concerning corporate real estate assets have significant effects on firm value' (p. 26). The impact of property decisions can affect share value directly; real estate and operational business managers beware.

This chapter links the ideas commonly associated with business strategy to the strategic management of property via the organisational objectives that strategy produces. Business strategy is a well developed subject area with a wide literature, some would argue dating back to the fourth century BC (Mintzberg, 1990). Consequently there are a variety of schools of thought as to how business strategy should be developed. This book does not aim to contribute to the development of business strategy theory. However, it is difficult to develop an effective property strategy without an understanding of business strategy.

While we acknowledge the variety of theories and schools that exist, we have elected to use Porter's contribution as the basis for our discussion here (Porter, 1998). Porter's work focuses on the analysis of a business and the industry within which it operates in order to identify the best means of establishing and/or retaining competitive advantage. Porter's work is widely acknowledged as one of the most influential in modern business management. Inevitably it is one of the most widely read. It is also sufficiently well developed and flexible to be capable of broad application across a range of different business types. This allows us to explore the property implications of a range of different strategies that might be applied to different organisations.

Organisational objectives

It is useful first to clarify some terminology. This chapter focuses on how property can contribute to the achievement of an organisation's 'objectives'. Objectives are statements of *what* we want to achieve. These objectives will normally be clearly articulated and may vary from the specific, e.g. 'to double the number of retail outlets within two years', to the general, e.g. 'to offer budget accommodation to young people of limited means', to take examples from case studies used later. In some instances the organisational objective might simply be to survive. The business strategy provides the means through which these objectives are reached, in light of the political–economic and industry-specific context. Strategies are statements of *how* we intend to achieve our objectives.

Both the organisational objectives and the business strategy developed to achieve them may change over time and in response to external influences. They therefore have to be dynamic and sensitive to change. Within the framework we provide for the analysis of the property strategy, this dynamism is reflected in the performance evaluation/strategy formulation loop. This section of the framework allows for a continuous process of learning from the experience gained through the operation of the property strategy. We believe that this iterative process of review and improvement is essential to good property strategy, and, we would suggest, to good business strategy too.

Strategy

We have used the term *strategy* in relation to real estate within this text to refer to a deliberate plan for the operation of an organisation's real estate portfolio. Within strategic business management, the term is used to describe a clearly defined plan through which a business will seek to optimise its operating capacity, developed in the light of a variety of constraining factors such as technology, available capital, market conditions. Unfortunately, as much of the literature points out, the two are not often seen together, even now. It is rare to find a business operating without an overall business strategy, but it is quite common to find one operating without a property strategy (Roulac, 2001).

This chapter gives us the opportunity to explore why a lack of property strategy is a problem for any organisation. We examine the impact a property strategy can have on a business strategy using a developed strategic business management theory as a basic framework. Through this we can try to make clear the very direct ways in which an organisation's property can be made to support organisational objectives. It is important to remember, however, that we are providing a framework, not a 'recipe'. Each business and real estate portfolio is different, and the same business may have very different property requirements at different times. They have to be assessed individually. As Gibson and Barkham (2001) identified in their discussion of what might constitute the 'best real estate strategy for an organisation:

> 'Best ... was ... best for that organization at a particular point in time from the perspective of the most senior corporate real estate manager'
>
> Gibson and Barkham, 2001, p. 110

The property strategy has to interpret, and align with, the business strategy, which inevitably changes over time.

Porter's theory of competitive advantage

As previously mentioned, this chapter is based on Porter's theory of competitive advantage, the management theory we are using. This theory is based on a dynamic but consistent system for analysing industries. The underpinning premise is that once an industry has been analysed, it is possible for an organisation within that industry to develop a competitive strategy to allow it to achieve its objectives (Porter, 1998).

Porter's theory is relatively straightforward. It simplifies the dynamics of any industry to five basic competitive forces:

- the threat of new entrants
- the bargaining power of suppliers
- the threat of substitute products or services
- the bargaining power of suppliers
- rivalry amongst existing firms.

This can be expressed diagramatically as in Fig. 6.1.

The intensity of these five forces sets the extent to which profits can be made within the industry as a whole, over the long term. Porter points out that in the short term, economic conditions will affect the profitability of companies within the industry but the overall structure will remain the same.

An analysis of these forces as they affect the industry within which your organisation operates will enable the development of an effective strategy to 'find a position in the industry where the company can best defend itself against these competitive forces or can influence them in its favour' (Porter, 1998, p. 4).

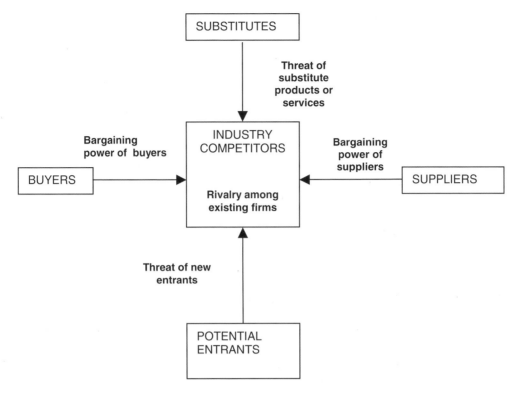

Fig. 6.1   The five competitive forces that determine industry profitability. Source: Porter, M. (1998) *Competitive Strategy*. Free Press, New York

This requires a clear understanding of the position of the organisation within its industry and its operating strengths and weaknesses. However, once such information is established a strategy that will enable an organisation to defend its position can be selected from one of three generics Porter identifies:

- overall cost leadership
- differentiation
- focus.

Analysis of the industry will enable an organisation to establish an organisational objective. Analysis of the business will enable the most appropriate of Porter's generic competitive strategies to be identified. Once these two are known it is possible to consider the way in which the property strategy can support the organisational objectives.

Property as part of competitive strategy

Whether the firm is a retail, industrial, office or leisure occupier, the property it occupies can be used to support whichever generic competitive strategy is adopted. If the role of the property is not considered it can seriously undermine even the most carefully thought through and well developed business strategy. This chapter goes on to look in turn at each of the three generic competitive strategies that Porter identifies. It explores ways in which the property portfolio can be used to support them, demonstrating why it is so important that a strategy is developed for the real estate which aligns with the objectives of the organisation as a whole.

Overall cost leadership

Overall cost leadership requires a substantial commitment from the organisation. In order to produce the cheapest product or service within a particular industry the firm must have identified and acted upon more efficiency measures and economies of scale than the next most efficient organisation, without compromising quality and standards. The firm must also undertake to maintain this competitive advantage, requiring a substantial investment in time and performance measurement. This is a tall order for any organisation.

The foundation of such a strategy is often favourable access to a supply of raw materials or a distribution network. If a business is operating in an industry in which the bargaining power of suppliers is a significant force, regular access to supplies at a stable price would make overall cost leadership a viable business strategy.

Given that real estate is often the second largest cost a business faces after labour, ensuring that the property strategy is aligned with the business strategy is essential. It is also essential that the property is approached strategically. It would be tempting in such a situation to see the property portfolio as a cost base that needs minimising, i.e., reduce cost by getting rid of property. But there are three issues to bear in mind here:

- if the business is still to operate it has to have some property (the cost is never going to be zero)
- divesting an organisation of property is often very expensive (disposals may cost a business more than retentions)
- trying to operate out of insufficient or inappropriate property will substantially undermine business performance.

A perhaps more useful (strategic) way to look at the property, is through the contribution it makes to the business objective. The corporate portfolio has to contribute marginally more effectively to profit maximisation than the closest competitors' property. The real estate strategy can seek to actively support this in a number of ways.

Optimising occupancy costs

Understanding the contribution a business makes to a location can provide opportunities to negotiate lower occupancy costs. A business pursuing a cost minimisation strategy may well be a high volume trader that produces related business for neighbouring occupiers. This presents a strong bargaining position at rent review or lease renewal. In a climate where shorter lease lengths and greater flexibility for the tenant are becoming commonplace, being willing to take a relatively long lease can provide the leverage to obtain a reduced rent.

Identifying the lowest cost locations in which to set up operations will clearly facilitate cost reduction but has to be considered in combination with other factors. Costs will not be reduced if:

- obligations under existing property are expensive to terminate
- the lowest cost location is one where no one wants to work, leading to a high staff turnover
- such a location is too far from the firm's market, leading to reduced demand.

However, location remains an important factor within a firm's competitive strategy. Where cost is the issue, consolidating activities in one location may improve a firm's negotiating terms by increasing the amount of space required at one site. If such consolidation is within the overall strategy, it may be important to consider the purchase of sufficient land for expansion, particularly where the firm's presence may increase land values itself, or where having to relocate or decentralise activities would be detrimental to the cost structure.

Whatever industry an organisation operates within, location issues will affect productivity. This is not just a customer base issue, it also relates to labour supply, supply of materials, access to a distribution network, commuting distances for staff and so on. A cost-based approach may identify a location as expensive and make a decision to move to cheaper space look attractive. A strategic approach would be to identify what that location brings to the business and whether losing it would cost productivity more than any reduction in rent would achieve. Once relocation expenses are also taken into account the decision to relocate can be very expensive.

A strategic decision can only be taken about a site if its contribution to the business is fully understood. This requires a location model that accurately reflects the factors affecting the business. For a retailer this is likely to be customer base, catchment area, demographics, retail mix and so on, for a manufacturer access to supplies, local labour force, transport network and access to market. Any such model should be able to identify the optimum location, against which any other location can be judged. If the model identifies areas where real estate is expensive, location is likely to repay its cost in improved profit margins and greater sales volumes. However, the level of supply and demand within the local property market will also have to be taken into account.

Workspace revolution

Reconfiguring existing real estate to improve capacity and the efficiency of the workforce can bring reduced costs and improved productivity. A clear understanding of how a worker actually uses his or her space is required for this. In a manufacturing context, design of new facilities and redesign of existing facilities to complement a production process can substantially improve productivity. Communication between different departments can be improved, 'ownership' of the production process by the whole staff can be encouraged, a smooth production system can be developed.

A property strategy seeking to support cost minimisation will benefit from taking a ground-up approach to this issue and studying the reality of what actually happens in a building. Performance data showing the number of people per square metre against cost per square metre and sales per square metre are undoubtedly valuable, but a study of what those people are actually doing in the space to make the sales is what identifies where effective space and cost savings can be made.

It is often tempting to consider new ways of using space or 'workplace initiatives' as an argument for reducing space requirements. It may well be that technological advances have liberated many office workers from their desks. However, it has not reduced the overall requirement for space. Space may be used in a more productive way and single offices are becoming less common, particularly in new office layouts, but space is still required and more may be required if extensive investment in technology is to take place in order to facilitate these workplace initiatives. A firm pursuing overall cost leadership would find a reorganisation of workplace practices an unsuccessful avenue for cost reduction as yet. However, it may find the reconfiguration of existing space to better reflect work patterns helpful.

Aligning interior environment with business activity

Ensuring the facilities and services within a building are appropriate for its use will again reduce cost and increase productivity. It might be tempting to take office space that is not air-conditioned, as being cheaper to rent and potentially cheaper to run. However, this will significantly reduce the capacity of a building, often making it a false economy.

Ensuring the facilities management system is operating at maximum efficiency will also have an impact: services are a substantial business cost and while ensuring the boiler is regularly maintained may be incredibly dull, it will make a difference to the running costs of a business. Service engineers will recount tales of traffic lights being run off a building's electricity supply and cleaners turning all the lights on at 6 a.m. and leaving them on.

Raising capital

Traditionally, firms not directly involved in the property business have been slow to identify the potential for the property portfolio in raising capital. Using the property portfolio as security can provide investment capital more cheaply than the money markets. The increased use of sale and leaseback arrangements is a manifestation of the greater awareness of the potential of this source of finance. However, this also needs to be considered in light of the business strategy. Short-term cash-flow might be eased by the sale of property but long-term property costs may increase. A building owned on a long leasehold interest or freehold which is sold and leased back at market rent will turn from an asset into a regular outgoing and may increase risk. If the capital raised is invested in plant and machinery that increases productivity above and beyond any increase in long-term property costs, the strategy will have worked; if it does not the long-term future of the business may have been jeopardised.

Maximise space devoted to the revenue raising function

To minimise costs an organisation has to make the most effective use of space within its portfolio. This means devoting as much of it as possible to the major fee earning activity of the firm. This has clearly been an element of the property strategy applied to most supermarkets. The major fee earning is done through the retail space so as much of the floor area as possible is devoted to presenting merchandise to the customers. The storage is minimal by comparison. They have been able to reduce the amount of space set aside for storage through the development of just-in-time delivery systems. However, this has simultaneously increased their reliance on transport networks and warehousing.

So, reducing the real estate portfolio is not necessarily an effective way to support a cost minimisation strategy, in fact it can cost more than it saves, and remember that an assigned lease can (and often does) come back to haunt a business. However, if the property strategy is developed with a view to cost minimisation, many opportunities can be identified to reduce costs while continuing to support the business function with no loss in performance. Given that the vast majority of businesses do not have a property strategy, you can develop some competitive edge almost immediately.

Differentiation

Differentiation as a strategy is based on developing a product or service that is clearly perceived as unique by the industry as a whole. The examples Porter (1998, p. 37) gives are:

- brand image
- technology
- customer service
- dealer network
- product features.

If a firm adopts differentiation as its competitive strategy, it has to strive to develop a unique product characteristic accepted across the industry and has to retain it. The firm's property portfolio can directly support this process.

Brand Identification

The development of 'brands' has been one of the major factors affecting businesses in the late twentieth and early twenty-first centuries. While it might be most clearly associated with retailers such as Nike and Gap, it has an impact across all the major industry sectors. Branding is often a significant part of a differentiation strategy and can be directly supported by corporate real estate.

An organisation's property is often its closest interface with its customer base. This is not limited to retailing. Offices provide the main meeting space for service provider and client, and be they former accountants, lawyers, advertising agencies or architects, the property will convey a strong message to the visitor. If the property is incorporated into the brand image, the message can be very strong.

Some of the most obvious examples in this area come from food retailing – for example, McDonald's golden arches and Pizza Hut's 'hut' shaped restaurant, are clear examples of a firm's property making a bold statement about brand identification. But they are by no means confined to restaurants. One of the earliest was the development of the Oxo Tower in London, (coincidentally now a restaurant) where the firm's brand logo was designed into the fabric of a very prominent building on the River Thames in order to circumvent regulations regarding advertising.

- the NatWest Tower in the City of London was designed to reflect the bank's brand logo
- the Elf Towers at La Defense on the outskirts of Paris have been designed to make a very dramatic statement about that firm
- Ikea stores tend to be visible from a long distance because of the distinctive blue and yellow livery.

Location, location, location

Differentiation may rely in establishing particular characteristics about the organisation which set it apart from others. This may be about image, for example in luxury retailing, where the location of outlets may be crucial. Where it is about convenience or having the most extensive network of locations, the property must be identified with accessibility preferably with complementary services on site.

Multiplex cinemas, for example, have adopted a strategy of differentiation by striving to be accepted by the cinema-goer as offering comfort, access, choice and additional services such as food. The property has to support this strategy as location is crucial in terms of access, parking and potential audience.

Customer service and product features

An organisation may seek differentiation by establishing itself as a market leader in terms of the services and products it offers its customers and clients. The property can often make a big contribution here, given that it is the major interface between business and client. The most obvious examples are within the leisure sector where hotels provide a bewildering range of services based on accommodation. This is not restricted to the luxury market, one budget operator will differentiate from another through location and provision of facilities.

Other examples include major airlines offering airport lounges to particular customers, supermarkets offering crèche facilities and universities offering accommodation to first-year undergraduates and overseas students. All of these services and products rely on the corporate real estate.

Proactive property strategy

Where the business strategy is differentiation, the organisation has to encourage the generation of new differentiation ideas. Given the importance of property in communicating with the client and customer base, the inclusion of the corporate real estate team within strategy development will support this. It is the real estate team that will have information on local property markets, the availability of space, the current efficiency of space use. Excluding this perspective from strategy development will translate into lost business opportunities.

Focus

The final generic strategy Porter (1998) identifies is focus. An organisation can defend its position within its industry from the five competitive forces by focusing on a narrow segment of the market. This may be a narrow geographical location, a type of customer or a variation within a product range, for example. The success of such a strategy is based on serving the particular segment of the market better than any other firm within the industry.

This strategy differs from the first two by not being industry wide in nature. Its very essence is to avoid appealing to the whole customer base in order to appeal more effectively to its target market. This can allow the firm simultaneously to achieve either cost advantages or market differentiation, giving further defence against the five competitive forces.

By adopting focus as a competitive strategy a firm is relying on its ability to identify, attract and retain a specific segment of a market. Corporate property will underpin a number of strategies here.

Geographical focus

If the focus is geographical, for example being the main provider of legal or accountancy services in a region, the property portfolio should be located to maximise local awareness of the firm. The property is likely to be the most striking communication of the organisation's brand image within its target market. This makes it crucial to the strategy that the message conveyed is positive and is maximised. Brand loyalty can be generated through the association of a business with a particular location, the characteristics of the organisation can be reflected and emphasised. The real estate has to be incorporated into the business strategy if the latter is to be effective.

Customer focus

If the focus is on a specific type of customer, the property must support the customer experience and reinforce the characteristics of the organisation that attracted the customer in. The service has to meet customer expectations, as does the environment. The property has to provide access to the customer and allow the product to be seen by its target consumer. Building design and location will be fundamental to these issues and will be supported by a detailed location model.

The most obvious example is luxury retailing, where the organisation is focusing on providing high-end goods to high-income clients. A bridal shop for example, may operate on an appointment only basis, allowing a single client full use of the store and the complete attention of staff for a period of time. The customer experience will rely on the quality of the environment as well as the service. The success of such a strategy will also rely on an appropriate location. The real estate decision is fundamental in this type of business.

Product focus

If the strategy is to focus on a particular product within a market, the property will have to support delivery of the product. This may require a bespoke manufacturing and testing system, or it may require a specific location, on the waterfront, for example. An obvious example is the luxury car market. The manufacture of hand-built specialist sports cars is a very focused operation if one compares it to the mass, standardised production techniques in the rest of the motor industry. The property has to accommodate a bespoke, hand-built car manufacturing process, precision engineering techniques and provide space for testing. It also has to accommodate the customer in an appropriate environment. As a major capital investment there has to be little risk of relocation. The corporate portfolio can only support this type of operation if the property strategy is developed in conjunction with the business strategy.

Whichever business strategy an organisation adopts, whatever industry it operates within, the corporate property at its disposal can be used in one of two ways: to support the strategy or not to undermine the strategy. It is not sufficient to say that having a property strategy aligned with your business strategy will make a positive contribution to the achievement of organisational objectives. It would perhaps be clearer to say that not having put such a strategy in place will hinder the achievement of organisational objectives and reduce competitive advantage.

This chapter concludes with a table (Table 6.1) outlining some of the ways in which corporate real estate can support a chosen business strategy. This list is

Table 6.1 Aligning real estate with business strategy

Competitive strategy	Property strategy
Focus	Identify customer base, place business close to customer base, support customer experience
Differentiation	Convey brand image, organisation characteristics, support business activity, identify property based differentiation opportunities
Overall cost leadership	Optimise occupancy costs, support business function, maximise space devoted to income generating function, reconfigure internal layout, identify potential for capital release

certainly not definitive and is inevitably limited by being general rather than specific, but we considered it helpful. However, the greatest difference can be made by having a detailed understanding of both the business and the real estate; this is where the support one can give the other becomes clear.

Exercise 6.1 Identifying generic business strategies

Consider the following questions with regard to an organisation you work for, or have worked for in the past.

- Which of the three generic business strategies best describes that organisation?
- To what extent does its real estate portfolio also reflect that business strategy?
- How could the real estate have been changed to better reflect the business strategy?
- Is the selected business strategy the most appropriate for that particular business?

References

Gibson, V. & Barkham, R. (2001) Corporate real estate management in the retail sector: investigation of current strategy and structure. *Journal of Real Estate Research*, **22** (1/2) 107-2.

Mintzberg, H. (1990) The Design School: reconsidering the basic premises of strategic management. *Strategic Management Journal*, **11**(3) 175-95.

Porter, M. (1998) *Competitive Strategy*. Free Press, New York.

Rodriguez, M. & Sirmans, C.F. (1996) Managing corporate real estate: evidence from the capital markets. *Journal of Real Estate Literature*, **4** 13-33.

Roulac, S. (2001) Corporate property strategy is integral to corporate business strategy. *Journal of Real Estate Research*, **22** (1/2) 129-152.

Further reading

Estey, R. (1988) How corporate real estate departments contribute to the bottom line. *Industrial Development* July/August 4–6.

Chapter 7
Understanding Property Markets – an Institutional Approach

Introduction

The aim of this chapter is to help you understand the property markets within which property managers must operate. By referring to markets, in the plural, we mean the property markets of different countries, regions and local areas as well as property markets operating for different types of property.

It is important to first understand the fundamental construction of property markets. We do this by introducing you to an 'institutional approach'. This is a generic approach that will help you to understand different markets around the world. It will do so by making you aware of the different rules and regulations that make up a particular property market. We refer to all these different rules as *institutions* and, when separate rules combine to form a complex network of rules, we refer to them as *institutional arrangements*. Ostrom (1986) defines institutions as: 'sets of working rules that are used to determine who is eligible to make decisions in some arena, what actions are allowed or constrained, what aggregation rules will be used, what procedures must be followed, what information must or must not be provided, and what payoffs will be assigned to individuals dependent on their actions.'

Institutions, either formal or informal, are different from 'organisations', which are collective bodies that exist under a framework of institutions. In this chapter, a collection of 'institutions', or rules, are referred to as 'institutional arrangements', to avoid confusion with those organisations operating in the financial market, which are referred to in most property literature as 'financial institutions' or simply, 'institutions'.

Understanding the institutional arrangements that underpin property markets helps the corporate manager to assess the costs involved in conducting a transaction in each specific market. We refer to these as *transaction costs*. When choosing between different property strategies, it is important for the corporate property manager to be aware of the transaction costs involved in each strategy. Making the transaction costs transparent can not only help the manager to choose between different strategies, but also act to minimise their transaction costs wherever possible.

We consider it important to provide some background on the origins of institutional analysis at this point. This will help to explain our starting point in the development of the strategic property management framework and, to some extent, our need to borrow from other disciplines in its elaboration. It will be useful for the reader to study this chapter before moving on to Chapters 8 and 9, where we use an institutional framework to explore property markets.

Institutions

The term 'institution' or 'institutional' can be confusing, because it is often used to mean different things. For example, it can be used to mean:

- an established group or organisation (e.g. the Church)
- a practice or way of doing things (e.g. surveying, accountancy)
- a specific organisation with standing within a local area (e.g. the university, hospital, or prison).

The institutional perspective adopted here refers to that of the new institutional economics.[1] This sees 'institutions' as informal and formal rules, including norms and conventions, and their enforcement mechanisms.

Informal rules, including social mores, are deeply embedded in the cultural heritage of communities. For example, in many cultures it is considered polite to stand up when a new person enters the room. This is a simple social custom that might be considered an 'institution'. Most informal rules have evolved to serve some sensible purpose. In the above case, standing when someone new enters the room provides a break in the conversation. This allows the new person to be introduced to everyone and brought up to speed on the current issues under discussion; it is designed to make the new person feel comfortable and immediately included within the existing group. Similarly, the convention of each man making sure that he dances with each woman at his table during a formal dinner dance, ensures that even the most retiring wallflower gets to dance.

Formal rules, on the other hand, are imposed by those with authority, and often carry sanctions if they are broken that are far worse than other dinner guests accusing you of being rude. Formal rules are often derived from informal rules, and are formalised into laws, bylaws or regulations when there is some consensus that they are good for society.

Formal rules might suffer from serious enforcement problems if they are at odds with informal institutions. For example, dropping litter in the UK is seen as a bad practice and convention suggests that people should place litter in bins. This has been formalised into law, and fines are payable for people prosecuted for dropping litter.[2] If the state were to impose a law that stated that people would be fined for wearing bright clothing, this would be seen as totally unacceptable in UK society and very difficult to enforce. There is no recent convention of wearing *only* dark clothing in the UK and such a new law would be at odds with our informal institutions.

Exercise 7.1

Identify an example of a 'rule' within your organisation. Try to think of one that is not apparent to anyone who is unfamiliar with your organisation.

Does lack of appreciation of the rule hinder their understanding of how your organisation functions?

Institutional arrangements

'Institutional arrangements' comprise *sets* of rules, both formal and informal, which govern choices that people can make. Nobel Prize winning economist Douglas North is credited with referring to institutional arrangements as 'the rules of the game'. When people refer to institutional differences, invariably they mean differences in the rules of the game.

A tennis player can devise different strategies to win a tournament and different tactics to win each game. His strategy might be to play safe, easy games early on in the tournament, saving his energy and skills for the more difficult games later on. Within each game, his tactics might change, but must do so within the rules of the game. For example, it is within the player's discretion to decide to play the first serve fast and, if that one does not clear the net, the second one more carefully, but slowly. What the player can not do is serve more than twice on one point score; to do so would involve a change to the rules of tennis.

Exercise 7.2: Strategy or tactics?

The rules of the game analogy draws attention to the difference between strategic and tactical thinking. Strategy is concerned with winning the game or tournament; tactics with winning the point. It is easy to become preoccupied with the details of the rules, and yet fail to see the 'big picture'. Similarly, focusing on the big picture without understanding how it can be transformed by the detailed rules can be just as dangerous. The ability to achieve strategic objectives is largely determined by the complexity of the 'decision route', from beginning to end. Think of a project you have recently been involved in: this might be a property project, or something personal like organising a party, holiday or house move. Look back over your decision route. You will see that you had a number of clear strategies and a choice of tactics in how to achieve each one. Why did you choose certain tactics? Was it because some had less uncertainty attached to them than others? Did you have to change tactics along the way?

The property manager of a hospital can devise different strategies to maximise the value of the property holding for the hospital. This might involve, for example, disposing of some buildings and redeveloping others. However, she must implement her strategies within the rules that pertain to the property market. Thus, if she decides to redevelop one of the hospital buildings, she must apply to the relevant authorities for permission to carry out the development. In obtaining such permission, she may employ different tactics. For example, she might decide to commission an architect's model of the new building, to help persuade the local planning committee of the aesthetic value of the new building. Alternatively, or as well as this tactic, she might decide to hold community meetings, to solicit the views of the local community and encourage them to back the new building. These tactics are all within the rules of the game in the UK. Playing outside the rules of the game would, for example, involve bribing some of the planning committee members to gain approval for her scheme.

Almost everything we do is influenced by rules of one form or another. The idea that individual behaviour is governed by the rules of society is not new. For centuries philosophers have debated the significance of social obligations. Most of the debates have been concerned with social obligations *within* specific societies. However, in the new international era of business and investment, the corporate property manager is just as likely to be concerned with rules and obligations *across* societies and cultures.

'Foreigners' or 'outsiders' can often be at a disadvantage when operating in a new environment. They are likely to be outside the internal social networks and lack the social and cultural clues that enable 'locals' to structure their search for information in an effective manner. In Chapter 5 we referred to the need to tap into networks in the local community, and in Case Studies 4 and 5 we see how two organisations are pursuing this objective through their place and the place of their employees within a local area.

In work conducted on the Beijing and Shanghai property markets, Cao and Edwards (2002) report on the effect, amongst other things, of the tendency for officials to conduct secret deals on development projects. The paper explains that such deals were facilitated by the presence of the social institution of 'Guanxi', a system of personal connections on which Chinese society operates. Understanding Guanxi is a fundamental requirement to understanding the institutional arrangements that govern property markets in China. The institution of Guanxi is both affected by and affects Chinese society.

Most organisations minimise uncertainty by operating in areas that they understand best. However, when faced with new institutional arrangements, with which they are unfamiliar, corporate property managers need to assess the extent of the uncertainty surrounding the unfamiliar institutions. They can then decide whether to proceed with dealings in a particular country. The same is true of familiar institutions that are likely to change.

The rules and conventions of social and economic interaction can and do change, sometimes frequently and sometimes infrequently. Some institutions appear resistant to change, even though they might appear outdated. Many of these rules are strongly influenced by cultural and political factors that vary from country to country. Just as there are similarities between soccer and rugby, there are similarities in the institutional arrangement of property markets throughout the world. However, just as soccer and rugby are different games, there are significant differences in the rules of the game from one country's property market to another

Difficulties can arise when dealing in foreign countries in deciding exactly whose institutions to follow. For example, in the USA, the Foreign Corrupt Practices Act prevents US companies involved in deals overseas from entering into any transactions that would be considered corrupt by US law, even if they are customary in the country in which the company is operating. Clearly, this can place a US company in an unfavourable position when competing with companies based overseas.

Markets

It is the rules, or 'institutions' that allow markets to operate with relative stability. As the subject of economics was first developing in the eighteenth century, Adam Smith and his fellow Scottish philosopher and political scientist David Hume were concerned with the structure of markets. In 1786, Hume pointed out that at least three institutions are fundamental to human progress and civilised society:

- guarantee of *property rights*
- *free transfer* of property by voluntary contractual agreement
- the *keeping of promises* made.

Kasper and Streit, 1998

At a simple level, 'market' is the term used to denote the grouping together of transactions of exchange, based on the similarity of the commodity concerned. This grouping is based largely on convention and informal rules, although, as markets develop, the rules may become more formal. Buyers and sellers seldom make a decision to 'participate in a market', they make a decision to buy or sell ('transact an exchange' – normally goods for money) and, in the process, participate in the market that encompasses those and similar transactions.

Property rights

Participation in a market requires certain conditions. In particular, the purchaser will wish to be confident that he is not simply receiving possession of the goods, but also the entitlement to them (and the entitlement to conduct a subsequent transaction).

Rules of entitlement constitute the authority to allocate resources, and under what circumstances. This introduces the concept of 'ownership' and associated rights and obligations. The power to allocate or 'transfer' resources rests with the 'owner' of the resource in question. Thus, if you currently 'own' a car, you have the right to give it away, or sell it. The concept of ownership can be relatively complex and the details of ownership might be obscure. In the case of the car, anyone you decided to sell the car to, or indeed give the car to, would expect you to also hand over documents, showing that the car is yours to transfer; showing that you have 'title' to it. In contrast, 'possession' is in most cases more self-evident. In many cases, possession and ownership are considered synonymous: reinforced by the maxim 'possession is nine-tenths of the law'. In practice, the distinction between ownership and possession can be surprisingly ambiguous.

The rules defining ownership under the English system of common law, developed over a span of a thousand years, are the most comprehensive in the world. The distinction between ownership and possession should be clear in property transactions in any market economies based on the rules of common law. Nevertheless, disputes still arise over issues of ownership and possession.

'Free' transfer

The institutions that determine the issue of 'title' are elaborate and powerful. They allow individuals and corporations to hold property rights with a clear understanding of what those rights confer. They have such a significant impact on the ability of market mechanisms to transfer property, that market economists bemoan the imperfection of property as a market commodity. The time and cost associated with the majority of property transactions mean that these transaction costs can actually affect sale and purchase decisions; sometimes making a transaction that seemed worthwhile simply too costly to execute (see Transaction costs on p. 99).

Nevertheless, without this sort of stability, markets can not operate effectively and the economic well being of the community is fundamentally undermined. For example, in economic environments as diverse as mainland China and Indonesia, the definition of ownership is less precise and the distinction between ownership and possession is fuzzy. The vagueness of the institutional arrangements generates an uncertainty for potential purchasers:

> 'If property rights are hard to define and/or enforce, then parties that create new value in property run the risk that some – perhaps much – of that value will leak out to or be appropriated by others.'
>
> Williamson and Masten, 1999

Keeping promises

The successful use of property rights depends upon a system that will uphold and *enforce* those rights. The institutional arrangements of a country will determine the way in which rights are enforced. In most countries, a transfer of ownership of a property, accompanied by the appropriate documentation, will be upheld by the legal system. For example, a new property owner might have trouble in obtaining possession of a property. The vendor, having transferred the legal title of the property to the purchaser, might refuse to vacate the building. The purchaser, or new owner, can rely on the judicial system in the UK to issue an eviction order. This might take some time and cost the purchaser a considerable sum in legal fees, but she can be confident that possession will eventually be obtained; her rights will be effectively enforced.

The operation of the market

Markets that are orderly and reputable operate according to rules and conventions that are respected and observed. Some of these rules are the result of government policy, which influences the way in which markets function at the operational level. Market rules are designed to address the following concerns:

- the risk of being cheated (e.g. being sold a property that does not exist in the form described on the sale particulars)
- the risk of unfairly opportunistic behaviour (e.g. vendors who have agreed to sell reneging on a deal if someone offers a higher amount – often referred to as 'gazumping' the original purchaser)
- a need for ordering procedures to facilitate market operations (e.g. an expectation that the property will be advertised, surveyed, negotiations made, etc., in that order)
- a need to ensure speedy, unambiguous transactions.

In new or emerging markets, the institutions tend to be informal and the conditions above cannot be relied upon. Two types of buyer tend to participate in such markets. First, emerging markets will attract the opportunistic, those people who are willing to speculate or 'gamble'. Second, emerging markets will attract those people who have very detailed personal knowledge of the way in which that particular market operates. The institutions appear to be vague and poorly expressed, and enforcement procedures might be very rudimentary. The cardinal principle in such a market is 'let the buyer beware'.

As markets mature, policy makers in positions of power and authority insist upon:

- accountability to stakeholders
- independent regulation (introducing a 'referee' to the game)

- transparency of information (making the rules, the commodities and the conditions clear).

At the beginning of the twentieth century, economists across Europe developed a comprehensive and systematic view of the way in which markets maintain price stability. They showed how this resulted from equilibrium between the supply of goods and the demand for goods. If the prevailing equilibrium were to be disturbed, participants on the market would act in a way that would restore equilibrium. If demand exceeds supply, suppliers will increase output to the point at which they reach short-term capacity. If demand continues to exceed supply, suppliers will increase price. All other things being equal and in the case of a 'normal' good, this will lead to a reduction in demand until supply and demand fall into equilibrium again. Note, however, that this is a much abbreviated description of the operation of the price mechanism, fuller details of which appear in standard economic textbooks, such as Lipsey (1997).

Economists' models of economic behaviour resembled this mechanical system, in which human interaction was almost coincidental: economic decisions were undertaken by firms, not people. The economists adopted assumptions and conditions for 'perfect' markets that would allocate resources in a manner that was 100% efficient. The analysis of economic behaviour at the operational level (the level of the 'firm') came to be referred to as 'microeconomics'. This model has dominated economic theory for over 60 years.

Microeconomics was developed on the assumption that economic behaviour can aspire to perfection. It states that the market is said to be 'perfectly competitive' when all firms can sell all they wish at the going market price and nothing at a higher price. The set of conditions that will guarantee this result are (Lipsey, 1997):

- homogeneous products
- many sellers
- perfect/full information
- freedom of entry and exit.

An important addition to this list is that in a perfectly competitive market, there are no costs associated with actually making a transaction (see Transaction costs below).

Only relatively recently have economists formally recognised that:

- markets are the collective result of individual transactions, which can be grouped according to some common characteristics, such as the type of commodity
- transactions are undertaken by human beings, whose behaviour is motivated by a *variety* of factors, not just maximising individual utility
- the parties to market transactions have certain expectations concerning the risk of being cheated, the speed of transfer, etc.

Such observations have helped to make the *transaction* the focus of analysis and, in turn, the costs of making that transaction. Commons (1961, p. 73) comments that:

> '... it is this shift from commodities, individuals, and exchanges to transactions and working rules of collective action that marks the transition from the classical and hedonic schools to the institutional schools of economic thinking. The shift is a change in the ultimate unit of economic investigation, from commodities and individuals to transactions between individuals.'

Transaction costs

Ronald Coase was awarded a Nobel Prize for his contribution to economic theory. The importance of his work lies in its recognition that the neo-classical model of economics only holds up under the severely restrictive assumption that there are no barriers to exchange. This assumption is an unrealistic one, as most people would recognise. In practice, the costs of undertaking a transaction can be sufficient to prevent the exchange being completed.

For example, you might have the choice of buying either a second-hand computer or a new one. The second-hand computer will be priced lower than the new one. However, first you have to find out about different models, work out your ideal specification, seek out a willing seller, negotiate a second-hand price, have it checked by an IT expert and arrange transport home. Should you decide to buy the new computer, this might involve visiting a computer store, accepting the free advice of the salesperson, selecting from a wide choice, paying for it and having the computer delivered to your door. Thus, although the second-hand computer is *priced* lower than a new one, the costs of buying it – of making the transaction – might be higher. These are what we refer to as *transaction costs*: not the price of goods and services, but those additional costs incurred in making the transaction. These might be monetary and non-monetary (such as effort, emotion and time). Eggertsson (1990, p. 14) defines transaction costs as: 'the costs that arise when individuals exchange ownership rights to economic assets and enforce their exclusive rights'.

Transaction costs are also incurred in non-market transactions, where goods might be sought and provided at public expense, or by the voluntary sector.

Uncertainty and institutional arrangements

Organisations and individuals accept that the world is an uncertain place, in which many events do not turn out as they expected. Uncertainty arises from:

- an implicit inability to know what the future holds *and*
- ambiguity about the rules of the game and the way in which they are interpreted and enforced.

If our view of the future proves to be wrong, we may lose some or all of the value of the strategy that we are implementing. In return for accepting the risk, we expect to be rewarded for getting it 'right', that is, making decisions that remain valid as the future unfolds. In this respect, we have a vested interest in reducing uncertainty. Most decision makers believe that uncertainty and its associated risk can be reduced by further and better knowledge and understanding. Thus, in Chapters 4, 5 and 6, we urge the property manager to obtain and analyse as much information as possible about the property, the property users, and the organisation's objectives, respectively. However, we must recognise that the costs of search for this information are transaction costs, which add to our overall cost structure in managing property portfolios.

The importance of institutional arrangements is that in determining the rules of the game, they also determine the costs of trading goods and services in the market. Institutional arrangements govern the choices that people make and can either support or impede market transactions. In the property market, transaction costs might involve not just searching for information about the property, but also obtaining property rights, enforcing those rights, seeking development consents, etc.

According to the *World Development Report* (World Bank, 2002), market-supporting institutional arrangements help to:

- transmit information about market conditions, goods and participants
- enforce property rights and contracts, to determine who gets what, and when
- manage competition in markets, by regulating entry and directing incentives.

In essence, they serve to reduce 'transaction costs' for market transactions. In contrast, those institutional arrangements that raise transaction costs hinder the development or even the establishment of markets.

The effect that the institutional arrangements have on the market might not be uniform across all players in the market. Sometimes the institutional arrangements for a particular market will have evolved in such a way that they result in reduced transaction costs for those players who are, in effect, less productive agents. At the same time, they might raise the transaction costs for the more productive agents. In such cases, the market is inefficient. On the other hand, if the transaction costs for the more productive agents are kept low by the prevailing institutional arrangements, the market operates more efficiently. Thus, an ideal institutional arrangement rewards the most productive agents by keeping their transaction costs low and so allowing them to retain more total net benefit in trading. In these cases, it might be said that the market is in 'static efficiency'.

In reality, few markets are static, and this *static* efficiency of institutional arrangements should be contrasted with *adaptive* efficiency. If institutional arrangements can be changed relatively quickly, a market that began with inefficient institutional arrangements may turn out to be more efficient over time, by adapting its institutional arrangements to more efficient operation.

The need for institutions to evolve and change

Institutional arrangements define the distribution of choice and incentives faced by individuals and groups. Institutions need to change as economic and social circumstances change: emerging problems require flexibility and innovation. Bromley (1985, p. 784) refers to the need for dynamism in institutions as the 'order–change antithesis', and recognises that:

> 'order creates expectations about secure futures, but there must also be mechanisms for mid-course correction. . . . Too much order and not enough change ensures revolution, too much change and not enough order ensures the absence of expectations, and hence stagnation.'

However, the costs of changing institutional arrangements can be considerable and there is a tendency for people to rely on others to pay for such changes in the rules of the game. We might refer to such people as 'free-riders', as they expect to benefit from the revised rules, but are not prepared to pay for getting the rules changed. If this is the case, and each person relies on another to pay, the bottom-up approach of institutional change is often very protracted, as each waits for another to act. Instead, the state, with its resources and authority, is in a better position to initiate institutional change. Therefore, the rules of the ruling party are of particular importance in the adaptive efficiency of a country (North, 1990). It might be helpful for you to consider institutions as 'nested', like a group of nested tables, whereby the rules of the ruling party, or government, influence and constrain the design and evolution of all other rules.

The importance that economists have placed on institutions has been echoed in political science. In modern political theory, political outcomes are perceived as a function of three primary factors: (1) preferences (interests) among the political actors; (2) the distribution of resources (powers); and (3) the constraints imposed by the rules of the game (constitutions). Each of these is treated as exogenous to the political system. However, new institutionalism argues that preferences and meanings develop *in* politics; as such they are dynamic and endogenous to the political system. Thus, political institutions affect the distribution of resources; the distribution is also partly determined endogenously. In turn, the distribution of resources affects the power of political actors, and thereby affects the political institutions. Finally, the rules of the game develop *within* the context of political institutions (March and Olsen, 1988).

Lobbying for institutional changes

If a particular group of stakeholders are likely to benefit from a rule change, then it is in their interests to organise themselves and initiate such a change. In this way, membership organisations, from unions and professional organisations to charities and interest groups will lobby government to bring about a rule change. This is often referred to as 'rent seeking', since the particular organisations seek to achieve a rule change which will leave them better off, and possibly some other group worse off. Demand for institutional change by the public and social groups with power is crucial to induce reform. Meanwhile, the political process must overcome the costs of institutional change. Therefore, institutional analysis that covers these aspects assists in the understanding of the evolution of markets, especially those markets undergoing rapid changes.

The property manager is a policy *maker*, who can decide what she wishes to do in terms of strategically planning the future of her portfolio. However, she is also a policy *taker*, constrained by the laws, regulations and sanctions of society, which have been determined by political mechanisms that reflect public opinion and values and by societal changes. In this sense, she works within a given institutional arrangement, which 'frames' (or 'constrains') the choices she can make in the ways in which she manages her property.

Interestingly, however, as a member of society, the property manager can attempt, through the democratic system, to influence government to bring about changes to the institutional arrangements and the institutions themselves, which will lead to more favourable rules of the game for her. She might also do this through the various groupings she belongs to, whether they are professional bodies and associations, interest groups or political parties.

Clearly, all other stakeholders in the property can also attempt to achieve rule changes that will favour their own interests. The scale of the rule change sought, and the point at which it is executed, might depend upon the strength of the group and the extent of their influence, but also upon the point at which they perceive the need for institutional change. For example, in response to the threat from the development of a large out-of-town supermarket on their doorstep, a group of market town retailers might choose to act in quite different ways, depending upon the size and authority of their group and its timing.

As a national group of independent retailers, they might lobby central government for revised Planning Policy Guidance, to favour in town development over out of town development (such as the published PPG 6).[3] As a regional association of retailers, they might seek to influence the county or regional development strategy, to favour market town development. As a small group of retailers from a specific market town, which is already faced with the development of an out of town supermarket, they might negotiate for their local district council to reduce or abolish car parking charges in their town car park, in order to encourage shoppers back to the market square. Car parking in town centres is often one of the problems of rejuvenating in town retail development (Kinsella, 1999).

Governments and institutional changes

Coase (1960) argued that policy makers in government should concentrate their attention on reducing transaction costs: acknowledging that it is the transaction costs that prevent an efficient solution being achieved. This perspective, which might be referred to as the *public choice* perspective, takes a narrow position concerning the role of government in altering the arrangement of institutions. Many public choice economists argue that the government's role should be limited to a precise definition and subsequent enforcement of property rights (Anderson and McChesney, 2003). Public choice theory asserts that if property rights are well defined and transferable, change should occur through market transfers. And if the market is not producing what people want, then people will change the market.

The public choice theorist's argument is that whenever the benefits exceed the costs of changing institutional arrangements, the invisible hand of the market will transfer rights to those positions where they produce most benefits. Any attempt to intervene in this process is perceived as *rent seeking*: rent seeking refers to efforts by interested parties to change institutional arrangements to their favour, thus enabling them to enjoy an economic surplus (or rent) associated with a particular institutional arrangement. Rent-seeking behaviour is not supported by public choice economists, first, because it favours a biased approach and second, because it creates uncertainty in the marketplace. Public choice economists are generally scathing of interest groups lobbying governments to change the rules of the game to ensure that they favour their particular interests.

Analysing institutions when managing property

As described above, mainstream economics does not provide a basis for analysing institutions, assuming them to be fixed and determining efficiency within that context. This neo-classical efficiency approach focuses on outcomes and is not concerned with the process that achieves them. It takes the existing set of institutional arrangements and concentrates on how trade might be improved within that given marketplace.

The public choice theory of economics develops the neo-classical approach to the extent that institutions become the subject of study. However, criticism of public choice theory identifies several problems with the public choice view of market institutional change. One of the most frequent of such criticisms is that the public choice view fails to see that the efficient evolution of institutional arrangements rests on the initial distribution of property rights. To this end, public choice theory ignores the fact that an individual's ability and willingness to pay depends upon the incomes resulting from the initial endowment of rights.

This has serious implications. The initial endowment of property rights governs *who* may exploit a particular resource and so gain benefit from that resource. For example, the owner of a quarry may extract gravel for financial gain. However, the use of the quarry might produce external costs, to other individuals, such as noise and air pollution. Public choice theorists would expect those individuals to negotiate and purchase 'property rights' from the quarry owner, and so govern the way in which the resource is used in the future. This might involve buying rights that ensure that the quarry is operated at a lower capacity and so reduce its pollution. In such cases the external costs may be dispersed among a large number of individuals, while the benefits are concentrated on the single owner of the quarry. This seems a simple solution, but it ignores two essential features. First, it ignores the costs incurred by the people who live near the quarry in getting together to negotiate a solution. According to Olson (1965), any group of people seeking a solution with widely diffused and collectively shared benefits is at a disadvantage when attempting to organise collective action. Clearly, the costs of organising the purchase of property rights in this instance may outweigh the benefits.

The second, and perhaps more important failure of public choice theory is that it does not recognise the importance of the existing institutional arrangements. Transactions (that is, property rights transfers), take place within the context of the existing law and therefore do not change the basic choices established by government policy. Whereas institutions refer to the 'rules of the game', property rights refer to ownership of certain rights obtained under a particular set of rules. In this respect, analysis of property rights alone will not reveal an understanding of broader issues concerning alternative institutional arrangements.

In our example above, you might have been questioning why the people living around the quarry should have to purchase property rights to reduce the amount of pollution they are suffering. Why should the quarry owner be treated so favourably? The answer lies in the institutional arrangements surrounding the ownership rights to quarrying. If by being the freehold owner of the quarry, the quarry owner has the *right* to extract gravel 24 hours a day, then the other affected parties must purchase some or all of that right from him in order to get him to curb the operation. Those are the rules of the game. However, the government might see this as a social injustice and decide to change the institutional arrangements in favour of the surrounding residents. They might change the laws ('institutions') governing quarrying, so that it becomes illegal for the quarry to operate for more than 12 hours per day. Alternatively, they might fine or tax the quarry for polluting the area and compensate the local residents in some way. In essence, the government has the ability to change the rules of the game.

The property manager, therefore, needs to be aware not only of the existence of the property rights which he is acquiring, but also the rules of the game that establish how those rights might be exercised. He needs to be aware that those rules can change.

Public choice theorists worry at this ability of politicians and public servants to change the rules of the game, and are concerned that they will be swayed in their value judgements by powerful lobbying:

> 'the fundamental dilemma of political economy is: once the state has the coercive power to do what voluntary (market) action cannot do, how can that power be constrained from being usurped by special interests?'
>
> Anderson and Leal, 1991, p. 17

Thus, public choice theorists argue that politically made changes in institutional arrangements are biased, destabilising, and create uncertainty (Livingston, 1987, p. 283).

Of course, governments can, and do, manipulate institutions to favour certain groups. Indeed, some governments will use this power to distort the rules of the game in favour of their own industries. Carried to extremes, this leads to what has become known as 'crony capitalism'; the result of institutional rather than economic weakness (Cao and Edwards, 2002).

Thus, an increasing number of political economists are recognising the importance of analysing the institutional arrangements governing decisions. Bromley (1985, p. 781) in advocating the analysis of institutional arrangements states that:

> 'Whereas the neo-classicist is interested in the maximising behaviour that occurs within predetermined choice sets, I am more interested in how those choice sets get determined.'

New institutionalists argue that the market is a subset of existing institutional arrangements, rather than vice versa. Individuals come together to negotiate the collective rules which will govern their individual and group behaviour by providing a structure of choice sets. In this respect, these bargaining sessions establish the working rules for interaction and *precede* any market transactions. Bromley (1985, p. 781) comments that:

> '... markets can only reflect a prior underlying structure of entitlements that indicate who has rights, duties, privileges, no rights, power, liability, immunity, and no power.'

Institutions are established by individuals' ability to come together and express, and agree to be bound by, conditions which will govern future individual and group action. As such, institutions define markets: the market is a real manifestation of a set of working rules. Ostrom (1990, p. 15) comments that:

'no market can exist for long without underlying public institutions to support it. In field settings, public and private institutions frequently are intermeshed and depend on one another, rather than existing in isolated worlds.'

Conclusion

While there appeared to be considerable interest in the study of institutions towards the end of the 1980s, there was little agreement on what the term 'institution' meant and, indeed, how to undertake a study of institutions. Ostrom (1990) identified several different interpretations of 'institutions' and concluded that 'we cannot communicate effectively if signs used by one scholar in a field have different referents than the same sign used by another scholar in the same field.' She advocates that the concept of 'rules', is used to symbolise the term 'institution'.

Rules do not directly affect behaviour, but affect the structure of a situation in which actions are selected: they rarely prescribe one action or outcome, but specify a set of actions or outcomes. Rules must be separated from behavioural and physical laws: theoretically, rules can be changed, whereas behavioural and physical laws cannot. This has important implications for understanding institutions: the fact that rules can be changed makes them interesting variables. Second, rules have a prescriptive force, so that knowledge and acceptance of a rule leads individuals to recognise that if they break the rule, other individuals may hold them accountable.

Property markets tend to have two particular characteristics. First, as a commodity, property is highly institutionalised: that is, it is very rule dominated. In this respect, it is significantly different from other commodities, such as moveable objects and shares, where the rules are less structured. In a common-law based market economy, transactions involving the transfer or allocation of property are dominated by legal rules: the institutional characteristics of land and buildings have become so formalised that they are now clearly seen as legal rules and not just informal rules.

In the second place, property markets are fragmented. This means that they can only be understood by analysing individual transactions. This is consistent with the heterogeneous nature of property. It also reinforces the point that market behaviour comprises a series of transactions. In this respect, property markets differ from markets in shares, which can be determined by the indices of share price movements, such as the Dow Jones Industrial Average or the FTSE index.

Perhaps the most important message for the property manager to pick up is that the institutional arrangements governing property markets will vary from country to country and from sector to sector. Comparing one country with another (e.g. the UK with China) or one sector with another (e.g. the agricultural land market with the office market), the institutional arrangements might appear to be the same. However, there might be significant differences of detail in the institutions – the rules of the game. Similarities can generate misplaced complacency and be more deceptive for the unwary than countries or sectors where the institutional arrangements appear haphazard and inefficient compared with the jurisdiction with which we are familiar.

Since rules constrain the choices we might make, we need to question the power of individuals and organisations to set and enforce rules and to bring about rule changes that will affect others. Within a given sovereignty, rules and procedures are developed at the constitutional level. However, in a market economy, resource allocation decisions are acted upon at the operational level. It is the operational level at which the property manager will focus her work. Nevertheless, it is useful to appreciate the complex structures and 'nesting' we have referred to in terms of institutional development. Complex institutional arrangements tend to adopt hierarchical structures. Kiser and Ostrom (1982) identify a three-level hierarchy of institutional arrangements for common property resources, which we find useful for all property:

- Level 1: constitutional
- Level 2: organisational
- Level 3: operational.

A certain amount of public policy is determined at the constitutional level, but a great deal more is simply formalised and empowered at this level. It is designed and implemented at the organisational level. Typically this might consist of local government, but also includes agencies (ministries or departments) and non-governmental organisations (NGOs). The organisational level also includes the administration of justice and the courts and tribunals that carry it out. The operational level includes the developers, investors, agents and occupiers participating within the property markets.

The next chapter establishes an analytical framework for examining the institutional arrangements of property markets and the effect the institutions have on the control and management of property. Figure 7.1 illustrates the different elements that comprise the institutional arrangement. It shows the different levels and shows how each level contains a set of rules, regulations or guidance to which the operation of the market conforms.

The essence of the structure and dynamics of institutional interaction can be explained by understanding the dynamic interactions that occur within and between the three levels. The constitutional level contains the foundation of the arrangement for each type of institution, which undergoes only limited change and normally in response to major cultural or economic upheaval. This is essential in providing stability to the system.

The second (organisational) and third (operational) levels within the arrangement have increasing levels of flexibility. The operational level requires flexibility in order for the market to operate efficiently by responding to the changing economic circumstances of the time. Just as the rigidity of the constitutional level provides stability to the institutional

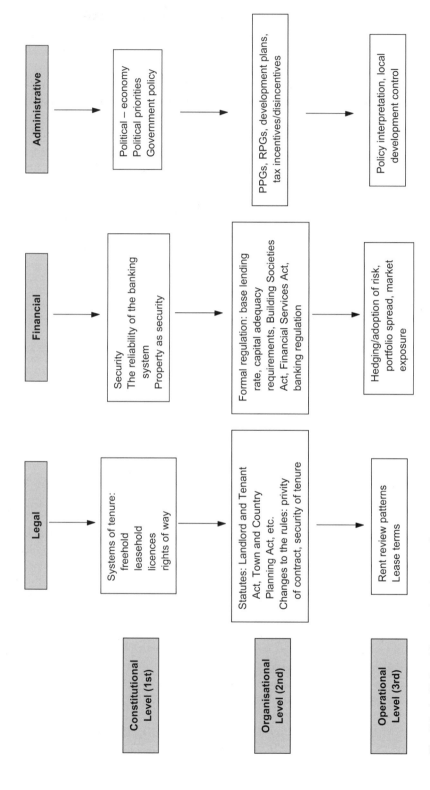

Fig. 7.1 Institutional frameworks: structure diagram

arrangement, ensuring that all market operators are clear about the rules and regulations their activities must reflect, so the flexibility of the operational level allows the institutional structure to accommodate and reflect the needs of the market.

It is wise to be aware that, in some circumstances, operational level institutions may appear to be more significant than institutions higher up the hierarchy. In the UK, institutional arrangements are very formalised, and most negotiations and economic decisions undertaken at the operational level are undertaken in the shadow of the law. However, in regulated economies and emerging markets, such as Indonesia, the institutions at the operational level might appear to be less formal. Less formal operational level institutions allow more freedom to the parties to negotiate their own positions, whereas the higher levels *imply* less autonomy. Nevertheless, supposedly freely negotiated arrangements might eventually require the approval of a referee or regulator, whose authority ultimately links the parties to the higher, more authoritarian levels.

Each level is explored in turn in the following two chapters through the examination of the administrative, legal and financial institutions which guide the operation of the property markets.

References

Anderson, T.L. & Leal, D.R. (1991) *Free Market Environmentalism*. Pacific Research Institute for Public Policy, Westview Press, Boulder.

Anderson, T.L. & McChesney, F.S. (2003) *Property Rights: Cooperation Conflict and the Law*. Princeton University Press, Princeton NJ.

Bromley, D.W. (1985) Resources and economic development: an institutionalist perspective. *Journal of Economic Issues*, **19**(3), 779–796.

Bromley, D.W. (1991) *Environment and Economy: Property Rights and Public Policy*. Blackwell, Oxford.

Cao, J. & Edwards, V.M. (2002) The Beijing office market: its current status and opportunities for international developments and investment financiers. *Briefings in Real Estate Finance* **2**(1), 42–60.

Coase, R.H. (1960) The problem of social cost. *Journal of Law and Economics*, **III** 1–44.

Commons, J.R. (1961) *Institutional Economics*. University of Wisconsin Press, Madison.

Eggertsson, T. (1990) *Economic Behaviour and Institutions*. Cambridge University Press, Cambridge.

Kasper, W. and Streit, M.E. (1998) *Institutional Economics*. Elgar, Cheltenham.

Kinsella, P. (1999) Rough road to easing traffic. *Property Week, Supplement*, February 1999, 27.

Kiser, L.L. and Ostrom, E. (1982) 'The three worlds of action: a metatheoretical synthesis of institutional approaches. In: *Strategies of Political Inquiry* (ed. E. Ostrom). Sage, Beverly Hills.

Lipsey, R. (1997) *An Introduction to Positive Economics*. Oxford University Press, Oxford.

Livingston, M.L. (1987) Evaluating the performance of environmental policy: contributions of neoclassical, public choice and institutional models. *Journal of Economic Issues*, Volume **XXI1**, 1.

March, J.G. & Olsen, J.P. (1988) The new institutionalism: organizational factors in political life. *American Political Science Review*, **78** 734–749.

North, D.C. (1990) *Institutions, Institutional Change and Economic Performance*. Cambridge University Press, New York.

Olson, M. (1965) *The Logic of Collective Action: public goods and the theory of groups*. Harvard University Press, Cambridge, MA.

Ostrom, E. (1986) An agenda for the study of institutions. *Public Choice*, **48** 3–25.

Ostrom, E. (1990) *Governing the Commons: the evolution of institutions for collective action*. Cambridge University Press, Cambridge.

Williamson, O.E. & Masten, E.E. (eds) (1999) *The Economics of Transaction Costs*. Elgar, Cheltenham.

World Bank (2002) *World Development Report 2002: Building Institutions for Markets*. Oxford University Press, New York.

Endnotes

[1] For further reading on new institutional economics, see Eggertson (1990), North (1990) and Bromley (1991).

[2] Interestingly, few such prosecutions for littering are made in Britain nowadays. This might be a reflection of limited resources for enforcement and priorities for those resources lying elsewhere (e.g. police time used to pursue theft and assault instead), or might reflect an underlying belief in society that fining for littering is an excessive penalty and should not be enforced. Once people realise that sanctions associated with a rule are not routinely enforced, then certain individuals will break the law, knowing that they will not be 'punished'. Lack of formal enforcement does not *always* lead to a breakdown in order, as other sanctions (especially peer pressure – other citizens openly criticising litter droppers) can act to maintain expected behaviour from individuals.

[3] Planning Policy Guidance 6 (PPG6) aims to: 'sustain and enhance the vitality and viability of town centres which serve the community as a whole and focus on retail development where proximity of competing businesses facilitates competition from which consumers benefit'; and to 'ensure the availability of a comprehensive range of shopping opportunities to which people have easy access and the maintenance of an efficient and innovative retail sector'.

Chapter 8
An Institutional Approach to Understanding Property Markets – Legal and Financial Institutions

Having looked at the background to institutional analysis and developed an institutional framework through which we can study the property markets, we are now going to examine the system in action. This chapter takes the first two of the three institutions, *legal* and *financial*, and explores how they manifest themselves at each of the three levels identified in Chapter 7. We will investigate what impact they can have on the operation of the property markets and how this might effect the strategic management of a corporate real estate portfolio. We start by looking at the legal institutions.

Legal institutions

The constitutional level

The operation of the English and Welsh property markets conforms to English law, which is rooted in *common law*, *case law* and *statute*. This establishes basic property rights in the form of freehold, leasehold and licences, plus less obvious rights such as rights of way and easements (see Chapter 4). These form the main institutions providing the framework within which our markets operate.

The longevity of the English land tenure system combined with the influence of Great Britain as a colonial power has led to land tenure being based on a similar system in many other countries. For example, Hong Kong, many African countries and Australia all have systems of land tenure rooted in the English system.

Proof of title

One of the most crucial aspects of the right of ownership is the ability to prove that you hold that right. Proof of title can be relatively complex but its reliability is the foundation of a stable property market. This is one of the reasons why transfer of property rights is a relatively cumbersome process in England and Wales. Separate (and arguably simpler) arrangements exist in Scotland, where the legal system is different. It is essential to be absolutely sure of the title being transferred and this can require extensive investigation. In some cases the system is becoming quicker with more extensive use of computer generated mapping systems and the updating of the land register. However, if a piece of real estate is historic and/or a number of legal interests exist within it, the process will inevitably be time consuming. This emphasises the need for any real estate strategy to be supported by comprehensive data collection for the portfolio.

The system of freehold and leasehold is important because it recognises the role of land and buildings as investment assets as well as operational assets. By allowing more than one party to have a legal interest in the same asset, the benefits that flow from the asset can be spread more widely and used much more efficiently. This would not be possible without a robust system for proving ownership of title beyond doubt.

These basic rights form the institutional arrangement that sets out how legal rights in property can be granted, held and transferred. From this institutional arrangement, rules have then flowed which govern the day-to-day operation of the market. These rules are flexible and subject to change. This is crucial to the system operating efficiently and responding to changes in the economic and cultural environment within which they exist.

Rules of engagement – the organisational level of the framework

The main rules affecting property rights are contained within the Landlord and Tenant Act 1954, which regulates the relationship between landlord and tenant of commercial real estate and clarifies the obligations of each to the other, and the Town and Country Planning Act 1990, which regulates the way in which the property held can be utilised, and clarifies obligations to the immediate community and wider society.

These rules allow liberal use of property as a resource, but limit the disadvantages that might flow from that use if it were unregulated. If a tenant were not obliged to leave a building in a good state of repair over the long term, the fabric of the building stock would be undermined. If there were no system for reviewing rent, leases would be unnecessarily short, reducing the business security that flows from certainty about the right to occupy the premises for an appropriate period, and the increased business value that flows from customers knowing where the business is located.

Regaining possession

An important aspect of the rules through which these legal institutions work relates to regaining possession of a building. For commercial property this is governed by the Landlord and Tenant Act 1954 and is well established. For residential property the rules governing regaining possession have undergone a number of changes and the markets have consequently been seriously affected. The private residential lettings market experienced extremely limited supply in response to changes in the law making it very difficult for landlords to regain possession of property they had let, and controlling the level of rent they could charge. This made it so unattractive to let residential property that very few private sector owners did, leading to a rapid shortfall in supply.

These institutional changes were applied to the market as a response to the cultural environment of the period and questionable behaviour by some private landlords, but had a detrimental effect on the operation of the market. They were changed in the 1980s with the introduction of assured shorthold tenancies. These form a different set of rules within the institutional framework of a lease and provide security for both the landlord and the tenant. As a consequence the private residential market is now more active than it has been for many years but recovery has been slow.

Privity of contract

One of the most important changes to property law in recent years relates to privity of contract. This was one of the fundamental rules underpinning the system of leases and in particular the assignment of leases. It allowed that if a person took a lease they were obligated under it until it expired through effluxion of time or mutual surrender. If she assigned the lease she remained obligated under it in the event of the assignee failing in his obligations. This allowed the granting of a lease to one person, safe in the knowledge that if the property was assigned, the landlord would have recourse to the original lessee in case of default on the rent or other obligations.

This system has now been removed and does not apply to new leases, although if it was in force when the original lease was granted, it remains. This represents a major change to the rules applying to the granting and transfer of leases. It has given rise to a new set of rules in its place. It is now common practice for a landlord to demand that a guarantor be provided by a tenant, who agrees to take responsibility for any obligations on which the tenant reneges, in particular payment of rent. It has become acceptable for a landlord to withhold permission to assign a lease if the guarantor is unsuitable, although this consent can not be unreasonably withheld.

This change in the rules was provoked in part by the economic downturn of the early 1990s. The number of business collapses increased the number of instances where tenants could not fulfil their obligations under a lease, leading the landlord to go back through the chain of assignees until they found one able to fulfil the leasehold obligations. In some instances this led to people being required to pay large amounts of rent and fulfil repairing obligations on property they had long since vacated and as a result of business decisions over which they had no control.

This latest development of the role of the guarantor provides an interesting example of the third level within the institutional framework of the property markets in action. It is this third level that gives the institutional structure its flexibility and allows it to moderate but not jeopardise the operation of a market within a mixed economy. Of course, this will bring with it transaction costs for that market. If these costs are too high the market will operate less efficiently and economic productivity will be reduced.

Flexibility – the operational level of the framework

These few examples provide ample demonstration of the importance of rules through which the institutions can be applied uniformly and equitably. They also demonstrate the impact that changes to the rules can have on markets. However, changes to these rules do not happen often and tend to result from major cultural or economic change or a problem coming to the attention of central government. Gibson and Lizieri (2001) identify 'inertia and friction' as a characteristic of the property markets. They identify the very structure of the market as responsible in part for slowing innovation and the wider implementation of new and changing business practices. What they are describing is the rigidity of the second level institutional arrangements and their resistance to radical changes. This is a dichotomy: it is the robustness of the institutional arrangements that allows flexibility within the 'rules of engagement'; however, that robustness is also inevitably an obstacle to radical change.

Rent review patterns

The third level can change much more quickly. There have been a number of examples of change at this level of the institutional arrangement but one of the most important, which very clearly illustrates the efficiency of this system in responding to economic change, relates to rent reviews. The length of time between rent reviews is not governed by statute and consequently has changed considerably over the years in response to negotiation between landlord and tenant.

In the early part of the twentieth century it was common to find leases without provision for rent review. It was not until the economic climate after the Second World War gave rise to inflation that the need for a periodic review of the level of rent was recognised. In the first place such reviews were provided at relatively long intervals, perhaps 14 or 21 years. As inflation rates rose and more regular opportunities were required to increase the rent to ensure a satisfactory return on capital, the period was reduced to 7 and then 5 years. The Landlord and Tenant Act 1954 still makes provision for a 14-year lease which suggests a natural cycle of a 7-year rent review pattern, where the courts are required to resolve a dispute between landlord and tenant over a renewal. However, it would be unusual for such a lease to have anything other than 5-yearly reviews.

While the upwards-only rent review may seem an onerous provision within a lease, recent research by Reading University for the Royal Institution of Chartered Surveyors (RICS, 2002) has identified this issue as less significant to corporate occupiers than might have been expected. While this is likely to be influenced by the relatively stable level of rents within the commercial markets at the time of writing (2003), it is nonetheless worth noting. According to this research the length of the lease term is much more of an issue than the rent review clause. This is another area in which the third level of the institutional arrangement has demonstrated sufficient flexibility to respond to changing demand from operators within the market.

Turnover rents

An increasing number of landlords are letting retail and leisure units on a rental basis that includes some element of 'turnover'. A unit will be let at perhaps 80% of open market rental value with an additional amount to be paid, based on the gross turnover of the store. This encourages a more active relationship between landlord and tenant, simply by transferring some of the risk of falling trade to the landlord. If the shopping centre or high street as a whole is not managed in such a way as to attract customers, the landlord's rental income will be affected. It has taken a long time for this type of lease arrangement to be offered in the UK but it is becoming more common (Heighton, 2002). This again reflects the potential for the third level within the institutional arrangement to accommodate the changing requirements of the market, without undermining the stability of the market.

Lease length

Lease terms have reduced considerably over the course of the twentieth and early twenty-first centuries and are undergoing a further period of change. The standard institutional lease became accepted as 25 years, being reduced from 35 years, in the late 1970s and early 1980s. Many occupiers feel that this is too long. They are looking for leases of 15 years or less, or with break clauses allowing flexibility on both sides. At the other end of the spectrum there has been considerable growth in the serviced offices market, offering space for terms starting at as little as an hour at their most flexible; Byrne et al. (2001) identified 442 serviced office locations in the UK alone.

This shift is in part in response to less certain economic conditions, but also to the change in the type of business driving economic development within the UK. The small and medium sized enterprise sector is now accepted as the driver of economic development. The property requirements for this sort of company are inevitably different from the large multinational organisations that had begun to dominate the economic landscape. Many small and medium sized businesses are not fully aware of their long-term property requirements and need flexibility built into the terms under which they hold property to allow change in the interests of efficiency and growth.

This requirement for flexibility can be accommodated only because of the stability that exists within the legal institutional arrangement governing the granting, holding and transfer of property rights under English law. New terms can be negotiated between operators at the third tier that will be upheld by the institutions, assuming they conform to the existing arrangement. Where the existing institutional arrangement becomes an obstacle to such flexibility, second level institutional changes can be made to change this, although experience tells us such change is very slow.

RICS Code of Practice for Commercial Leases in England and Wales

A very interesting example of the interaction of the three levels within this institutional arrangement is currently developing in respect of changes within the commercial lease. A great deal of UK based corporate property is held on what is commonly referred to as an 'institutional lease' (in this instance the word 'institutional' is referring to the investment institutions who the lease is designed to serve). Such a lease will be recognisable by:

- a relatively long term, 25 years being the norm
- regular rent reviews, usually every 5 years, at which the rent can only stay the same or go up, not down
- the tenant being responsible for the maintenance of the fabric of the building – full repairing and insuring terms.

Clearly, this is a very effective set of conditions if you are an investor who wants to collect rent on a building and minimise management costs.

One of the unfortunate consequences of this lease has been the development of a very distant relationship between the investor and the asset, and between the landlord and the tenant. Over the long term this has been seen to undermine the productivity of that relationship and the fabric of the building. While the occupier is charged with a repairing obligation, not having a long-term interest in the building mitigates against investment in capital equipment and major improvements (Weatherhead, 1997; Edington, 1997).

It has also become apparent that this rather rigid leasing structure is simply inappropriate for the modern economy in which we now operate. The vast majority of businesses in the UK, particularly the SMEs, as identified above, do not want a 25-year lease and often need something more flexible than a standard institutional grade office building. The lease terms are, of course, negotiable and it has been usual in the past for the term to be reduced and break clauses to be included in order to provide more flexibility. However, the extent to which a tenant has been able to negotiate these sorts of change has been dependent on a range of variable factors including, particularly, the level of supply and demand within the market.

This type of negotiation is typical of the third level of this institutional arrangement, but there is currently the possibility of legislation being enacted to change the nature of the commercial lease in the UK (change within the second level). This is being strongly resisted by operators within the market (third level) and a Code of Practice has been published (RICS, 2002) as a means of forestalling what is seen as a potentially prescriptive and unnecessary move. The property industry has argued vociferously that voluntary measures are sufficient. The government has demanded evidence of change in practice if it is to be persuaded not to legislate.

This issue provides an excellent example of the three levels of the institutional arrangement of the property markets in operation. Players at the first level, essentially government and its agents, want to encourage economic development through the SME sector, and see the provision of more flexible terms and conditions of occupation of space as one way of doing this. It seeks to do this by amending the institutional arrangement at the second level. The market operators respond by offering to introduce greater flexibility at the third level, where they are active. If they can avoid a change in the institutional rules at the second level they retain more flexibility in their operation of the market.

From the perspective of the corporate occupier, these legal institutions are perhaps the most significant of the rules of engagement within the property markets. A real estate executive who understands how these institutions work will identify the potential for occupancy cost savings or opportunities for expansion through negotiation. Without this depth of knowledge a real estate portfolio risks paying too much rent and accepting lease terms and conditions that do not fully support the business strategy.

Financial institutions

The second institutional arrangement we will study is the financial framework from which the rules and conventions governing the operation of the UK finance sector flow. These institutions are fundamental to property rights for three reasons:

(1) property rights normally have financial value which must be capable of clear and unequivocal assessment
(2) property rights are commonly held as investments and are therefore to some degree financial instruments in their own right
(3) property is commonly used as security to raise capital.

For all these reasons, and more, if the financial institutional arrangement is not robust and reliable the stability of the economy will be undermined.

It is worth reiterating at this stage what is meant by 'institutional arrangement'. We are focusing on institutions in the sense of an openly acknowledged system through which something, in this case the property market, operates. It is important not to confuse this meaning with the common reference to insurance companies and other large financial organisations as 'institutions'.

The constitutional level – ensuring financial stability

One of the most important structures within any market or mixed economy is a reliable banking system. It is the banking system that provides the conduits for transferring capital from one area of the economy to another. Without it, or without complete investor confidence in it, investment and the transfer of capital is slow and inefficient. This inevitably leads to economic inefficiency. The reliability of the banking system is thus paramount and is protected by the institutional arrangement governing the finance sector. The problems that can flow from an unstable banking system are most graphically illustrated by the Wall Street Crash. The depression that characterises 1930s America was partly due to the collapse of the banking system. Lack of confidence in the system led to account holders demanding to withdraw their money on the basis that if they did not have it now, they would lose it. This created a 'run on the bank' in many towns, and an insufficiently organised support network for those banks meant they were unable to repay deposits, resulting in many of them collapsing and many people losing all their money.

Maintaining confidence in the system

While minimum levels of liquidity are enforced that allow banks to cover depositors' withdrawals, the level of liquidity in modern times has fluctuated between 0.25% and 1%. If all depositors decided to withdraw money at once the system would collapse. Maintaining confidence within the system thus becomes a necessity and contributes to the system's own stability.

Changes were made to the banking systems in different countries to try to avoid a crisis occurring again. In the UK, if a bank is in danger of collapsing, the Bank of England takes steps to support it, if it is felt that allowing it to collapse would endanger the whole of the banking system. This is known as the Bank of England's role as 'the lender of last resort'. It was last necessary to use this system in 1974 when so called 'near banks', set up to avoid restrictions on the creation of credit, made high-risk loans to property companies. The companies suffered severe financial disaster when property values fell substantially.

This event is well documented but other incidences of banking collapse have been seen since, mainly as a result of fraud of one kind or another rather than more widespread economic problems. A notable example is that of Barings Bank, an investment bank, which collapsed in 1996 as a result of the irregular activities of one of its dealers. The Bank of England did not protect it as, while a problem for the larger investors, its collapse was no threat to the banking system as a whole. The use of taxpayers' money to protect it was therefore unwarranted. Investors of relatively small amounts are protected against the loss of most of their money.

The organisational level – encouraging vigilance

Since 1992 the capital adequacy requirement mutually agreed between bank regulators from around the world has required banks to maintain capital of at least 8% of their assets. This is in addition to 0.5% liquidity for UK banks currently to be kept with the Bank of England, to ensure sufficient funds are available to cover withdrawals, and 0.5% liquidity to service daily transactions between the banks. This still allows banks sufficient flexibility to make money through the granting of loans and the financing of investments to the tune of £10 for every £1 deposited with them.

These occurrences and the rules that have developed as a result of them, help to illustrate the way in which the institutional arrangement operates to ensure efficiency within the system. If all depositors were protected from losing their money there would be no incentive to maintain a watchful eye on the operation of the banks or for the banks to behave responsibly. If depositors of smaller amounts were not protected, the vast majority of the public would have little confidence in the system, again reducing efficiency. So the institutional framework has been allowed to develop a system which protects the depositor of smaller amounts while encouraging the depositor of large amounts and the bank itself to support that protection through vigilance.

The banking system operates through the creation of credit on the basis of deposits held. However, economic development does not continue without investment and this requires a reliable system through which we can transfer credit from one form of capital into another. This system relies on using valuable assets as security, often in the form of real estate. (For a full discussion of the flows of capital, see Harvey, 1985.) This is where the third level of the institutional arrangement takes effect.

The operational level – facilitating investment and entrepreneurial activity

In the case of many small enterprises, the entrepreneur's house will provide the security for money raised to finance the business venture. In the case of larger organisations the value of the property portfolio is often used to raise capital.

The basic system is sound and is supported by market incentives. In order to raise capital the asset has to be identified as having value. The lender has an incentive to ensure accurate assessment of the value of the asset and the reliability of the proposed investment. The borrower has an incentive to ensure the success of the proposed investment in order to avoid losing the original asset.

Open to negotiation?

Within this basic framework, flexibility can then be applied in the form of negotiation between the lender and borrower. This will be prompted by the opportunity that each sees to make a profit and the level of risk they identify within the market. In situations where high levels of profit have been identified lenders have been willing to take on high levels of risk by lending to unproven companies or individuals or on less than prime assets. This has led to spectacular results, both positive and negative, for the parties concerned.

In the case of property companies this has gone so far as developers raising funds for the next development project on the value of the previous development project, which is retained and let. This is risky as it exposes the property company and, more particularly, the lender of the money, to the property markets twice. If property values fall, the value of the security will be undermined as will the value of the development project. This happened in many instances in the late 1980s. The exposure of the banks to the property markets at that time was significantly larger than it had been in the 1970s property crash. However, the institutional arrangements put in place to avoid banking collapse helped to retain confidence in the system. A number of banks made losses for some years and had to write off considerable sums in bad debts to the property sector, but none collapsed.

Big Bang – deregulation of the British banking system

The most important change to the institutional arrangements governing the financial markets in recent years was the deregulation of the banking and building societies sector in 1986. This allowed both banks and building societies greater freedom of operation and gave them the opportunity to compete with each other. The mortgage market expanded and the commercial lending operations of the building societies also expanded. In the short term this led to much greater levels of lending on property and was a contributory factor within the property crash of the early 1990s.

However, this was because of the way the changes were utilised by the market operators. The same arrangement is in operation today but the market operators have adopted a more cautious approach to lending. The property market crash of the early 1990s is a good example of 'market shock' as a response to a change in the institutional arrangement through which it operates. Equally good examples can be seen in countries undergoing major changes, such as deregulation of banking systems and the introduction of a market oriented institutional arrangement that is open to global influences and exchange rate markets. Charles Goodhart, an adviser to the Bank of England, has even gone so far as to say the removal of exchange controls and banking constraints in China will lead to a major market shock in the form of a financial collapse in the next few years (Goodhart, 2000). We will have to wait and see if he is right.

Thus it is clear that the institutional arrangement that defines the operation of an economy's financial system underpins the smooth operation of that economy and its ability to experience economic growth. Any changes to the arrangement will have a direct impact on the economy and in the short to medium term that impact may take the form of market shock. However, it is also clear that the institutional structures must allow sufficient flexibility for the markets to respond to changes in the economic and cultural climate, just as we saw in the legal arrangement. Only by market operators being able to amend their approach to risk in different markets can capital be allocated to the most efficient sector of the economy.

For the corporate occupier, these financial institutions enable capital to be raised through the portfolio or the portfolio to expand through the use of someone else's capital. Crucially, a stable and robust set of financial institutions significantly reduces the risk inherent within this type of arrangement and hence transaction costs. A comprehensive understanding of these financial institutions and their operation will enable a real estate executive to make the best use of the capital asset a property portfolio represents. Incorporating this type of expertise within the development of business strategy for the organisation as a whole is the only way of ensuring opportunities are not missed.

Exercise 8.1

(1) Consider the impact that the following institutional changes might have on the property market:

    (a) An increase of stamp duty to 2% on house purchases of over £250,000

    (b) Release of green belt land for development

    (c) Introduction of Development Land Tax.

(2) How would the changes to the Use Classes Order affect property held as an operational asset?

(3) How would the introduction of Enterprise Zones and Urban Development Zones impact upon a property investment portfolio?

References

Byrne, P., Lizieri, C. & Worzala, E. (2001) *The Location of Executive Suites and Business Centres: an exploratory analysis, Final Reseach Report.* Real Estate Institute, Bloomington.

Edington, G. (1997) *Property Management: a customer focused approach.* Macmillan, London.

Gibson, V. & Lizieri, C. (2001) Friction and inertia: business change, corporate real estate portfolios and the UK office market. *Journal of Real Estate Research*, **22** (1/2) 59–79.

Goodhart, C. (2000) Keynote speech at RICS Cutting Edge Conference, 6–8 September, London.

Harvey, D. (1985) *The Urbanisation of Capital.* Basil Blackwell, Oxford.

Heighton, M. (2002) Turn over the issues. *Estates Gazette*, 2 March 214–215.

Lizieri, C. (2001) New players, new markets: has the property industry really changed? IPD/IPF Property Investment Conference, 29–30 November, Brighton.

RICS (2002) *A Code of Practice for Commercial Leases in England and Wales.* RICS, London.

Weatherhead, M. (1997) *Real Estate in Corporate Strategy.* Macmillan, Basingstoke.

Further reading

Gibson, V. & Lizieri, C. (1999) New business practices and the corporate property portfolio: how responsive is the UK property market? *Journal of Real Estate Research*, **16** (3) 201–218.

Rydin, Y. (1993) *The British Planning System: An Introduction.* Macmillan, Basingstoke.

www.commercialleasecodeew.co.uk

Chapter 9
An Institutional Approach to Understanding Property Markets – Administrative Institutions

Introduction

This chapter looks at the last of the three institutions we identified in Chapter 7.[1] The administrative institutions are formed by government, its agencies and the policy mechanisms that flow from them. Property is subject to considerable regulation, most of which flows from the administrative institutions. The fundamental role that land and buildings play in the everyday working of the economy, combined with the high financial value they represent, make it inevitable that their use will be subject to a complex and changing set of rules, forming the major administrative institutions.

This chapter examines how these institutions, or rules, impact on the operation of the property markets and the implications they might have for the operation of a corporate property portfolio.

Constitutional level

The first level within the institutional arrangement is set by the political economy of the day and will reflect the priorities of government policy. These tend to reflect the main macroeconomic objectives of price stability, economic growth, employment, balance of payments stability and maintenance of the environment. This basic agenda remains more or less unchanged whatever the political persuasion of the party in office. What changes is the priority order of the list.

Real estate and the property markets are implicated in some way in each of these macroeconomic objectives. Consequently they are utilised by government to implement policy either directly, such as through government funded development, or indirectly by providing the conduit through which policy takes effect. This interface between property and the national administrative system is relatively fixed. The only major change that has taken place since the Second World War period has been the addition of 'maintenance of the environment' to the list of macroeconomic objectives. Consequently, the way in which government decides to implement policy and the objectives it decides to target will inevitably impact upon the operation of the property markets.

Economic growth

One of the most important areas of government policy relates to the promotion of economic growth. This tends to be generated through government spending which forms an injection into the circular flow of the economy. It has been particularly important in the past in generating growth nationally during periods of recession and more locally in areas of economic decline. It is common for this type of government spending to be directed through property, mainly through construction and building development programmes, primarily because construction has been identified as the most efficient means of getting investment expenditure to flow round the economy as a whole.

The government house-building programme following the Second World War and the development of the country's motorway network in the 1970s are two of the most important government investment projects of the twentieth century. They both used the property markets as the conduit through which the government policy objective of economic growth could be implemented most effectively. They both led to, amongst other things, substantial increases in economic growth for the country as a whole.

For the property markets themselves, this has important implications. Major government projects increase the demand for labour and materials, which can, if capacity is insufficient, lead to higher production costs for the rest of the industry and a slow down in private sector development. Equally, during a period of recession, this sort of government project can inject much needed demand into the private sector, sustaining companies and individuals within the industry through an economic downturn and thereby ensuring capacity is available for the economic growth which will follow.

Public–private partnerships

Since the mid-1990s, Government policy has been inclined to reduce public sector spending by passing the financing of major infrastructure projects and social housing projects to the private sector. These policies are grouped under a policy known as Public–Private Partnership Programme (4Ps), which includes the Private Finance Initiative. This policy shift also has implications for the property markets. The private sector has different funding decisions from the public sector. While collectively having access to a much larger pool of funding, private companies are unlikely to embark on a programme as ambitious as an entire national motorway network. The problems encountered by the UK rail network are a vivid manifestation of the difficulties inherent in transferring this type of capital spending programme from the public to the private sector.

Public spending

The early years of the twenty-first century have seen a significant increase in the level of public spending, particularly investment in hospitals and schools. Much of this spending has targeted building works and the impact on demand and supply within the construction industry has been widely reported. The shortage of skilled labour, particularly electricians and plumbers has led to substantial increases in costs, as has shortages of materials. The knock-on effect in building cost inflation is easy to see and this ultimately impacts on the whole economy. The short-term impact of increased public capital spending might be beneficial but the long-term impact of increased building and therefore occupancy costs, increases risk within the economy as a whole and this should not be ignored.

Environmental responsibility

The one change we noted within the list of macroeconomic preoccupations, was the addition to the agenda of 'maintenance of the environment'. This is an objective that is becoming embedded within all areas of policy and, inevitably, has a significant impact upon property. It manifests itself most significantly through development control but is not limited to this area. Strict regulation exists to control pollution and contamination of land. This increases the risks associated particularly with industrial corporate occupiers who need to take measures to ensure their activities do not contaminate their own or adjoining land or waterways.

More recently, the environmental debate has given way to the broader debate surrounding 'sustainable development'. Environmental and social responsibility is becoming embedded within public policy where it is becoming an expectation that issues of sustainable development are considered within the development and implementation of policy. This is matched in the business sector where corporate governance and corporate social responsibility have risen up the boardroom agenda surprisingly quickly.

The constitutional level within the administrative branch of the institutional arrangement comprises:

(1)   government macroeconomic objectives, which rarely change
(2)   political priorities, which change according to the state of the economy
(3)   government policy, which changes over the long term but again tends to be constrained by economic circumstances.

Each of the above will have an impact on the property markets, which are used, either directly or indirectly, to implement policy. Policies will be implemented through a variety of mechanisms including statutes, consultation papers, policy guidance and incentives, all designed to influence behaviour. These mechanisms form the second level of the arrangement. They are characterised by greater flexibility than the first level but are ultimately driven by the policy objectives of the central administration (central government). Policy interpretation and implementation at the local level and the operation of the property markets have to reflect their content.

Organisational level

The organisational level within the framework provides the context within which the property markets operate. The most important elements for the property markets include issues of tax and development control. Both are used as means of increasing or reducing development and directing development to specific areas or property types and both are currently under review.

Taxation

There are a variety of taxation issues in relation to property which are far beyond the scope of this book. This section examines those tax issues we consider to be most pertinent to the corporate property occupier, local property taxes (rates) and the potential for taxing development land.

Local property taxes

Property taxes have long been used as the main local form of raising revenue. In the UK they are based on the rateable value of the building, which is based on an estimate of its annual rental value, and levied annually at a centrally set rate (the Uniform Business Rate). This element of taxation normally forms a significant element of occupancy costs. Some occupiers, charities for example, can obtain relief from a portion of it. This may make a substantial difference to business costs and any potential of this relief being lost or jeopardised by a change in business activity should be viewed carefully.

Suggestions are sometimes made that additional revenue should be raised from local businesses to resolve particular local issues. Such schemes have been used successfully in the USA to fund Town Centre Management schemes. They tend to be resisted in the UK but, from a corporate occupier perspective, such suggestions should be monitored. They may increase occupancy costs but if the revenue is effectively used in improving an area, this could be money well spent.

Taxing development

There are two main areas where the possibilities of a form of 'development tax' are explored:

(1)   where value is increased through the granting of planning permission
(2)   where value is increased as a side effect of public sector investment, particularly in relation to transport links.

The windfall profits accruing to developers as a result of gaining planning permission tend to be taxed through the system of planning obligations that are currently negotiated between the development control officers (organisational level) and the developers (operational level). This is discussed below under Development control. Attempts have been made in the past to place a tax on development, most notably Development Land Tax, but they have tended to be unsuccessful, leading to a reduction in the supply of development land and the identification of ways around the system.

The increase in value that accrues to a landowner as a result of public sector investment is more difficult to assess. If development of a new London Underground line, such as the Jubilee Line extension, can double the value of commercial real estate within its vicinity, it seems logical that some of this increase should come back to the taxpayer. Of course, an element already does, as the local property taxes payable on a building (rates) are likely to increase. However, this increase will be smoothed out to some extent across all the property in the area so it only addresses the windfall in part. Perhaps more importantly, the occupier of a rented building who receives none of the benefit of the increase in capital value will normally pay the rates.

It would be difficult and highly controversial to introduce a tax on this kind of gain, but the possibilities are currently being investigated (ATIS REAL Weatheralls and UCL, 2002). Whether or not organisational level institutions are changed to allow for it remains to be seen.

Development control

Development control provides the framework within which our use of real estate is organised.[2] For the developer, this is the main area of interaction with organisational level administrative institutions and a significant transaction cost in the operation of the development market. On the government (both local and central) side of the equation, it provides a mechanism for encouraging or discouraging different types and levels of development as a means of pursuing policy objectives.

For the corporate occupier, development control will impact on

- the potential for changing the use of property within the portfolio – increasingly important to SMEs which expand quickly and have a range of functions their building must support
- the potential for expanding the portfolio through development
- the maintenance obligations it places on the owners of building with heritage value, i.e buildings protected through listing.

Proposed legislation

The 2002 Planning and Compulsory Purchase Bill seeks to make changes at the organisational level. The main objectives of the Bill (which is expected to receive Royal Assent in mid-2003) are to improve the development control process by, amongst other things:

- speeding up the decision-making process for planning applications
- removing the option of 'twin tracking' (submitting two similar applications simultaneously to avoid delay if one is rejected)
- replacing structure plans, local development plans and regional planning guidance with local development frameworks, local development documents and regional spatial strategies
- introducing 'local development orders' which may ultimately replace outline planning permission, although it has been the case that the latter perform a very useful function within the development process, and as such will be retained
- reducing the normal life of a planning permission from five to three years, after which it is not longer valid if it is not acted upon
- replacing planning obligation (section 106 agreements) with a more structured and transparent system of fees
- strengthening the local development authorities' powers of compulsory purchase
- increasing the level of compensation payable where compulsory purchase takes place.

This is by no means a definitive breakdown of the provisions of the Planning and Compulsory Purchase Bill (there is a useful commentary on it in Guyat (2003, and at www.law-now.com) but it gives an indication of the impact of changes in the institutional arrangements under which the property markets operate. Viewed in institutional terms, the objective of this proposed legislation is the reduction of the transaction costs created by inefficiencies in the development control system. By making the system work more smoothly it is anticipated that the market will work more efficiently, particularly in relation to the provision of development seen as desirable at the organisational and operational levels.

Planning gain

Perhaps the most radical proposals are those relating to planning obligations, otherwise known as section 106 agreements. The planning obligation system has long been used by local planning authorities to extract some gain for the community from the granting of planning permission to a private developer. This may take the form of a new access road to improve traffic flow, a green space, or a contribution to a community project. The difficulties within this system are seen to lie in the lack of consistency with which it is applied in different areas. Guidance is given as to 'reasonableness' in relation to a development but application across the UK is still variable.

The suggestion has been made that the system be replaced by a scale of fees, to be set locally and levied according to the size of the development. While this may not reduce the monetary cost to the developer of obtaining planning permission, it would reduce the transaction costs created by the uncertainty and length of negotiations that take place under the current system. The proposals have been indicated in the Bill but only in outline, at the time of writing (early 2003). A more detailed proposal is expected imminently.

Operational level

The third level within the administrative institutional arrangement is where the developers, the development control officers and the community all interact. This level is manifest in policy interpretation, community consultation, for example in the drawing up of local or unitary development plans, and negotiation between public and private sector property market operators.

The interpretation of policy at the operational level may reduce or increase the amount of development or investment that takes place or direct development or investment to a particular area or even site. Development control is essentially a system of policy interpretation and implementation and thus it allows flexibility to be incorporated into the operation of the system. It also allows for inconsistency to develop in the application of policy across different regions. Whether this inconsistency is a positive or negative characteristic of the system is difficult to say. One could argue that it allows local development control officers to reflect local needs and requirements within planning decisions, improving the efficiency of the market. One could also argue that it creates unpredictability within the market, increasing risk and thus transaction costs, reducing the efficiency of the market.

Housing

The current (2003) shortage of housing, particularly in the south-east of the UK and London, has led to the implementation of local development control policies to encourage development of low cost housing. A private sector housing development of 15 or more houses within some local planning authority areas, will have to provide some low cost or social housing on site. In some instances this has led to positive relationships being formed between developers and housing associations or other social landlords. The developer obtains planning permission for the site and in the process provides housing which is usually handed to a housing association for management. This effectively represents a tax on the developer, but the site will not be developed if it is not profitable net of the effect.

The downside of this system is the distortion created within the property development market. Sites that may have been suitable for development of between 15 and 20 houses are simply not developed, or if they are, 14 units are developed. This inevitably reduces the efficiency with which the resource is being used and where proposals exist to increase the requirement to 50% social housing, in London for example, this is likely to get worse.

This system of extracting social housing through planning obligation also relies on the value of housing remaining high. If house prices reach a plateau, or fall, residential development sites with these conditions attached to planning permission will quickly become uneconomic to develop, reducing the supply of all forms of housing. The difficulties inherent within this system and the inconsistency with which it is applied is one of the arguments behind the removal of section 106 agreements and replacing them with a more transparent system of a scale of fees as discussed above.

Property-led economic regeneration

One of the most far-reaching examples of the administrative branch of the institutional arrangement at work is its application within development-led economic regeneration. This was used substantially in the 1980s to encourage development in areas of industrial decline, such as the dockland areas of London and Liverpool. There was an identified requirement for economic redevelopment and growth, particularly in inner city areas, and government policy dictated that this would be most effectively brought about through increased private sector development activity across the country as a whole, but with an emphasis on areas of specific need.

Two major institutional changes took place to facilitate this policy.

(1) The development control system was effectively deregulated, becoming more efficient and sympathetic to the demands of private sector developers:
  - maximum time periods were set down for development control decisions
  - the development plan system was reviewed with the objective of making it clear to developers what schemes would be acceptable in different areas
  - a presumption in favour of planning permission required that permission be granted unless there was a particularly good reason for withholding it (this policy was reinforced through the appeal system)
  - conditions attached to planning permission and the use of section 106 agreements were reviewed to making them more 'developer friendly'
  - the use classes order was reviewed and a new class of B1 introduced which could be used for light industrial or office uses.

(2) Urban Development Corporations and Enterprise Zones were established in areas that demanded the highest levels of economic regeneration. These gave tax incentives to property development and deemed planning permission to have been granted, thereby removing local development control powers within the boundaries of the schemes.

These changes were implemented within the organisational level of the institutional arrangement but their impact was felt within the operational level. They were manifest in documents such as planning policy guidance (PPGs), regional policy guidance (RPGs) government circulars, development plans and the use classes order (UCO). However, their impact was felt in the increased level of development activity in the EZs and UDCs, the increase in the number of planning applications and appeals made and the rapid spread of B1 office space across areas that were initially occupied by light industry.

How much has changed?

It is interesting to note the similarity between these changes, made in the early 1980s under a relatively radical programme of government policy, and the changes suggested within the Planning and Compulsory Purchase Bill, 2002. There is a greater emphasis on community involvement and the changes to planning obligations will perhaps be taken further, but the basic institutional arrangement remains unchanged.

The current climate is one of greater caution with regard to the granting of planning permission, particularly in relation to environmental consequences and thus development has slowed down. Regeneration is also less likely to be entirely property-led and will reflect local economics and community initiatives. However, the political–economic objectives remain unchanged and many of the mechanisms for implementing those objectives are the same as they were in the 1980s. The market is interpreting and using the mechanisms in a way that reflects the current economic context. It is essential that the institutional arrangement allows the market to do this.

Implications for the corporate occupier

For the corporate occupier, this type of policy can provide useful cost savings. Location in areas targeted for regeneration can attract tax incentives and considerable flexibility in terms of the use of space. The 2002 Planning and Compulsory Purchase Bill enlarges a little upon the existing concept of simplified planning zones, referred to now as Business Planning Zones, which retain many of the liberal development control features of the Enterprise Zones. The objective is to attract business to an area by providing appropriate space and environmental conditions, i.e by reducing transaction costs. This type of policy instrument can be useful for a corporate occupier, as long as the location fits with the rest of the business strategy.

Within the context of the strategic management of corporate property, an understanding of these institutions and the impact they have on the operation of the property markets is invaluable. It provides the depth of understanding that enables a real estate professional to interpret the likely impact political–economic changes may have on a portfolio. This makes it possible to prepare a defence or capitalise on an opportunity. Perhaps even more importantly it may prevent him from being taken by surprise.

References

ATIS REAL Weatheralls and UCL (2002) *Land Value and Public Transport*. RICS, London.

Goodhart, C. (2000) Keynote speech at RICS Cutting Edge Conference, 6–8 September, London.

Guyat, R. (2003) The Planning and Compulsory Purchase Bill: proposed changes to the development control regime. *Planning Law Journal*, 10 Feb.

Rydin, Y. (1993) *The British Planning System: An Introduction*, Macmillan, Basingstoke.

Endnotes

[1] It is helpful to read Chapter 7 before reading this chapter.

[2] For a comprehensive text on development control in the UK see, for example, Rydin (1993).

Chapter 10
Formulating Strategies for Property Management

Introduction

The first nine chapters of this book have analysed the property markets, and the management issues particular to property within the context of those markets, in some detail. The approach has been to analyse the elements that form the property markets by section, enabling us to examine and understand each one in detail. The aim is to develop a consistent but dynamic management strategy that can be applied to any type of property holding in order to maximise the contribution of the real estate to the objectives of the organisation of which it forms part. This chapter begins to piece this jigsaw puzzle of property rights and obligations back together again and, in doing so, explores the management strategies that are currently being applied to real estate.

The application of institutional analysis

Chapters 7 to 9 developed an institutional approach to the analysis of the property markets, exploring them from the perspective of the major decision-making structures that influence and shape them. It is important that this perspective is retained when strategy for managing real estate is developed, particularly given the impact new decisions or priorities within those institutions have on the property markets. Weimer, writing in 1966, was very graphic about the fundamental influence government has on real estate:

'Except for narcotics, no commodity is affected by government to a greater extent.'

Weimer, 1966, p. 108

Weimer points out that rights in real estate are a product of government, which they in turn rely on for enforcement, and therefore continued existence. His list of government initiatives relevant to the operation of property is not exhaustive but illustrates the extent to which real estate and the process of government are intrinsically linked:

- full employment policies
- income tax
- depreciation allowances
- monetary policies
- urban renewal and transportation programmes
- supervision of lending institutions
- guarantee and insurance of mortgages
- local taxation
- zoning
- building codes.

Although Weimer was writing in 1966 and focusing on real estate in the USA this list has surprisingly strong relevance today. This current relevance demonstrates the continuity and strength of the relationship between property and the institutional arrangement of power.

In developing a real estate strategy for any organisation it is essential that the administrative framework is taken into consideration and the political-economic context is established. It is this that provides the barometer we use to reduce the uncertainty surrounding decisions based upon future productivity and economic buoyancy. It is the constitutional level within the institutional arrangement that provides the rules under which the markets operate and which thus provides the context for any property strategy.

In Chapter 8 we examined the legal and financial institutions within which the property markets operate. We touched on the large proportion of invest-ment which real estate often represents within an organisation and the potential it holds for financing options. When an organisation develops a real estate strategy it has to consider how it wants to finance the investment. When there is simply rent to account for the strategy is straightforward. When capital investment is required it is less so.

It might be possible to raise finance through a mortgage, based on the value of the real estate asset to be acquired, or on the value of existing real estate. This might be cheaper than a conventional loan secured on the income of the organisation. Where a bespoke building is necessary or a new building required, a joint venture may be the best option for financing, incorporating an investor to provide long-term funding in return for a geared rent and a portion of equity in the building. The conventions surrounding property financing can be complicated but have to be incorporated in a real estate strategy if it is to support the management strategy of the organisation effectively.

The third institutional arrangement examined was legal; the context pro-vided by the legislative institutions that form the framework of property ownership. This legislative context is often characterised within strategy for-mulation by the buy/lease decision but it can be misleading to simplify the myriad forms of property rights and obligations so. Decisions relating to the form of property rights an organisation adopts will reflect a number of different factors.

Organisational factors

The following section explores some of the organisational factors that drive property decisions. The discussion is arranged as a series of questions that could be asked about any organisation. The discussion they generate illustrates the extent to which each of the three institutions we have examined govern the alternatives available for real estate strategy.

What stage of development has the organisation reached?

The start-up organisation is unlikely to want long-term property rights, opting for the flexibility of a relatively short lease, or perhaps a longer one with a break clause. A more established business, which has a more highly developed understanding of its markets and better information on which to predict the future, is likely to opt for property rights that will support the further development of its stability, perhaps by guaranteeing a particular geographical location for a minimum period.

It may be that the organisation as a whole is well established but is seeking to extend operations by moving into a new market, or needs space for a specific project or enterprise that has a set life span. This will influence the organisation's decision with regard to taking on property rights, which are likely to be short term, for that specific area of activity.

Does the organisation want the responsibility of property management that comes with the freedom to improve and use the property as it wishes?

This question is connected to the first question. The answer will depend to some degree on the stage of development the organisation has reached. A start-up organisation is unlikely to be concerned with the potential for improving or changing the property it occupies, so will be content to acquire relatively short-term property rights giving it limited obligations, a licence for example.

An organisation that is established and expanding is much more likely to be concerned with its freedom to use and improve and, perhaps even more importantly, the potential to increase its floor space. As such it is critical for an organisation that is expanding to involve property management in its organisation's management strategy. This avoids expansion plans being undermined by insufficient space being available or only being available at high cost. The most appropriate space is unlikely to be acquired if insufficient time is allocated to search and negotiation.

An organisation that is well established may require long-term rights over property holdings. Where the organisational objective is consolidation of operations, to improve operating efficiency or strengthen competitive position, securing a presence in a particular location may be important. The ability to make changes to property, which complement a developing business strategy, may become more of an issue. Such rights only come with the obligations and responsibilities of effective property management.

What real estate options are available to the organisation?

This will reflect the state of the market within which the organisation is seeking space. A market characterised by high demand and restricted supply will present limited options for the organisation. This will be reflected in the terms and conditions under which property can be obtained as well as the price. If space is only available on terms that are unattractive this may make the operation too risky to pursue.

This question also allows the real estate strategist to consider the wider context of property options. Could the organisation benefit from space availability in another region, country or continent? Could the organisation use existing space more efficiently in order to free up capacity? Could the organisation adopt innovative space strategies to use space more efficiently?

What financing options are available to the organisation?

Corporate real estate management literature has identified financing options as an area commonly neglected by corporate executives in the past. This was one of the catalysts behind the asset stripping of the mid to late 1980s. One business organisation identified the value in another's real estate portfolio, purchased the company, closed it and sold the real estate for a profit. This precipitated a rapid learning curve as businesses realised the importance of correctly valuing their real estate assets. Most organisations now at least understand that their property holdings are valuable assets that should be reflected in the balance sheets.

However, the idea that these property holdings could be used as a means of raising relatively cheap capital took a little longer to dawn. If an organisation already has extensive property holdings, it is important to explore the possibility that finance could be raised through them for new property requirements. The usual alternatives will be through bank credit or retained profits. Whichever avenue is explored, the investment in property has to be cost effective, so if the financing options are expensive this may also make the venture too risky.

How crucial is the real estate to the organisation?

Real estate can be crucial for a number of reasons. A long established organisation, which is associated with a particular building, will seek to retain that building as a central plank of its management strategy. The world famous retail store Harrods would suffer considerably if it lost its famous Knightsbridge location in London. A central tenet of its management strategy will be the protection and optimum use of this building.

An organisation whose principal activity is land based will also see its real estate holdings as crucial, seeking to protect, and in some instances extend, those holdings. A farm, for example, relies on the quantity and quality of its land for productivity and profitability. If a farm decides to extend its land holdings it will want to acquire rights for a relatively long period of time, if not in perpetuity.

Other organisations have far more ambivalent approaches to their real estate holdings and consequently can apply a much more flexible management strategy that can produce least cost solutions for the portfolio. Back room tasks can move to locations where accommodation is cheap and labour cheap and plentiful. The most extreme examples of this type of strategy so far seem to be the call centres set up in India to take calls from the UK and USA.

Whether the requirement for space is short term, long term or indefinite, an established organisation may require additional space for a short-term enterprise or project. In such a case, the strategy may be to acquire short-term rights, offsetting the increased facility management costs of site identification and negotiation of terms and conditions against the benefit of an early release once the project or enterprise is complete. Lettings are available for as little as one hour in some serviced office complexes, but the price is inevitably higher than for a conventional rights package such as a lease or licence. For a short-term project, it may be equally appropriate to utilise spare capacity or create additional capacity within existing space holdings. It will only be possible to identify this as a potential least cost solution if the executive with responsibility for real estate has input into the management strategy for the business and, most importantly, has access to sufficient information about the existing estate.

Where the requirement is for long-term or indefinite space, for example where a factory plant or engineering works is being developed for a particular process, it is essential that rights to the property are secured for sufficient length of time for any investment in plant and machinery to be recovered. Again, real estate strategy has to have input into the business strategy for this to be ensured. Securing property rights for an indefinite period leaves an organisation with obligations for the same indefinite period. This considerably increases the risk inherent within a venture if that real estate is taking a significant chunk of investment capital.

Do investment or fixed costs need to be minimised?

An organisation's investment in property may represent a considerable proportion of total fixed assets.[1] It is therefore important to consider whether this is the best use of capital or whether some of the capital should be liquidated. Sale and leaseback agreements and outsourcing contracts can transform capital tied up in real estate into working capital, such as for plant and machinery, to improve production. If the real estate is not critical to the organisation's performance and productivity and investment capital could be put to more productive use through application of new technology or research and development, reducing investment in real estate could significantly improve the performance of the organisation.

Minimising costs requires the productivity associated with real estate to be the driving force behind the decision to continue occupation. Such a strategy has to be supported by careful and detailed market knowledge coupled with a fundamental understanding of the operational requirements of the organisation. This enables decisions to be made to take on cheap space on short-term arrangements, taking advantage of fluctuations in market factors.

An example of such a strategy was the policy of National Car Parks (NCP) to purchase bomb-sites in London after the Second World War. The very unusual circumstances of the time produced sites that were derelict and available in the short term relatively cheaply. The rapid expansion of car ownership that followed provided demand for the product, which could be provided at a relatively low price thanks to the cost minimisation strategy of the organisation.

A cost minimisation strategy may, however, undermine the quality of the space provided, so can only be effectively employed where surroundings have a limited impact on productivity. An organisation that is knowledge based or driven by face-to-face contact with its customers may find taking cheap space to be a false economy. Utilising more expensive space in a cost effective and efficient way that supports the business function is likely to be a more effective strategy.

Any organisation can ask these questions of itself and use the answers to begin to develop a real estate strategy. Understanding the role of institutions within the property markets will assist in the analysis of potential options and the identification of opportunities. However, ultimately, the underlying function of a real estate strategy is to support the operational aspect of a business. To understand how to best align a real estate portfolio in this way requires a basic understanding of the overarching objectives and management strategy of the organisation itself, and for those responsible for developing these objectives and strategies to have an appreciation of the role of property.

The application of management strategy

The corporate property management literature has, for some years, reported a lack of interest amongst corporate executives in real estate[2] (Veale, 1989, Nourse and Roulac, 1993). The standard approach was to apply the classic question 'what business are we in?' and answer it 'we are not in the real estate business'. Of course this is nonsensical; any organisation, from a commune to a multinational business, has to use real estate in some way. Thus they are all in the real estate business at some level. Nonetheless, this approach seemed to legitimise the view that real estate had no active role to play within the development of a management strategy for the organisation as a whole. It was seen as a passive resource, supporting overall business strategy as cost effectively as possible.

This attitude is waning, particularly amongst organisations that take their management strategy seriously. Research conducted in the 1980s identified at least 25% of corporate property assets as being in real estate, and reported instances of companies estimating their real estate to be worth 50% of total assets. In some cases the property holdings were felt to be worth more than the book value of the company as a whole (Zeckhauser and Silverman, 1983). Nonetheless the research estimated that at that time only 40% of US companies 'clearly and consistently evaluate the performance of their real estate; most treating property as an overhead cost like stationery and paper clips' (Zeckhauser and Silverman, 1983, p. 111).

Thus, many non-property oriented organisations are not simply in the real estate business, but in it to a larger extent than a lot of property companies.

While these figures are historic, real estate has been identified as becoming increasingly expensive over time (Ball, 1994), so it is safe to suppose that the real estate values are likely to be increasing, rather than decreasing. This is supported by Bootle and Kalyan (2002), who estimated corporate real estate assets to be worth £400 bn in the UK, 34% of total business assets. One would expect to have seen a dramatic change in the corporate attitude to property strategy over the intervening period, but their research and that of others suggests this is not the case. Work carried out in 1993 and 1995 identified corporate real estate executives experiencing frustration in their attempts to integrate a corporate property strategy into the overall business strategy (Manning and Roulac, 1996).

Annual research carried out by the Corporate Real Estate Management Research Unit at Reading University since 1993 identifies fluctuations in the share of assets represented by real estate. The sharp fall in property values in the mid-1990s inevitably reduced the impact real estate had on book value, seeing this fall to approximately 10%. The subsequent recovery in the markets has seen this rise to 25–30% and the share of property in total costs has risen to nearer 35% (Bon and Luck, 1999).

Attitudes to corporate real estate can be equally affected by the fluctuations of the property market and business cycle. During the early to mid-1990s, when poor real estate decisions made at the end of the previous market peak were having a major impact on corporate bottom lines, the idea that 'every organisation that occupies space is in the real estate business as well' (Bon and Luck, 1999, p. 173) gained increasing approval. Once the problems associated with real estate began to abate with the upswing in the business cycle and the next round of negotiations at rent review and lease renewal, the same idea lost currency (Bon and Luck, 1999).

The importance of a property strategy to the overall management strategy seems to begin to slide down the corporate agenda as the problems that a poor property strategy can create become less obvious. Of course, this is the worst approach to take to the management of such a significant proportion of an organisation's assets. It suggests that the next time the importance of the organisation's property is acknowledged will be the next time poor management results in the organisation having a major property problem; not a strategy anyone would really recommend.

This tradition of taking a myopic view of property within an organisational portfolio context can be explained to some degree by the unique characteristics of property as an asset class and a business resource:

- the physically inflexible nature of buildings
- property's illiquidity as an asset
- the apparent time scale required to make radical changes to the portfolio
- the perception of property and the property markets as complex, risky and beyond the remit of business management
- the properties an organisation occupies often being the product of historic decisions in some cases made by senior management figures long since buried

These are all characteristics that add to the tendency for a disconnection between an organisation's senior management and its property strategy. In addition, the mismatch between the timeframe of business strategies and the timeframe of real estate makes reconnecting the two more difficult still. Whereas businesses tend to operate on a 3–5 year strategy, as O'Mara (1997) suggests, Gibson (1994) identifies 5–10 years as a more meaningful timeframe for property decisions. This obviously makes incorporating real estate into the organisation's management strategy problematic but it simultaneously makes it essential.

So how do we reconcile strategic decision making with something about which we apparently have very little choice? Initially by improving our understanding of the primary objectives that drive an organisation. This can then be more logically followed by a consideration of how the property portfolio can contribute to this organisational objective. This is supported by the development of a clearer understanding of real estate and its markets, facilitating identification of those aspects of the portfolio over which management does have a choice in the short term and the extent and nature of management's choice over property in the longer term.

Porter (1998), as discussed in Chapter 6, provides a common framework through which an industry can be analysed and a competitive strategy developed for an organisation within that industry. Nourse and Roulac (1993) take this a stage closer to the organisation. Using Tregoe and Zimmerman (1980) as their guide they provide a range of 'strategic driving forces ... that determine the future product and market scope that define a business and provide a framework for guiding operating decisions' (Nourse and Roulac, 1993, p. 476). While Tregoe and Zimmerman acknowledge that more than one of the strategic driving forces are likely to be important to a business, they argue that one will be the most important and will therefore drive the strategy of the organisation as a whole. These are represented on the next page alongside a brief analysis of the real estate issues that will be central to each one.

Once a property manager identifies the drivers behind the business organisation, he can begin to identify the real estate considerations that may support those driving forces. This sets up the possibility of a proactive real estate strategy, which feeds directly into the management strategy. While we have defined the strategic driving forces in sufficient depth for our purposes here, we have only begun to address the role of property. The next section explores

Strategic driving forces	Real estate considerations
Products/markets	
(1) *Products offered:* focus is on the product, ways of improving the product; the organisation is geared towards the development, production, promotion, sale, delivery and servicing of those products.	Real estate must promote and support product development and all support functions. A range of types of building will be required supporting R&D, production, sales and delivery network. Interface with customers may be necessary. Geography, accessibility and building design will be important. Changes/improvements within the production process must be accommodated within the real estate portfolio making flexibility and possible potential for expansion further considerations.
(2) *Market needs:* focus is on a particular segment of the market and the identification of products that serve that market. The organisation is geared towards needs analysis and the development of new products to serve identified needs.	Needs-analysis and product development require space which promotes creativity, data collection and communication. Location must give access to an appropriate work force and buildings must attract and retain staff. Final production is likely to be outsourced, having little impact on the real estate.
Capabilities	
(3) *Technology:* the focus is on the organisation's technological expertise. This is used to develop new products and services so the organisation is geared towards research to find new applications of its technology.	Research and development space will be crucial for such an organisation. These types of company were the target market for the B1 use class introduced to England and Wales in 1988. Real estate must be located and designed to attract and retain staff. Location close to similar companies will often be an important consideration, for example Silicon Valley in California and the Cambridge Science Park in the UK. Acquiring sufficient real estate to allow for expansion without relocating may also be a consideration.
(4) *Production capability:* the focus is on the production capabilities of the organisation and the identification of new products and services that utilise those capabilities. The organisation will be geared towards the improvement of the production process and the search for products it can be used to create.	Real estate must support the production function and will often be designed specifically and owner occupied. Such real estate can be very difficult to accurately assess in terms of market value. Access to suitable labour will be a consideration. Proximity to a required raw material may be crucial. These types of consideration make it important that the real estate is secure for the long term.
(5) *Method of sale:* The focus is on a specific method of sale, which the organisation strives to perfect, and uses to persuade customers to purchase certain types of goods. The organisation will be geared towards the identification of goods appropriate to this method of sale and the improvement of the method of sale. The sale of Ann Summers lingerie via parties in agents' homes is a good example of this strategic driving force.	Real estate may have to support the sales function directly but is more likely to have to support training and communication functions. Location will be an issue in terms of transport links rather than markets and will be weighted equally in importance with IT facilities. Short-term use of conference facilities or serviced office suites may be a strategy for this type of organisation, with headquarters' functions alone requiring long-term accommodation.

(6) *Method of distribution:* the focus is on the provision of goods and services via a particular distribution system. The organisation will strive to identify and develop products which can be delivered via the distribution system it operates and will seek to perfect this system. The development of telephone based products by BT and by cable television companies is a good example here.

Real estate must support the distribution system and provide access to customers. If the distribution system is physical, home delivery of goods for example, the portfolio will contain warehouses in a variety of locations. These can be cheap but must be close to transport hubs. Where the distribution system is technological, such as the telephone or cable network, the real estate must support the technology. Access will be continuous and internal environmental considerations as well as physical space considerations must be accounted for. Access to customers may be via telephone rooms that can be located anywhere in the world. A cost minimization function can be applied to this aspect of such an organisation.

(7) *Natural resources:* the focus will be on the provision of products and services derived from an organisation's rights over a natural resource. The organisation will be geared towards the development of new products based on that natural resource and its maintenance and protection. An organisation providing and managing access to a national park or natural feature is a useful example here.

Real estate is likely to be integral. It has to support the exploitation of the resource and efforts to conserve and protect the resource. This may be via strategic development to control access or by reinstatement of the land following exploitation. Agriculture exploits the natural resource but the real estate strategy is to reinstate and replenish the resource almost simultaneously.

Results

(8) *Size/growth:* The focus will be on fulfilling new growth objectives and identifying products and markets that can fulfil this. The organisation will be geared towards the identification of new opportunities. Virgin could be cited as an example in this context.

Real estate has to support the attraction and retention of key staff and knowledge-based work. Such an organisation's image is often also important, both in demonstrating market share and supporting a negotiating position. Real estate can be central to this. The real estate portfolio as a whole may be extended to exploit new opportunities so awareness of existing provision and potential for expansion is vital. Real estate must be a fundamental part of the management strategy within such an organisation.

(9) *Return/profit:* the focus will be on the identification of products and services with the potential to provide a return above a certain level. The products and services are not necessarily related. The organisation will be geared towards maintaining the rate of return required and identifying opportunities that will yield a similar return.

The portfolio of such an organisation can be very mixed and locationally diverse. It may incorporate assets purchased via merger and acquisition. The real estate assets of another organisation may be central to the return it produces. Corporate real estate management must be central to such an organisation and examined with every product and service under consideration.

Source: Adapted from Nourse and Roulac (1993)

the role of property within an organisation more closely, as we begin to get into a little more detail about the development and adoption of property strategies.

The role of property within the organisation

If we are to develop a strategy to maximise the contribution of property, we need to establish the role it plays within the organisation. O'Mara, 1999, reduces the role of real estate within an organisation's portfolio to two fundamentals: providing space in which the activity of the business is carried out AND presenting an image to the external world. Buildings 'help get the product out the door better, faster, or with less cost' (O'Mara, 1997, p. 5). While this is accurate, it is not terribly specific. Other research helps us to examine the role of real estate more specifically, in terms of its generic function but also in terms of the primary function of the specific organisation. Nourse and Roulac (1993) provide a list of questions that address this aspect of the property portfolio directly.

- What contribution does property make as an input to the production and service delivery function of the business?
- Is property central to distribution of the company's products?
- What role does geography play within the business?
- How important is interpersonal interaction between workers within the organisation?
- What amount of space per worker is required for the type of work done by that function?
- What message or image is the organisation trying to send via its property to its employees, suppliers, customers, the financial markets and the wider community?

Nourse and Roulac, 1993, p. 479

While they are working from a business-oriented perspective, the basic questions are applicable to any organisation with real estate holdings. A car plant will have a specially designed production system housed in purpose-built factories. The property is central to the production process. By contrast, a factory that produces computer components is affected far less by its property, although the design will have an impact on productivity. The property strategy each organisation adopts will reflect the different levels of importance attributed to the actual buildings held.

Property tends to be central to the distribution of retail goods. The shop is the traditional means whereby retailers connect with existing customers and find new ones. Consequently the location, design and fittings of the property unit are crucial to a retailer. However, if the retailer does not operate via this traditional network but uses e-commerce or catalogues as its main system of distribution, the real estate portfolio is important in a different way. Strategic planning of the property will contribute to a cost minimisation strategy within an e-commerce or catalogue based retailer by identifying the cheapest distribution warehousing with the best transport access. It will contribute to a strategy of focus among a traditional shop based retailer by identifying property in locations with favourable demographics.

The primary manufacturing industries of the UK were defined in many ways by geography while themselves shaping the geography of the country. Coal mining, steel making, shipbuilding, textiles, ceramics all became located in specific areas of the country because of certain geographical features, the most obvious being the proximity of a raw material such as coal. The decline of these industries and the growth of secondary and particularly tertiary sectors within the economy have freed business organisations from these geographic restrictions. However, the importance of geography to an organisation still has to be considered.

An organisation that provides and manages access to a national park or monument is tied by geography. An organisation with an intangible product – insurance, for example – is not. Some organisations are not tied by geography but have a distinctly regional presence, which is an important part of their management strategy. An example of this is building societies that focus their business on the region within which they were set up and after which they were named.

It is clear, therefore, that management strategies have to be applied to the property portfolio of an organisation if it is to achieve its operational objectives efficiently. This requires the development of a real estate strategy. However, it also requires the development of a coherent overall business or operating strategy, with clear organisational objectives. It is into this that the property strategy must feed.

The last section of this chapter looks at the issues that are currently important to the corporate property community. Research carried out since the early 1980s has led to the identification of a long list of factors that impact upon the effective management of real estate as a corporate or organisational resource. Certain key factors come up repeatedly.

(1) *A property inventory:* an up-to-date, accessible, standardised record of all properties over which the organisation has rights and obligations.
(2) *A formal property strategy:* a plan which allows for acquisition, development and disposal, needs assessment, financial analysis, planning, and management (which supports the organisation's management strategy and feeds into that strategy).
(3) *Formal inclusion in the management 'loop':* routine two-way communication and consultation between the corporate/organisational real estate management team, the individual business units or departments within the organisation and senior management.
(4) *Cost transparency:* an internal renting system for property space that is economically rational and commonly understood.

Zeckhauser and Silverman, 1983; Pitman and Parker, 1989;
Gale and Case, 1989; Schaefers, 1999; Carn et al., 1999

Although these key factors can be seen as generics for strategic management of the real estate resource within an organisation, they are sufficiently dynamic to be able to reflect the issues or considerations which impact upon the organisational property requirement over time. Research carried out in the USA suggests the major issues currently facing this area of management are globalisation, technological change, productivity, benchmarking, and flexibility (Carn *et al.*, 1999).

The globalisation of economic activity is increasing competition between operators and forcing organisations to strive for greater productivity. Given the large proportion of an organisation's assets often invested within property, if productivity is to be improved the utilisation of real estate as a resource for the organisation has to make efficiency gains. This is clearly linked to the second issue, technological change.

It is widely accepted that the impact of technological change on the use and operation of property is a major issue facing corporate property managers. However, there is often a misunderstanding of how and why. The commonly held belief that technological change is reducing the requirement for space as people change their working practices is erroneous. Technological advance tends to increase the amount of space an organisation requires. Research has been carried out on integrated work place strategies, looking in detail at new working practices and what implications they have for the use of space. This suggests a reorganisation of space and the identification of new work place settings as major issues facing real estate now and in the future, but does not suggest space requirements are going to fall (Becker and Joroff, 1995). Furthermore the upgrading of space to accommodate technological change arguably increases space costs.

Carn *et al.* (1999, p. 287) identify within their sample group an expectation that while the application of new technologies to work place settings will continue to increase in importance, 'the traditional space requirements for other types of corporate operations will continue to apply'. The way in which work space is used and defined will change over time but it will be driven by factors beyond simply technology. Human resource issues, sociological issues and environmental issues will all have an influence.

This suggests that corporate real estate should perhaps be looked at as part of a composite set of business support services alongside human resources, IT and finance. Pottinger (2000) cites research by the IDRC (1999) suggesting this approach is being developed and will be spearheaded by telecoms, health, business services and consultancy services. The more recent downturn in the business sector may, however, slow this trend.

Productivity and benchmarking can be looked at together here. As already identified, productivity will be a concern for the corporate property management community as competition increases and all areas of the organisation have to keep striving for efficiency gains. The development of effective benchmarking systems will be central to achieving greater productivity. What is crucial is that they should be meaningful for the resource being measured which, in terms of strategic property management, can not be simplified to numbers alone. While the tradition within the real estate community has been to judge real estate on financial performance, this is not the tradition in the strategic property management community which, although being concerned with financial performance, has also to consider the effectiveness of property in supporting the business function as a whole. Benchmarks have to be developed which measure property performance qualitatively as well as quantitatively.

The speed with which technology changes and the potential for application that each change brings have reduced the lifecycle of many products. Production processes, sales methods and the range of products and services provided by all areas of the economy have driven a requirement for greater flexibility within all factors of production, including space. The property in an organisation's portfolio has to accommodate and facilitate these types of change, often over a time scale which does not suit the 5–10 year cycle on which property tends to work. This increased demand for corporate property to be sufficiently flexible to respond to and actively support the continual change and development within an organisation's activities is a major strategic management issue.

This chapter has begun to piece together the framework we have created and examined in the previous chapters. It has looked in more detail at the types of strategy that might be appropriate for different types of organisation to adopt. Having examined the institutional arrangement, the strategic management issues involved, and the key factors that comprise effective strategic property management, this chapter brings this section of the book to a close. We will go on in the second half of the book to look at the theory in practice as we examine practical examples of a wide range of organisations and the issues and problems that arise with the strategic management of their real estate.

References

Ball, M. (1994) *London and Property Markets: a long term view*. Research paper, South Bank University, London.

Becker, F. & Joroff, M. (1995) *Reinventing the workplace*. International Development Research Foundation, Narcross, GA.

Bon, R. & Luck, R. (1999) Annual CREMRU-JCI survey of corporate real estate practices in Europe and North America: 1993–1998. *Facilities*, **17** (5/6) 167–176.

Bon, R. (1994) Ten principles of corporate real estate management. *Facilities*, **12** (4) 9–10.

Bootle, R. & Kalyan, S. (2002) *Property in Business: A waste of space?* RICS Books, London.

Carn, N., Black, R. & Rabianski, J. (1999) Operational and organisational issues facing corporate real estate executives and managers. *Journal of Real Estate Research*, **17** (3) 281–99.

Evans, M., French, N. & O'Roarty, B. (2001) Accountancy and corporate property management: a briefing on current and proposed provisions relating to UK corporate real estate. *Journal of Property Investment and Finance*, **19** (2) 211–223.

Gale, J. & Case, F. (1989) A study of real estate resource management. *Journal of Real Estate Research*, **4** (3) 23–33.

Gibson, V.A. (1994) Strategic property management: how can local authorities develop a property strategy? *Property Management (UK)*, **12** (3) 9–14.

IDRC (1999) Corporate infrastructure resources management: an emerging source of competitive advantage, Research Bulletin No. 22. International Development Research Centre, Atlanta.

Manning, C. (1991) Leasing versus purchase of corporate real property: leases with residual equity interests. *Journal of Real Estate Research*, **6** (1) 79–85.

Manning, C. & Roulac, S. (1996) Structuring the corporate real property function for greater 'bottom line' impact. *Journal of Real Estate Research*, **12** (3) 383–396.

Nourse, H.O. & Roulac, S.E. (1993) Linking real estate decisions to corporate strategy. *Journal of Real Estate Research*, **8** (4) 475–494.

O'Mara, M.A. (1997) Corporate real estate strategy: uncertainty, values and decision making. *Journal of Applied Real Property Analysis*, **1**(1) 15–28.

O'Mara, M. (1999) *Strategy and Place: Corporate Real Estate and Facilities Management*. Free Press, New York.

Pitman, R.H. & Parker, J.R. (1989) A survey of corporate real estate executives on factors informing corporate real estate performance. *Journal of Real Estate Research*, **4** (3) 107–119.

Porter, M. (1998) *Competitive Strategy: techniques for analysing industries and competitors.* The Free Press, New York.

Pottinger, G. (2000) *Occupational Futures: corporate real estate restructuring and refinancing.* College of Estate Management, Reading.

Schaefers, W. (1999) Corporate real estate management: evidence from German companies. *Journal of Real Estate Research*, **17** (3) 301–320.

Tregoe, B.B. & Zimmerman, J.W. (1980) *Top Management Strategy: what it is and how to make it work*. Simon and Schuster, New York.

Veale, P.R. (1989) Managing corporate real estate assets: current executive attitudes and prospects for an emergent management discipline. *Journal of Real Estate Research*, **4** (3) 1–22.

Weimer, A.M. (1966) Real estate decisions are different. *Harvard Business Review, Nov/ Dec*, 110–112.

Zeckhauser, S. & Silverman, R. (1983) Rediscovering your company's real estate, *Harvard Business Review*, **61** (1) 111–117.

Further reading

Duckworth, S.L. (1993) Realizing the strategic dimension of corporate real property through improved planning and control systems. *Journal of Real Estate Research*, **4** 495–509.

Estey, R. (1988) How corporate real estate departments contribute to the bottom line. *Industrial Development*, July/August 4–6.

Joroff, M. (1992) *Management Strategies for the Next Decade*. Corporate Real Estate 2000, White Paper, Industrial Development Foundation, Norcross, GA.

Joroff, M., Louargand, M., Lambert, S. & Becker, F. (1993) *Strategic management of the fifth resource: corporate real estate*, Industrial Development Research Foundation, Norcross, GA.

Nourse, H.O. (1986) Using real estate asset management to improve strategic performance. *Industrial Development*, June/July 1–7.

Pottinger, G. (2002) Occupational Futures? Divesting real estate and corporate PFI. *Property Management*, **20** (1) 31–48.

Roberts, S. (1991) How property can help organisations achieve their objectives, *Facilities*, **9** (3) 7–12.

Roulac, S. (2001) Corporate property strategy is integral to corporate business strategy. *Journal of Real Estate Research*, **22** (1/2) 129–152.

Silverman, R.A. (1987) *Corporate Real Estate Handbook: Strategies for Improving Bottom Line Performance*. McGraw Hill, New York.

Endnotes

[1] See Evans *et al.* (2001) for a discussion of the impact of real estate holdings on corporate accounts.

[2] This literature is largely American and based on USA experiences, but the literature that focuses on Europe reports a surprisingly similar approach.

Section II
Case Studies

Case Study 1
Borders UK

Introduction

This case study focuses on a retail organisation. Although property could be seen as secondary to the core function of a retailer, it is inextricably linked to that core function in a more fundamental way than is the case with most other business activities (Gibson and Barkham, 2001). The property management function has a direct impact on the success of the business as a whole. It might be logical to assume, therefore, that analysis of the property management strategy of retail organisations is an area that is well rehearsed and researched in real estate and management literature. Surprisingly, this is not the case.

The following study therefore provides a relatively rare opportunity to examine the property strategy of a single retailer, Borders UK, in some depth. In particular we are able to apply the framework developed in Section 1 of this book to property management information within the context of the company's business strategy. This enables us to examine specifically the way in which the property function has been developed to underpin the core business activity.

Background

Borders UK is a subsidiary of the American book retailer Borders Group Inc., an international business selling books, music, video and periodicals. The company was set up by two brothers, Tom and Louis Borders, in the early 1970s. One, a computer specialist, developed a stock inventory system which enabled sales to be tracked and the stock to become more tailored to the customer base. Having initially purchased a single large book store in a university town, the success of the system in increasing profitability allowed the company to expand. Borders now operate well over 1,000 book stores in the USA, over 400 of which are classed as book superstores.

Borders retail strategy in more recent years has had two strands:

- the convenience book store, based in high pedestrian flow areas, airports, shopping malls etc., focusing on the convenience shopper, and

- the *book and media superstore*, usually based on a retail park or similar, in an accessible but often out-of-town location, focusing on the destination shopper.

Expansion in the number of convenience book stores was undertaken in the US through the acquisition of Walden Books, a company that had an existing portfolio of book shops in town centre areas. Borders still uses the Walden Books name for its smaller retail outlets in the US.

The second element of the retail strategy, the media superstore, was a new avenue in book retailing and was undertaken at some risk. However, its success in the US persuaded the company to pursue a similar strategy in the UK and other predominantly English-speaking countries. The arguments against the strategy working are persuasive. In particular, book purchases tend to be convenience rather than destination purchases, making it unlikely that consumers will travel out of town to purchase them. However, experience has shown this not to be the case. The company has found both in the US and in the UK that out-of-town stores are much more attractive destination stores than anyone could have predicted.

When the decision was made to enter the UK market, Borders adopted a similar strategy to the one working for them in the US. They identified a book retailer with a chain of small but well positioned outlets, Books Etc., and purchased the company. They then began to identify suitable locations for their book superstores.

As the company embarked upon its expansion strategy within the UK, it quickly became clear that property decisions are key to the strategy's success. Borders UK has consequently been careful to make sure the property decisions in themselves support and enhance the overall business strategy. The first store was opened on London's Oxford Street in 1998. At 40,000 square feet this was a bold entrance into the market and had repercussions for other book retailers.

The remainder of this study focuses on the application of the framework established in Section 1 of the book, in an analysis of the management of Borders UK's property strategy. While the whole property strategy and its relationship with the overall business strategy is examined, the case study focuses primarily on the development of the book superstores. We start with a consideration of the characteristics of Borders UK as a property user.

Property user characteristics

Development of the company

Borders UK is a relatively new company (although clearly not a 'start-up') going through a phase of rapid expansion, opening 8–10 superstores each year. Using the categories developed by Nourse and Roulac (1993) the 'strategic driving force' behind the organisation is *growth*. As Nourse and Roulac point out, this is not a sustaining driving force. It can only be in place until the organisation has reached the target size, at which point the strategic driving force will change. Nonetheless, while growth is the aim, the property decisions have to support that strategy. With a cash rich parent company driving the expansion, Borders UK has to keep expanding until it has sufficient sales volume in the UK to support its operating costs and expected return on capital. The property function is clearly imperative to this. The strategy will be undermined if the rate of expansion is slowed because of a lack of appropriate property opportunities or a real estate function that fails to support the business strategy actively. However it is important to balance rate of expansion with profitability – slower but profitable growth is preferable to rapid unprofitable growth.

Management structure

It is well established that good communication links between those responsible for the property and those responsible for executive decision making for the business as a whole, are fundamental to a truly embedded and supportive property function (see, for example, Zeckhauser and Silverman, 1983; Pitman and Parker, 1989; Gale and Case, 1989; Schaefers, 1999; Carn, Black and Rabianski, 1999). The management structure within Borders UK has been allowed to develop as the company has grown. As a result the communication links have remained strong. The property decisions are agreed between the property director, the chairman, the managing director and the operations director.

The property director is now supported by a construction manager and a site and facilities manager. Originally the property director carried out these two roles. Consequently he understands the processes each involves. The operations director is supported by two operations managers and twenty store managers. Again, these roles have grown as the company has expanded. The operations director initially had direct liaison with the store managers.

This 'organic' development of these roles has fostered an environment of open communication and learning from experience. The pace of development has necessitated a culture where lessons are learned quickly and experience capitalised upon at once.

Business strategy

As a business strategy the organisation has chosen market differentiation in its book superstores and specialisation in its convenience book stores. The development of the book superstores is a clear example of a means of selling the product which is unique to the market and sets Borders apart from the rest of the industry. The overall offer from the superstore is a 'media package' including café and many in-store events. This sets the tone as a social place as well as a retail outlet. The evidence suggests that this has allowed the organisation to expand through tapping into a growing market for books in addition to competing with other book retailers for existing market share among the traditional town centre customers.

Having two elements to its business strategy gives the organisation the flexibility to be able to tailor its competitive strategy to the individual market. Competing head-to-head with another book retailer with an established pitch can be expensive and clearly increases the risk inherent in opening a store. The dual strategy gives Borders the option of avoiding such a contest. Opening a book superstore in an accessible out-of-town location is, proportionally, sometimes cheaper and can provide access to a geographically larger and demographically more diverse market.

The expansion strategy target is to open a retail outlet in each of the top 70 population centres of the UK. The identification of those top 70 centres, however, has to reflect the market for books. Borders' customers are office workers, students and academics, tourists and leisure shoppers. The centres are therefore assessed on weighted shopper population, taking into account:

- population size
- education
- socio-economic grading.

This allows identification of a list of potential store locations. At this point the property strategy is brought into the decision-making process. An assessment has to be made of the property market in a location if an informed decision about store location is to be made.

As a retail organisation, Borders' stores are crucial to its business success. Its real estate is an operational asset which has to promote sales *and* the selling process. The company has to consider the location of each store in terms of catchment area and market as well as pitch if informed decisions about store location are to be made. They then need to respond to shopper behaviour.

As with any retailer, the shop forms the interface with the customer. However, book purchase as an activity is often different to other kinds of retailing. The customer will tend to want to browse and the likelihood of increased purchases will improve if they are able to browse in comfort. This makes the retail environment crucial to the success of each store. While books are not part of the luxury goods market, the retail environment is as important as it is for goods in that market. It also means customers can spend a considerable amount of time in the store.

Aware of these factors, Borders make their stores attractive and comfortable as destination stores. All the stores contain cafés and regularly hold in-store events such as book signings and band showcases. They have also found a ready market in some of their book superstore locations for book retailing beyond normal shopping hours.

To recap, Borders UK has the following major characteristics:

- a retailer with a cash rich parent company
- market differentiation as a competitive strategy
- growth as a strategic driving force
- in-town and out-of-town outlets
- retail environment/shop fittings of key importance.

The main strengths of the organisation are its cash rich parent company, the success of its book superstores and the expansion of the book market. It is effectively combining and building on these strengths by using the cash to expand the differentiated market it has found and build market share.

Property characteristics

Borders UK currently has 20 book superstores and 37 convenience book stores in the UK. Each one is an operational resource, providing an interface with the customer, housing the profit generating activity of the business and advertising the brand.

The smaller stores still trade as Books Etc. and, focusing on the convenience end of the book retail market, are located in airports, major cities and the provinces. These stores are to some extent clustered around the south east but this reflects the outlets in place when Borders purchased the company.

The Books Etc. stores are between 54 and $900\,m^2$ (600 and 10,000 square feet) in size and stock approximately 20,000 titles. They focus on the sale of books and consequently have a higher proportional profit than the superstores. This allows them to support the higher rental levels in the locations they occupy. This only works, however, on small premises. As the outlet size expands, the turnover reduces in proportion to the volume of stock held and the rents in town centre sites become uneconomic.

The book superstores are between 2000 and $3000\,m^2$ (20,000 and 30,000 square feet), stock between approximately 100,000–140,000 book titles, 30,000 music and video titles and 2,500 periodicals. All have a café and stationery concession. Interestingly, a decision has been made to outsource the operation of the cafés. They add an important dimension to the retail experience in store and will be retained as a feature but run by a specialist food and drink retailer.

The cafés and stationery concessions reflect the extent to which shopper requirements have been considered within the configuration and fitting out of the stores. The superstores will be on no more than two levels if possible. If it is essential to go to three levels the composition will be basement, ground and first floor, giving only one floor to travel in each direction. The stores often incorporate a mezzanine, constructed at the tenant's expense. This can give up to 50% more space and an improved retail environment while enabling Borders to contain the initial rent and exposure to rental growth. This is particularly appropriate in retail parks where the unit sizes and ceiling heights are generous and rental growth can be difficult to predict.

The specification of each unit has to be sufficiently high for the customer to be comfortable spending relatively long periods of time in store. Air-conditioning is standard in the superstores, as are toilets, unusual in anything other than the larger department stores.

Organisational objectives in relation to real estate

As identified above, the business strategy is differentiation and the strategic drive force is currently growth, using expansion through acquisition to enter new markets. The target is to capture 20% of the UK book market, having an outlet in the top 50–70 markets within the UK. Underpinning all this is a basic business aim of making highest possible sales at lowest possible cost.

This business strategy currently means the company may increase its retail space by up to 50% each year. The rate of expansion has been increasing as the property team and the business team have become more experienced. In particular, experience has allowed them to improve efficiency through cost reduction. Equally importantly they are also learning constantly about the particular characteristics which will allow a town or city to support a new store. Interestingly, the company is finding that smaller towns than they initially expected are able to support book superstores, helped partly by the expansion of the market for books.

While the business strategy is well developed it is nonetheless reliant upon an effective property strategy. The identification of the top 70 towns for a shop is not necessarily followed by identification of a suitable, available retail unit. The company's business strategy will only work if the units it takes are the right ones and the 'deal' is right. This will incorporate:

- the initial rent
- whether it is a turnover rent
- the rent-free period offered
- the specification of the store and
- any capital contribution by the landlord.

It is by getting this aspect of the decision making right that the property team underpins the company's organisational objectives.

To get the final deal right, the real estate decision will have to factor in the specific characteristics of the local market:

- supply
- demand
- rental levels
- total occupancy costs
- quality of space
- accessibility
- terms available.

In addition to these fundamentals, the decision must be based on the team's knowledge of and understanding of what has made their existing stores work. As the company expands and existing stores move into profit, the factors contributing to each store's success become a little clearer and this area of expertise contributes more and more to the decision-making process.

A balance must be struck between the attractiveness of the location, the availability of space and the cost of space. It is often the case that the best locations simply do not have appropriate units available or these are not offered at an acceptable price. Book retailers traditionally operate at a margin of approximately 40% on sales of £250–£500 per square foot of space. They will consistently be outbid by higher volume, higher margin retailers such as fashion stores operating on a 60% margin and £350–£600 sales per square foot. Compromising on the town often makes better sense in the long term than compromising on the size, pitch and deal negotiated on the store itself or taking space that is simply too expensive for the store to support. It is often the very tight town centre supply in the highly desirable locations that makes out-of-town retail sites an attractive option.

The institutional arrangement of the property market

Whatever real estate decisions are made, they have to reflect, and use to best effect, the existing institutional arrangements of the UK property markets. For an expanding retailer seeking to establish a solid market presence this necessitates balancing flexibility with security within the confines of a market that tends to be determined by the requirements of investors.

Each Borders UK store has to achieve a target rate of return (IRR) over 10 years, cover its own staffing costs, rent, rates, fitting out, refurbishment cost and other overheads. If this is not achieved or does not look likely to be achieved, the company needs sufficient flexibility to be able to move or close, depending on the factors causing the problem. In this context a 25-year standard 'institutional' lease is overly restrictive. However, this potential requirement for flexibility has to be balanced against the need to establish and maintain a presence in a specific site, a crucial consideration for a retailer, particularly a destination one.

Borders have balanced this in the main by opting to take 15-year leases with break clauses and the option to sublet. They also negotiate turnover rents wherever possible. By transferring some of the risk to the landlord, turnover rents benefit the retailer in two ways. First, it reduces the hurdle each store has to clear to hit its targets successfully. Second, it increases the landlord's stake in the retail success of the property, thereby increasing their incentive to make the location work as a retail environment. This has obvious knock-on benefits in terms of the physical appearance of the property and maximising footfall. It also has more subtle benefits in promoting good landlord–tenant relations and communication.

The lease versus purchase debate is not relevant in this business case. While the purchase of freeholds would protect the organisation from spiralling rents, particularly on out-of-town retail parks that become successful over the course of their occupancy, it simply ties up too much capital for a business expanding this fast to withstand. While it may give security of tenure, it also fails to meet Borders' flexibility requirements and balance the risk inherent within a relatively untried pattern of book retailing.

The leasing option itself is also not without risk. The strategy exposes the company to the possibility of significant future rent increases which may not be reflected in increased sales. It may be that in the next stage of business development, likely to be a consolidation phase, Borders UK will begin to reconsider the buy/lease decision on those stores it considers particularly important to the business. The climate of the property market at the time would be a pivotal factor within such a decision.

The book superstore strategy brings Borders UK into contact with developers as well as institutional investors as landlords. Taking space on new out-of-town retail sites means negotiating with the developer in the first instance. This can be enormously helpful, particularly with regard to store layout and negotiation of rent. As a destination store beginning to establish itself more solidly in the UK market, a pre-let to Borders Books is an advantage for a developer who will often be willing to negotiate on rent as a result. This recognition of the company's value to the tenant mix is important, as is an understanding on the part of the developer or landlord of the economics of the book retail sector. However, the tendency for developers to tailor a development to their perception of institutional investor requirements can limit their willingness to negotiate on terms and conditions.

The external world

An organisation's business strategy and the property strategy which underpins it have to reflect the context set by external world factors over which the company has little or no control. Consequently, a constant process of monitoring goes on within the management team to identify external factors – local, regional and national which will impact on the business strategy. The current political–economic climate (early 2003) is relatively positive for retailers within the UK. Interest rates and inflation are low in historic terms and employment, earnings and consumer expenditure strong for the most part, although this will change (possibly even between the time this is written and publication). The crucial factor for a retailer is, of course, the level of sales.

The problem these positive factors create for the company is the increasing cost of its retail outlets. While the opportunity cost of borrowing is relatively low, rents have risen substantially. Even allowing for the stability created by 5-yearly rent review patterns, the first book superstores opened in the UK are due for rent review. Each store is going to have to look for ways to improve its performance in terms of sales productivity if it is to be able to maintain profit levels following rent review.

This exposure to rent review is a product of the company's decision to lease rather than purchase space, which is clearly the correct decision at this stage in the company's development. However, the management team is aware that it represents an important area of risk. To defend the company against this risk, the management team has utilised the superstores' popularity as a destination store to strengthen its negotiating position at rent review and subsequently at lease renewal. Other tenants have identified benefits arising from having a large, comfortable book store, with a café, in the retail park, providing a natural meeting point for leisure shoppers. Becoming a preferred tenant in an out-of-town retail park in this way is a significant negotiating tool and could in the longer term turn a weakness into a strength. The ability to negotiate rents to less than market value on the basis of the store's importance to the success of a retail park would be a significant strength within the business as a whole in keeping space costs lower than those of a competitor.

One of the most vexing issues for many retailers in recent years has been the increased use of the internet for retail purchases. The successful, high profile establishment of the on-line book retailer Amazon has made this a particularly pertinent issue for all book retailers. Questions have to be asked about the impact e-retailing is likely to have on sales and the best way the organisation can interact and utilise the internet. However, realistically, given the scale of the book market, which is expanding, and the very small proportion of that market taken up by the major e-retailers, the threat to sales is limited for Borders UK. The impact on the property strategy is nil. The business objective is not changed.

Evaluation

As the strategy is put into operation and progress is made in achieving the number of stores and share of market targets, both the property and business strategies are improved through evaluation. From the business perspective this is done on a store by store basis. After three years of operation each store is expected to move into profit. Each will be assessed in terms of:

- total sales
- sales per customer
- sales per square foot of space
- sales across different periods of time.

As longitudinal evidence is developed, the characteristic sales pattern of each store becomes clear.

An important aspect of the business performance evaluation of each store is the knowledge the management team develop of the performance of all the stores within the group. Evaluating and monitoring each store as it fulfils its potential gives the management team greater knowledge to apply to each new store. This is invaluable in setting realistic sales targets for new stores, identifying stores which are underperforming and gauging what occupancy costs a store can withstand. For instance, if the team knows a store in a particular type of retail market can achieve a turnover of £5 million, it is much easier to determine whether it will be able to afford the prevailing market rent.

The property team also specifically evaluate the performance of each unit as a property resource. The team seeks to achieve the best value for money it can get from each store. This requires not simply the lowest possible rents but getting the greatest possible efficiency from the store in terms of:

- construction costs
- tenant mix
- pitch
- optimum store size
- optimum layout.

Greater efficiency in construction costs has been achieved through experience and through establishing uniformity within the stores. While not going to the extremes of the regulation Burger King or McDonald's restaurant, having a standardised fitting out requirement brings efficiency gains. This is partly through the increased buyer power it gives over suppliers of construction materials. The number of stores the company is planning to open, combined with a predictable set of materials required for each, gives the construction manager much greater negotiating power with contractors.

As the existing stores have begun to mature and reach their market potential, the impact of different high street pitches and tenant mixes can be assessed. In the out-of-town locations, the longer trading hours Borders operates and the comfortable environment provided by each store has brought unexpected benefits. For example, where a mix of retailers is present, families are using Borders book superstores as a meeting place. This is valuable for Borders but also useful for the other retailers on the site, particularly if they too are offering longer trading hours. This type of information is extremely useful in negotiating rental and lease terms where new units are taken on and, as established earlier, will be vital in rent review negotiation.

The store size and store layout are also products of evaluation of the property function. It is through the evaluation of existing stores that the basic requirements of a large, highly visible space with regular shape and a limited number of floors has been developed. Fewer floors mean fewer staff are required, energy costs are reduced and customers are close to the full range of merchandise. Interestingly, when Borders started in the UK they thought they needed 3000–4000 m^2 (30,000–40,000 sq. ft) of space for each store, depending on market size. The team have learned through experience and the evaluation of the different stores that a full package can be provided in 2000–2500 m^2

(20,000–25,000 sq. ft). This clearly has significant implications for the business and will feed into property decision making for the future.

While the existing strategy has benefited from ongoing evaluation, the Borders UK management team still feel they are learning from each store they open. This continuous process of feedback, application and review is essential to the application of their property strategy and to the achievement of the organisational objectives that strategy underpins.

Conclusions

The success of Borders UK's business strategy is reliant in large part on the successful implementation of its property strategy. The delivery of both has been supported by some key features within the management structure and the overall approach to their property.

- The management board identified at an early stage the importance of a property specialist in acquiring new sites. While it is perfectly possible for a non-property specialist to acquire retail units as part of an expansion strategy, using a specialist brings a much improved negotiating position simply through the higher level of understanding of the institutional structures that make up the property market. The potential for making efficiency gains and improving value for money is enhanced and these have reaped dividends for the company.
- The company understands the importance of its retail units as operational assets, but is also aware of the limitations posed by the external world in the form of the property market. This allows the property director to compromise in some areas in order to make the best overall deal for the company.
- The 'organic' growth of the management structure has led to an understanding among the personnel of the different roles people perform. This in itself is helpful in informing decision making but it also encourages communication.
- Having a relatively small team responsible for implementing property strategy engenders a culture of communication, evaluation and improvement of performance. This is increasingly valuable in informing each set of decisions relating to the next store opening. The efficiency gains and performance improvements it underpins have allowed the expansion rate to increase with no loss of performance in each new store.

Information for this case study was obtained directly from Borders UK through its property director, Geoff Robotham.

References

Carn, N., Black, R. & Rabianski, J. (1999) Operational and organisational issues facing corporate real estate executives and managers. *Journal of Real Estate Research*, **17**(3) 281–99.

Gale, J. & Case, F. (1989) A study of corporate real estate resource management. *Journal of Real Estate Research*, **4** 23–34.

Gibson, V. & Barkham, R. (2001) Corporate real estate management in the retail sector: investigation of current strategy and structure. *Journal of Real Estate Management*, **22** (1/2) 107–27.

Nourse H.O. & Roulac, S.E. (1993) Linking real estate decisions to corporate strategy. *Journal of Real Estate Research*, **8** (4) 475–494.

Pitman, R.H. & Parker, J.R. (1989) A survey of corporate real estate executives on factors influencing corporate real estate performance. *Journal of Real Estate Research*, **4** (3) 107–119.

Schaefers, W. (1999) Corporate real estate management: evidence from German companies. *Journal of Real Estate Research* **17** (3) 301–320.

Zeckhauser, S. & Silverman, R. (1983) Rediscovering your company's real estate. *Harvard Business Review*, **61** (1) 111–117.

Case Study 2
Clifford Chance

Introduction

Clifford Chance is currently the largest fully integrated legal practice in the world. The business is organised as a limited liability partnership consisting of approximately 680 equity partners. Turnover is currently approximately £1 billion per annum. This case study focuses on the firm's London based practice.

Being a partnership, all the decision makers within the firm have a very close engagement with its profitability. A fall in profits directly impacts on the equity earnings of each partner. This very direct relationship between partner earnings and the continued vitality of the firm affects the way in which it is managed. It augments a strong culture of encouraging communication and innovation at all levels and areas of the business as the best way to continue to grow fee income.

Property user characteristics

As a professional firm, Clifford Chance relies on the development and communication of knowledge and problem resolution for clients to generate fees. At the broadest level this defines the type of space the firm will require. The key functions are research, development of existing knowledge, communication and negotiation. These are the functions that the corporate portfolio must support.

Management structure

Clifford Chance is a global firm with offices spread throughout the world. However, it is the London based practice which forms the focus for this case study so the corporate structure explored here relates to that practice rather than the organisation as a whole.

Strategic and operational decision making are the responsibility of a management committee comprising: the regional managing partner, partners from each practice area, the general manager and representatives of all the support services, including property.

This corporate structure gives the practice a small management 'loop', supporting the firm's philosophy of open and active communication. Such a system has the benefit of keeping all employees in close touch with the decision-making structure, encouraging and maintaining staff engagement with the organisation as a whole, and consequently encouraging staff commitment. This is reinforced by all partners in management positions being elected by their fellow partners.

Having the real estate team represented within this management structure ensures two things:

- the property implications of business decisions can be considered early in the decision-making process
- any support the real estate team can give to a business decision or strategy can be factored in to the decision-making process.

Business decisions will reflect the capabilities and opportunities represented by the corporate property holdings and the corporate property strategy can be designed to respond to the changing needs of the business strategy over time.

Business strategy

The driving force of the business is the product offered, i.e. legal services. Nourse and Roulac (1993) would argue that growth of the business therefore requires a strategy which incorporates a continuous effort to seek out new markets for those services and to improve the services offered. In this instance the strategy focuses on the integration, improvement and development of services offered to clients.

The firm's expertise is delivered through several specialist practice areas. Each practice represents a specific area of legal work such as banking and finance, corporate, intellectual property, litigation and dispute resolution and real estate. Within each of these lie specific areas of expertise. For example the corporate practice has teams which focus on communications, media and technology, corporate finance or financial institutions. The expansion of the partnership has taken place partly through organic growth, partly through mergers with other firms, and partly through lateral growth: new partners joining and bringing their legal teams with them.

A key aspect of the firm's strategy is the smooth integration of services across geographical borders, the objective being that the client receives the same standard of legal service and the same quality support services in every office across the world. While this will clearly be driven in the first instance by the lawyers and support staff, it has to be underpinned by appropriate property.

Property user community

Clifford Chance has two major stakeholders within the user community for its property: the clients and the lawyers. The firm strives to optimise its client services and, as explored above, the current business strategy is one of integrating quality and efficiency across geographical borders. The clients are thus clearly identifiable as key stakeholders as users of the corporate property.

The firm strives to be innovative, having a culture of encouraging communication between the lawyers, partners and support staff, and the development of ideas generated by its partners and all its employees. It also seeks to adopt strategies to improve the efficiency with which its legal services are provided, enhancing the fee driven basis of the business.

This commitment to innovation has led to a number of quite radical strategies for the management and organisation of the space the firm currently occupies. It has also placed new demands on its properties in terms of the technology it can support. Many legal meetings are paperless with all parties present working on laptop computers. This creates demands for power points and supply but also places great pressure on air-conditioning systems. Video conferencing is widely used but with cabling systems that date from the early 1990s, the firm is finding it hard to support the use of the very latest and most effective communication systems available for this type of facility from its premises at 200 Aldersgate Street.

Clients can now access their client files and relevant information on-line. This is an innovative service which clients find useful but which makes new demands on space and the IT systems. Clearly such a service requires a dedicated IT team but it also requires increased capacity on servers and other hardware, all of which places new demands on the quantity of physical space available and the IT capability it can support.

The London based practice employs over 2,700 full-time staff. Adding the large complement of contract staff takes the total employed in the London practice at any one time to around 3,000 people. Apart from the basic physical requirements of space per person this places on the buildings, the way in which the firm organises its staff creates additional challenges. There are three aspects to this: the accommodation of the rotation system for trainees, the creation of new teams for specific jobs and, as an added complication, the creation of 'Chinese walls' between teams working for separate clients on particularly large jobs.

Each year the London office takes in two groups of trainee lawyers, approximately 65 in March and the same in September. These trainees are then rotated around four 'seats' during the course of their two-year training. After qualifying they move to whichever specialism they have chosen. This means that approximately 400 people and their attendant files, books and other effects, move offices every March and September. This has to be completed over a single weekend.

Being driven by the requirements of clients can mean putting a team together specifically for a job. If this happens, the new team will need to be relocated to be able to work together and have access to client records and information. This again, requires a high level of flexibility within the work space. It can require the reconfiguration of space within a building at relatively high speed. In some years there have been over 2,000 people moves in 12 months.

The traditional pattern of occupation is for two lawyers to occupy an office, with administrative staff outside. Each office is approximately 6 × 3 metres and has the usual office furniture plus both lawyers' sets of documents and records. Each lawyer builds a comprehensive set of bound files and documents that have to be available to them in their main work space. These will soon be transferred to an electronic storage and search medium, to reduce space needs, improve access for the lawyers and clients and improve the business continuity resilience. There are also shared knowledge and information areas in each practice group.

However, it became evident to the property team that this system was not supporting the teamworking nature of the business as effectively as it might. A space audit found that 50% of lawyers were away from their desks for 50% of their working day. The nature of their work requires the lawyers to meet with other members of the team, clients, other lawyers and this does not take place in 6 × 3 m offices.

The property team therefore suggested changing the configuration of the space. Two team rooms capable of accommodating eight people plus breakout space could be created where four offices had been. This increased the capacity to 16 people rather than 8 and was much more effective in accommodating the sharing of information, meetings, discussion, etc. It also reduced the amount of data storage required as documents could be provided per team room rather than per lawyer.

Other unexpected benefits also materialised from this new configuration of space: the trainees became more quickly involved with the teams they were learning from and experienced the operating practices of a range of lawyers rather than just one or two. The secretarial staff also reported being more involved and connected with the activities of the team, increasing their effectiveness in their role.

This new space configuration was introduced slowly and with maximum involvement of the staff affected, right down to choosing colour schemes. A number of issues were raised as potential problems, particularly noise and privacy. Interestingly, the rather different way in which people work in group space than in private space meant noise never became a problem. Privacy was dealt with by installing screens with a curved top edge, providing privacy in some areas and easy communication in others.

Some legal teams adopted the system, others did not. Roll-out was inevitably limited to some extent by the configuration of the overall building. The increasingly tight squeeze, plus some teams moving out entirely as pressure on space has grown, has also reduced application of this system. However, it remains in place in the real estate legal practice team, and the other teams who adopted it found it beneficial, not least because of the reduction in space costs on the profit and loss account. There have also been significant improvements in the client service levels by this change in working arrangements/methods.

For particularly large jobs, where conflicts between the different teams might arise, 'Chinese walls' are established. This is standard practice in many professional firms, not just legal practices and they are implemented through working practices, systems and structures embedded within a firm's operations and through the training of the professional staff. However, the property can provide a useful support system for this process where it is possible to track employees within a building and to restrict access to different areas. These are relatively unusual demands to place on corporate space, but the capability adds to the way in which space can support a particular business use effectively.

Property characteristics

Clifford Chance's London based practice currently occupies approximately 54,000 m^2 (600,000 square feet) of space in and around the City of London. This is spread between six different buildings. The largest building by far is 200 Aldersgate Street, which provides 39,060 m^2 (434,000 square feet) of space and is the main office in London.

When Clifford Chance took this building in 1992, it provided sufficient space for the firm's needs and allowed them to introduce additional client services. It was ultra-modern space, capable of supporting the latest technology available at the time and the facilities offered the level of services required to attract the best legal teams. Quite apart from office space, conference rooms, data storage space and a library, the building has a fully equipped, externally managed gymnasium, a swimming pool, a lecture theatre, restaurant, delicatessen, and shop.

In 2003 the Aldersgate Street building still looks well designed and the services remain of a high standard. However, the speed of change in terms of the demands business make on their space, means the building no longer fully meets the company's needs, particularly in terms of technology and services. Perhaps more importantly, this is preventing the introduction of new innovations within client services. This undermines the firm's ability to strengthen and consolidate its market position and, if not addressed, would ultimately weaken the business as a whole.

The increased size of the legal team has also rendered 200 Aldersgate Street inadequate in terms of physical space. The short-term strategy to alleviate this problem has been to take extra space in the City of London area.

This has led to the firm now occupying six different sites. This strategy of taking extra space in the vicinity could always only be temporary and this is reflected in the flexible lease terms negotiated in each case. The property management team has been careful to identify clear exit strategies in each case. These include short lease terms, break clauses and flexible assignment and subletting clauses.

The difficulties the business is experiencing in terms of its corporate space are now three-fold:

(1) the fragmentation into different locations is not conducive to optimum business efficiency

(2) the Aldersgate Street building is in need of updating in terms of technological capability

(3) the total space they occupy is inadequate for the firm's needs – they have simply out-grown it.

Organisational objectives in relation to real estate

The objectives of this firm have been identified as focusing on quality and efficiency of the service offered. This requires maintenance of existing standards and continued innovation in terms of the services offered to clients. The current space occupied by the London partnership has been identified as simply insufficient to effectively support these objectives within a twenty-first century organisation.

Strategy formulation

There were two alternative strategies available to the firm to resolve this situation.

Strategy One

Strategy One was to keep the Aldersgate Street premises and take additional space on London Wall. The benefits to the firm were:

- consolidation of its presence in the City
- rationalising of the property portfolio
- underpinning of a strong relationship with the Corporation of London, which the firm considers it important to maintain
- remaining in an area heavily populated by existing and potential clients.

The strategy also had negative aspects. Taking an additional building, even if located close by on London Wall, would have the poor psychological effect of splitting the working environment of the firm. However close, having to visit another building for meetings or presentations is not the optimum solution. Apart from being an inefficient use of staff time, it would also have required a doubling of the services provided, particularly data storage and research facilities.

This strategy also required the refurbishment of the Aldersgate Street premises, while the firm was in occupation. The cabling is outdated and would have had to be completely replaced. Other refurbishment would also be required, such as the lecture theatre. The air conditioning and power supplies would have to be upgraded to provide sufficient capacity for new technology to be really embedded within the legal services offered; an important facet of the business strategy.

Strategy Two

Strategy two was to take a much larger building, which could accommodate the firm completely, and vacate the Aldersgate Street premises. This presented the combined difficulties of identifying a sufficiently large building in an appropriate location and maintaining some presence in the City. One solution was to look outside the City for a building large enough to accommodate the firm and provide some element of future-proofing.

This would mean giving up a prestigious and established address. While location is not as important in this case as it might be for a retailer, it is still a significant issue for a high profile legal firm. Many of Clifford Chance's existing and potential clients are based in the City, and moving out of the vicinity could result in inconvenience for them.

The positive elements to this strategy were also strong. The firm could take advantage of the financial benefits of looking outside the City to acquire significantly more space at very high specification. This would give it the flexibility and capacity to add new client services that would be less cost effective in a City based building. The potential downside of losing contact with the City of London Corporation and a base in a client-rich area could be mitigated by retaining some level of presence there, even if it is smaller.

Finding a suitable building

The second strategy became very realistic when the new development at Canary Wharf became available. This presented Clifford Chance with the opportunity to take just over 90,000 m^2 (one million square feet), at significantly lower rents than those offered in the City. Being a new development it also offered the firm the possibility of input into the design, effectively tailoring the building to suit its business needs. Clifford Chance was in a strong negotiating position with regard to the lease, particularly given the amount of space it was prepared to take and the high profile name and strong covenant it brought to the scheme. As a result, Clifford Chance has negotiated flexible terms into its commitment to take extra space in Canary Wharf over the next 10 years.

The negative issues relating to Canary Wharf also had to be considered. The main one seems to be that of access, particularly once all the new towers are fully occupied. It is anticipated that the daily population will be to the order of 90,000 office workers. This will dramatically increase pressure on the Jubilee tube line and Docklands Light Railway, inevitably creating commuting difficulties for some staff. However, the positive aspects of this strategy have been identified as significantly outweighing the negative, making it the better strategy to adopt.

Strategy selection and implementation

Having made the decision to take the space at Canary Wharf following the signature of an agreement to take up the lease in 2001, a small Project Executive was set up to oversee the management of the move. The move to Aldersgate Street, in 1992 was managed by a much larger group including partners, external project managers, the architects, an IT team and internal support team. The existing team found this an ineffective way of organising such a project.

This time the team is much smaller, consisting of the regional managing partner, business manager and the head of business services and facilities management. While this may seem autocratic in a firm that encourages communication, decision making is much easier and the project more manageable. Partners and staff have been part of a full consultation and information process to ensure they are informed at all stages as to what is happening and the progress being made.

The Project Executive has been involved with the developers since the decision was made to take the space. This has given them a tremendous opportunity to have input into the design of the new building, leading to the inclusion of numerous features engineered specifically to support the business function. The Project Executive had to commit to providing detailed design information in accordance with a critical date schedule so that the developers could maintain the construction timetable.

Clifford Chance has taken approximately one million square feet of space over 30 floors. Of these, four will be sublet, two floors for five years and the remaining two for ten years, thereby protecting the firm's expansion space. There is potential to extend the South Tower by four floors if necessary. One of the key features the Project Executive has wanted within the building is flexibility. Experience has shown that managing the volume of spatial change routinely occurring within the firm requires flexibility within the built space. Having a large rectangular shell with relatively clear floor plates around a central core and good light helps.

Over 70 client meeting rooms are provided, each of which can support 1.5 laptop computers per person. 'Deal zones' have been incorporated into the design. These are areas where a group of client meeting rooms can be syndicated to provide a deal zone, secretarial support, business services support and breakout rooms. All can be effectively sectioned off, establishing privacy and a focused environment for a major job.

A 250-seat auditorium has been incorporated to support training and facilitate both internal presentations and those to clients. There are also four 80-seater 'classrooms' that can easily be reconfigured into eight 40-seater rooms laid out in any style (lecture, theatre, boardroom, etc.), as well as twelve purpose built IT training rooms.

Interestingly, the firm has decided to move away from the tradition of providing a large central law library. Looking very realistically at the working practices of the lawyers, it became clear that a series of smaller libraries close to each legal subgroup would be a more effective way of providing necessary research facilities. The expansion in availability of law reports and other legal data on-line makes it much more convenient to be able to access a library close to workstations.

As was established earlier, the main driving force behind the business strategy in this case is the provision of client services. The firm wants to retain its reputation for innovation in the services it offers to clients. However, it has to balance this against the value for money that clients demand. Clifford Chance feel they have achieved this in the new building with the provision of a client-support 'business lounge'. Clients sometimes spend very long periods with lawyers; negotiations will routinely go through the night. A great deal of this time can be spent waiting for responses or redrafts of documentation, for example. The business lounge is designed to provide clients with space in which to work or relax while this is happening, with information technology and other communication links, along with relaxation space and refreshments. It is this sort of innovation that Clifford Chance believes can make a difference in keeping the partnership ahead of the competition.

This is a useful example of the way in which carefully planned and managed space can provide a significant support to the business function of an organisation. The decision to take space at Canary Wharf rather than a City location has enabled the firm to provide an innovative extra service, at no extra cost to the client, without compromising profit levels.

The institutional arrangement of the property market

Clifford Chance's corporate property portfolio has to reflect the existing institutional arrangements of the property market. It also has to reflect the characteristics of the firm. At the time of writing (2003) the firm does not expect to expand as rapidly over the next 10 years as it has over the last 10 years but neither will it remain unchanged. The business strategy is one of innovation in the development of new services to offer clients. This strategy puts pressure on the corporate space to accommodate new functions and services. Ultimately, as a flexible and innovative firm Clifford Chance is unlikely to want to commit large amounts of capital to tie itself to a building that may be unsuitable for its needs 10 years in the future.

Consequently the buy or lease assessment has, to date, always resulted in a decision to lease property. This inevitably exposes the firm to certain risks, in particular rising rents, lease obligations and a commitment to space for a specific period of time. The property team are very aware of these risks and have been careful not to expose the firm to any lease without an exit strategy – no less than one would expect from a legal firm.

This has been crucial in allowing Clifford Chance to initiate its short-term strategy of taking small amounts of space as overspill. As the firm starts to move to the new building (expected in August 2003) it will exercise these exit plans – the target being to vacate five of the six sites at little or no cost.

The exposure to market rents also has the effect of ensuring the firm is continually aware of the real cost of the property it occupies. While it is absolutely necessary to occupy expensive, high specification space, it is also important that each team is aware of how much this costs. Hiding the true cost of the space occupied by a business reduces the incentive for efficiency.

Clifford Chance has taken the lease at Canary Wharf for 25 years, on FRI terms with 5-yearly rent reviews: the type of standard institutional lease we are beginning to expect occupiers not to want. In this case, however, it suits the firm very well. They are expecting to remain in the building for at least a significant portion of the lease term, so no purpose would be served by negotiating a shorter one.

Given this, and the availability of relatively cheap capital, it could be argued that the firm might be at a financial advantage if they invested in the freehold, or at least a long leasehold interest in a building like Canary Wharf. The property team would disagree. Being a limited liability partnership, making such a major capital commitment to the corporate property portfolio would fundamentally change the relationship between the firm and its buildings. Furthermore, their willingness to take a 25-year lease strengthens their negotiating position in other areas. This has been used to full advantage in the negotiations over Canary Wharf.

The firm always self-manages its buildings if possible. Having no service charge to pay is obviously a bonus and having a service infrastructure capable of managing the property internally allows it to keep the costs down. There is also the complication of the frequent changes in configuration and layout of space, and space requirements. To carry out these tasks with the necessary efficiency, an experienced in-house team is the only effective solution.

The external world

The external world tends to have its greatest impact on Clifford Chance's corporate property through:

(1) the potential it provides for new client services and new clients
(2) the rising cost of space.

These factors place new demands on space and drive the firm to make as efficient use of it as possible. A major driver of changing space demands is technology. Rapid technological development creates new opportunities for greater efficiency in the interaction between lawyer and client. The increased use of videoconferencing, on-line access to files and computer-based meetings represent just a few of the changes driven by technology. The implications for the corporate property portfolio are important. The buildings have to provide a much higher capacity and specification of technology and larger quantities of electronic data storage. These factors put new pressures on the building infrastructure and, in the longer term, effective provision can often only be made by moving to more modern premises.

In some businesses, technological developments have led to new working arrangements, such as hot-desking or hotelling. In many cases these are efficient uses of space. In this case, however, such innovations are simply impractical. While the extreme flexibility with which their corporate space is expected to perform has been explored in this case study, and innovations have been introduced, each lawyer has to have a specific location for the duration of each case or project. The volume of hard copy material required simply demands this. While on-line access for clients is being introduced, it is not yet possible for all the legal work and records to be electronic.

Evaluation

Clifford Chance's corporate property portfolio is evaluated in terms of performance on a number of different levels:

- space costs against fee income
- efficiency of space usage
- client satisfaction.

First, because property is the second largest business expense next to salaries, the firm monitors cost very closely. Each of the legal specialisms within the London based partnership is charged for each square foot of space they occupy. This has changed from a system where each specialism was charged for space according to how many people it employed. This penalised efficient use of space, particularly by larger teams. The new system is much more effective at demonstrating to each subgroup the real cost of space used and thereby encouraging efficiency. The cost includes rent, rates, and all services and management costs. It is included within the subgroup's profit and loss account.

Second, the space is evaluated on the basis of efficiency of use. The property team has a target of at least 95% space usage at all times. This is imperative to the profitability of the business given the very high cost of space. There is a constant drive towards achieving better value for money through efficiency in the use of space, be it through a reduction in the rent liability, more efficient configuration, or better support for the legal teams.

Client and lawyer satisfaction is the third area of evaluation for the space and perhaps the most important criterion. The firm seeks a balance between the provision of the best facilities for its clients and lawyers, in functional, well designed space, without appearing profligate. It is crucial that in any innovation or design specification, the functionality for the client is clear. However, there is an expectation among both staff and clients that the space meets certain standards. This is not an area in which the partnership seeks to economise beyond acceptable levels of business efficiency, which tend to be sufficiently driven by the space-charging system in operation. The imperative to monitor space and squeeze its efficiency in terms of cost is not as strong as it might be in, for example, a sales-oriented business.

Benchmarking

Clifford Chance has carried out a benchmarking exercise, albeit relatively informally, with similar types of business. It found this informative to some degree but not to the extent that it has driven any changes in the way in which space is occupied or the property managed. The support services the firm provides give the impression of a high level of space per capita. However, they are imperative to the business function. To measure the space on this basis and find it wanting would be inappropriate. This reinforces the point that strategic property management has to take account of the business strategy if it is to effectively support that function.

The developer of Canary Wharf (Canary Wharf Group plc) has been careful to include sustainability into the design of the buildings, including making efficient use of rainwater for example. Its close proximity to public transport should reduce the requirement for car journeys, if capacity is sufficient. However, the sustainability issues relating to the building are not factors that necessarily attracted Clifford Chance as an occupier. Given the amount of energy resources such a business uses it might be construed as at best pointless and at worst hypocritical for the firm to claim environmental sustainability credentials. However, given the increase in companies that do have and want to retain such credentials Clifford Chance may have another reason to be pleased to have taken this building in the future.

Conclusions

Clifford Chance's business strategy relies on the ability to present clients with a better and/or more innovative service than another legal firm, at the same or similar cost. The property portfolio is necessarily a large expense in such a high profile business where it supports the interface between lawyer and client. However, for the property to really be performing at its best, it needs to make a positive contribution to the lawyer–client relationship, not simply a passive one.

The real estate team are very aware of this, and work hard to make the property an asset to the operational side of the business. They see the buildings as having to support both lawyers and clients, who have different needs. We have seen above the many services offered by both the existing head office and new offices at Canary Wharf to both the firm's employees and its clients.

- For the staff:
  - high quality staff facilities
  - lecture theatre
  - flexible space
  - meeting rooms with optimum technological capabilities
  - team rooms when required

○ video conferencing facilities
○ library and research facilities.
● For the clients:
  ○ a high quality service environment
  ○ dedicated project space when required
  ○ client dedicated business lounge
  ○ an accessible location
  ○ on-line access to client files.

And, of course, there is also the reassurance that comes with a legal firm sufficiently successful to be able to afford a premium building and sufficiently forward thinking to manage its property to best effect.

For the property to perform effectively as an operational asset, however, it has to perform effectively as a cost base. The property team again strive to make sure the property provides value for money through:

● a rational system of internal charging that encourages efficient use of space
● innovative use of space to better support working patterns
● internal management of the space to keep servicing as cheap as possible
● building on and valuing experience in the property services team responsible for moving lawyers around the building
● seeking a minimum target of 95% space usage at all times
● providing the best possible services to clients in the building.

Avoiding exposure to liabilities under existing leases and, in particular, leases taken as part of the short-term strategy to alleviate space, has been an important focus for the real estate team. They have been very successful in using the strong negotiating position presented by the status of the firm and their willingness to take long leases in particular circumstances, and to agree exit strategies where they perceive their space requirements to be short term.

The success of the Clifford Chance property portfolio in all these areas is ultimately dependent on the approach senior management takes to the role of the real estate team. The high priority that this team place on communication about strategy and involvement in decision making provides a vital foundation for proactive property decision making. This is combined with the firm's culture of innovation and communication between all levels and the good practice of reflecting on its own working practices in order to improve client services. These factors have enabled strategic property management practices to be established which actively support the overall business objectives and strategy of the partnership.

Information for this case study was obtained directly from Clifford Chance through its head of business services and facilities management, Keith Toms.

Reference

Nourse, H.O. & Roulac, S.E. (1993) Linking real estate decisions to corporate strategy. *Journal of Real Estate Research*, **8** (4) 475–494.

Case Study 3
The Youth Hostels Association
of England and Wales

Introduction

The Youth Hostels Association (YHA) is a charitable organisation. Real estate is a secondary activity to the YHA but fundamental to its function. It was set up in 1930 with a broad but clear aim:

> '... to help all, especially young people of limited means, to a greater knowledge, love and care of the countryside, particularly by providing hostels or other simple accommodation for them in their travels, and thus to promote their health, rest and education.'
>
> YHA, 2000

This aim remains today and forms the basis of the strategic and operational decisions the YHA takes. From the perspective of strategic property management, the YHA provides an interesting case study. The property contributes directly to its charitable objectives but also contributes substantially to running costs. Only if it is effectively managed, maintained and developed will it continue to support the operational objectives of the organisation, but this places a substantial burden on cash flow. The property strategy must be clearly aligned with the orgainsation's strategy for the property portfolio to support the YHA effectively.

This case study provides an opportunity to examine the decisions and decision making process of an organisation with an unusual objective, an extensive and highly heterogeneous property portfolio, for whom property is a non-core activity and a considerable organisation cost.

Background

The concept of youth hostels and youth hostelling emerged from Germany in the first half of the twentieth century. It became popular in the UK as a way of making countryside recreation available to ordinary people. Small groups of enthusiasts acquired a suitable property and renovated it to provide basic affordable hostel accommodation. The properties were usually located in rural

177

areas and as they increased in number it became the practice to walk from one youth hostel to the next.

The setting up of the YHA in 1930 provided an informal structure linking the numerous hostels that had been formed in the UK. Management remained dispersed to the individual hostels but membership of YHA was required for visitors to stay in one of its hostels. The YHA brand began to emerge as a unifying identity and marketing device.

Forming the YHA also allowed a more fully considered aim to be developed for the movement and, importantly, led to the granting of charitable status. The principal objective of the YHA is clear: the provision of budget accommodation, particularly to young people. However, there are additional objectives within the stated aim, pertaining to education and access to the countryside and these also have to be addressed in the management of the property portfolio. The major objectives driving the YHA can thus be identified as:

- provision of accommodation
- education
- access to the countryside

all with an emphasis on young people of limited means.

The breadth of the aim is important. It has allowed the YHA to keep up with the rapidly changing recreational demands of modern society while adhering to the set of principles it represents and maintaining its charitable status.

It is clear from the aim, and the objectives that flow from it, that property is fundamental to the YHA's successful achievement. If we refer back to the functional spectrum discussed in Chapter 1 we can see that the YHA would be placed towards the right hand side: it can not achieve its operational objectives without its property and that property needs to be in appropriate locations. The buildings do not define the function and can be replicated elsewhere, but the extent to which the buildings and locations are interchangeable is limited.

In order to fulfil its objectives and survive, the YHA has at least to break even, making sufficient money in the process to maintain the real estate, support the staffing structure and central office and take the business forward. A clear business strategy has to be developed to operationalise the charitable aim, in a way which exploits the existing asset base to its full potential and allows the YHA to grow as an organisation.

Furthermore the market for budget accommodation has changed completely since the inception of the YHA and, over recent years competition has become stiff. Budget hotels have entered the market, other hostel organisations have set up, catering to a specific sector of the market, such as group travel or backpackers, and foreign destination holidays have become accessible for the majority. The YHA therefore has to continue to develop its own product in order to remain competitive.

These competing factors make the management of the YHA perhaps more complex than the management of a private business entity. This in itself makes it even more important that a clear organisational strategy is developed which is supported by an equally clear strategy for the property portfolio, and which reflects the current requirements of the portfolio and the potential for future expansion.

Since the year 2000, changes have been initiated which very much reflect this view. The management of the operational functions of the business have been centralised at a head office in Derbyshire. This has provided the opportunity for a reappraisal of the organisation, its assets and management systems and its business strategy for the future. A review of the property portfolio was initiated at this time.

The YHA real estate portfolio is its most valuable asset in financial terms, valued currently (2003) at approximately £100 million, and underpins all its activities. The real estate function has to be aligned with the business function for the operation as a whole to be effective.

The following study uses the framework developed in Section 1 of this book to fully explore the operational management of the YHA property portfolio. This gives a very useful insight into the opportunities and obstacles posed by a real estate portfolio that must work effectively as a corporate asset while still fulfilling a range of charitable objectives.

Property user characteristics

Driving force

The YHA is a membership organisation with an annual turnover of approximately £30 million. It is a charity and not directly supported by government or any other funding body. If we look back at Nourse and Roulac's (1993) driving forces we can see the YHA is driven predominantly by market need but that it is supported in this by its rights over natural resources. The market it has found is 'young people of limited means' and it seeks new ways of providing them with accommodation; making initial contact with them as school children via its educational role, through families and during early independent travel. The YHA has been successful in this strategy for many years and has had sufficient flexibility to identify and respond to new demands within its target market.

The natural resources at the YHA's disposal are embedded within the unique real estate portfolio it owns. Without the land attached to many of its hostels, the YHA would not be able to fulfil its educational agenda, without the variety of locations, it would not be able to provide access to the countryside. Furthermore, the limited capital outlay that has been necessary to acquire these rights, most of which are long-term in nature, makes it possible to provide accommodation cheaply. The property portfolio thus underpins the whole operation.

Income sources

The YHA's income is derived from four main sources:

- charitable donations
- membership fees
- overnight hostel stays
- grants.

Overnight hostel stays, the main trading activity of the YHA, make the biggest contribution to revenue. However, this operational activity also creates the largest overheads and is run at relatively narrow profit margins. This creates the major complexity at the heart of YHA management strategy: keeping the price of the accommodation low enough to meet the charitable objectives, but raising sufficient surplus to maintain the asset base and cover operational costs.

The identification of grant funding has become significant for the continued successful operation of the YHA, in particular in relation to the development of new properties and investment in the existing stock. The board of trustees is personally liable for the organisation's borrowings, and is thus understandably reluctant to increase its debt burden. Financing property acquisitions through borrowing is only practicable in very limited circumstances.

The YHA has been very effective in obtaining grant funding as a means of resolving this problem. Grants have been obtained from the European Union, local authorities, the Heritage Lottery Fund, the Millennium Fund and English Heritage. Very little of this funding would be available without charitable status, making the continued fulfilment of the charitable objectives key to this income source. However it also requires the YHA to position itself as an appropriate organisation to receive this type of funding. The breadth of its charitable objectives has again assisted here; having a mission that encompasses children, education, the environment and accessibility raises the potential for access to funds from a wide range of organisations. Being within the not for profit sector is another key factor.

The charitable fundraising activities of the YHA raise approximately £600,000 per annum. While this is small in relation to total turnover, it is still a significant figure. Historically however, charitable donation has shaped the YHA we know today: many of the properties in the property portfolio were left to the YHA by members. This type of giving continues today although it is more likely now that property bequests would be sold and the proceeds used to support existing plans.

Management structure

The management structure of the organisation itself is complicated, mainly as a result of its historical nature. The structure has evolved over 70 years and has been shaped by the wide variety and backgrounds of the stakeholders involved.

Figure CS3.1 shows the management structure of the YHA. It is complex but has very open communication between different types of staff. The Board of Trustees has ultimate responsibility for decision-making, and is accountable for any debts the organisation holds. They are supported in this by a chief executive with a team of directors, and a property manager. The chief executive is responsible for developing a business strategy, in consultation with the directors. The property manager is responsible for developing the real estate strategy to support this business strategy in consultation with one of the operational directors who holds responsibility for the real estate input at board level.

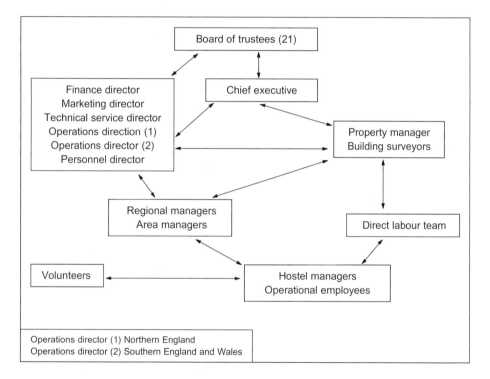

Fig. CS3.1 Management structure of the YHA

The management of the organisation has been split into areas that reflect government administrative regions. This facilitates the development and consolidation of relationships with local, regional and central government and related agencies. The regional managers all live within their regions and may have area managers working alongside them, and the hostel managers, particularly where there are a large number of YHA hostels in the vicinity.

The membership

Being a membership organisation gives the YHA an important stakeholder group who are not clearly identified within the management structure but are in some ways the most important property users. The volunteers could be described as a subset of the membership but they are not representative of the membership as a whole. This sets the YHA apart from other recreational accommodation providers, such as hotels and bed and breakfasts; YHA customers are often more engaged with the organisation as a whole.

Clearly not all the stakeholders and not all the groups represented in the diagram have input into the business or property strategies. However, the hostel managers and volunteers in particular are key staff who have developed considerable expertise and experience over the years. Part of the real estate strategy includes utilising this expertise to manage the estate more effectively.

Target market

The YHA is fortunate in that it has developed capacity to cater to three different recreational accommodation markets:

- educational and youth groups
- overseas visitors
- individuals and families.

Each of these forms approximately one-third of the YHA customer base, providing valuable diversity in the target market and thus reducing operational risk. This has proved particularly valuable since the events of September 11, 2001 reduced overseas visitor numbers. However, it also means they have three different types of customer and it is becoming increasingly necessary to separate these to some degree. This has driven some significant changes in the way the real estate is managed at operational level, but has also influenced some of the more strategic business and property decisions.

So, to recap, the property user characteristics can be listed as:

- a not-for-profit organisation with distinctive charitable objectives emphasising young people, education and the environment
- a provider of budget recreational accommodation currently achieving 2.1 million overnight stays each year
- a mature organisation with a complex management structure but good communication
- a turnover of approximately £30 million per annum
- a property portfolio valued at approximately £150 million
- a successful track record in achieving grant funding from a wide range of organisations
- a membership of approximately 300,000
- a broad group of stakeholders.

Having established a clearer picture of the property user characteristics, we can now examine the characteristics of the real estate portfolio and consider the extent to which one supports the other.

Property characteristics

In 2003 the YHA had 226 properties in locations spread across England and Wales. The properties range from castles to cottages and incorporate protected heritage buildings and purpose-built accommodation. This varied and interesting building stock underpins the major function of the YHA. While one can see that a retail unit is important to a retailer in terms of location, pitch, layout etc., one can also see that for a provider of recreational accommodation, the buildings within the portfolio are everything.

In this case the organisation seeks to provide a particular type of accommodation (budget) and fulfil two other objectives relating to education and the environment. The portfolio has evolved over time to support all three of these interrelated functions effectively. To develop such a portfolio from scratch would be almost impossible today. The portfolio as it exists is thus unique and without it the YHA could not exist. It is from this viewpoint that one has to consider the strategic management of this operational estate.

Accommodating different markets

Traditionally, the YHA has provided accommodation in dormitory style rooms with bunk beds and shared facilities. The use of bunk beds has been entirely practical; it raises overnight stay capacity to a level which allows YHA to charge low prices while simultaneously meeting certain quality standards. This has proved a successful formula in the past, but YHA management are aware that the requirements of their target markets are changing and the three types of customer: children, backpacker, family/individual, often do not naturally mix.

This has led to the development of greater diversity in the accommodation offered. More small group rooms are offered, some with en-suite facilities and family rooms are becoming standard at many hostels. This is beginning to allow the YHA to channel their customers into the type of accommodation most appropriate for them, reducing the problems created when backpackers, large parties of school children and individual hostel members are accommodated side by side.

The gradual process of refurbishment combined with a review of their target markets has allowed the real estate to underpin this process of targeting different market sectors. YHA can now focus its educational facilities and expertise on the sites most appropriate for school parties and other educational groups. Education is an important aspect of the YHA's charitable objective and is taken very seriously by the organisation. The YHA's portfolio directly supports its educational objective. Certain properties have sufficient space and access to activities and sites of special interest suitable for a range of age groups. It is important that these hostels are allowed to focus on this type of activity, developing expertise in the local staff and capitalising on experience. This also enables the property to be maintained, refurbished and developed with this particular target group in mind.

Business v. charitable objectives

Inevitably some of the most valuable properties in the portfolio are located in London and the south east. Two of the seven hostels in London are held freehold, three others on long leases. Only Oxford Street and the City of London hostels are on standard length leases. These seven hostels are also the most productive in terms of turnover. They routinely achieve 98% average occupancy and as such contribute substantially to the organisation's cash flow.

The hostel in Rotherhithe in London's Docklands is a new development designed to cater for educational groups and families. With 320 beds it is the YHA's largest hostel in London, generating 77,916 overnight stays in 2000–01 (YHA, 2002). The building is owned freehold and represents a sizeable investment for the YHA. However, the cash flow that this hostel produces, alongside that of the other London hostels, ensures that further investment can be made across the rest of the hostel network.

Inevitably not all the hostels manage such successful figures and it is estimated that approximately 25% do not break even. This is where the charitable objectives of the organisation influence the property strategy. A for-profit business occupier would review the 25% of hostels running at a loss and if it were not possible to make them run at a profit, dispose of them.

The options for the YHA are not quite so straightforward. While it will always look for ways to make a hostel at least break even, if one runs consistently at a loss it may still be retained if it contributes to the charitable objectives of the organisation. The 25% that do not break even must be contributing in a significant way to the charity's objectives, making it rational to support them through revenues raised by other, profitable, hostels.

Setting of rents

The property review undertaken by the YHA in 2001–2003 was relatively predictable in its findings. There were limited data available in accessible form, most of the information being held in files dating back to 1930. The rather ad hoc way in which the portfolio has developed meant a variety of forms of title were held and where leases had been taken they were often on rents that bore little relation to the market.

Setting of rents on the type of property held by the YHA is difficult. Hostels are rarely traded on the open market, but even where transactions have taken place, the special characteristics of any hostel in terms of its location, facilities and accessibility to trade render comparable evidence of limited use. Without recourse to the market, the usual alternative would be to a profits method valuation for this type of property. However, the YHA operates on a not-for-profit basis and some of the hostels run at a loss. It would be unlikely that another occupier would want to take such properties over, and change of use can be difficult to acquire. Placing a value on these properties is thus fraught with difficulty. Nonetheless it has to be done for those held on leases.

The property management team at the YHA have resolved this problem by taking a very rational approach to the setting of rental value. They know the turnover each hostel produces and the conditions of the local property market. This gives some indication of the value of the property to the YHA and what it might achieve in the open market. This gives a firm basis on which they can negotiate with the landlord.

Cost of capital

Rental issues are in some ways less problematic than finding a means of accounting for the opportunity cost of the capital invested in freeholds. This accounts for approximately 80% of the estate, including some of the London hostels and is confused further by many of the freeholds being bequests and thus requiring no capital outlay. A profit-driven business would make a strict financial appraisal based on a target rate for the capital invested in the asset and the return being made by the hostel. However, the YHA has to incorporate its charitable objectives into this equation. While they can establish a target rate of return for their capital invested, if a hostel does not make that target rate, but contributes substantially to the charitable objectives of the organisation it will not be appropriate to dispose of it.

Capital investment

A more immediate problem for the long-term future of the portfolio and a major concern of the property manager is the tendency the organisation has (along with most others) to underinvest in this crucial asset base. We are looking at two different types of investment here and it is important to differentiate between them:

(1) investment in the maintenance and refurbishment of the existing stock
(2) investment in additional stock to expand the portfolio.

Repair and maintenance

The manner in which the portfolio has been established, i.e. gradually over time and often at zero or minimal capital outlay, has an impact on the approach taken to the property by the operational management team. As is often the case, the property is seen as a cost base to be managed, rather than as an asset to be exploited but simultaneously protected and developed. This approach, in combination with limited data collection and management systems, has led to a long period of underinvestment in the maintenance and refurbishment of the portfolio and unrealistic estimates of the level of future investment required.

Where the property is so important to the function of the organisation, this type of underinvestment is unsustainable: nor is it enough simply to maintain and repair the buildings. The competition in which the YHA operates has expanded substantially in recent years. Unless the real estate is capable of providing modern accommodation suitable for today's traveller, it will be unable to maintain existing demand levels, let alone expand. To do this requires a continuous programme of planned maintenance and refurbishment.

This portfolio has an additional burden in that such a large proportion is of historic or architectural importance. This makes refurbishment more costly, maintenance more problematic and redevelopment extremely difficult. This in itself will often make an organisation reluctant to take on the problem of investment. It is often difficult to develop a rational basis on which the investment should be spread across such a large and heterogeneous portfolio. Given the large sums this type of investment can involve it is important that the money is spent in the most effective way possible, but often difficult to work out exactly what that is.

Having reviewed the portfolio, action was taken to increase the amount of money allocated to investment in the portfolio, and to develop a rational model for the allocation of funds. What became clear was that maintenance and repair budgets were being drawn up on imperfect information in the form of estimates rather than actual expenditure. These budgets were allocated across the regions making it difficult to target particular problems and projects, particularly where these might involve considerable expenditure.

In the course of carrying out the real estate review it became clear that the best information on repair and maintenance costs was available at a local level, from the hostel managers. A programme has been set in motion to gather this information by requesting that the hostel managers prepare a short, standardised report on the actual expenditure on repair and maintenance over the course of a year. This will then provide better information, from those best placed to know, as to what level of investment is actually required to repair and maintain the portfolio. Once this is in place, a more rational system for allocating investment funds can be implemented and specific projects anticipated and targeted. It is anticipated that this will happen in the 2004/5 financial year.

Refurbishment, redevelopment and expanding the portfolio

The second type of investment, that required to expand the portfolio, often needs much larger sums and careful forward planning. Given that the YHA is reluctant to take on more debt, expansion of the portfolio requires funds to be drawn in from elsewhere. Two main methods of financing this type of investment have been developed by the YHA:

- grant funding
- partnerships.

As identified earlier, the organisation's charitable status and broad aims make it attractive to a variety of grant agencies and funding partners. This has enabled it to lever sufficient grant aid to finance substantial refurbishment projects with limited capital outlay of its own. Hartington Hall in Derbyshire, for example, is a seventeenth century Grade 1 listed building which has recently undergone substantial refurbishment funded by the National Heritage Lottery Fund and a members' appeal. This has combined the protection of a building of historic interest with the upgrading of an important piece of YHA real estate, without making any substantial increase in the organisation's debt burden. The effectiveness of these types of arrangement in expanding the portfolio are explored below.

Organisational objectives in relation to real estate

The current prime objectives for the organisation as a whole is expansion. There are approximately 300,000 existing YHA members but the target is to expand this to 500,000 by 2008. Simultaneously the YHA wants to increase hostel use from 2.1 million overnight stays per year to 3 million. These are ambitious targets, particularly for an organisation that has a deep rooted traditionalism, a strong stakeholder interest group within its membership and an original structure that devolved management of the hostels down to the local level.

There are two strands of this expansion strategy.

(1) *Acquisition of new sites:* Each regional team has identified local areas it considers appropriate for hostel accommodation. This might be family accommodation, backpacker accommodation or educational group accommodation, depending on the location and market. This type of strategic planning utilises the local expertise of the regional teams, and their experience in operating hostels to best effect. It provides a rational basis upon which expansion and location decisions can be based, allowing reflection upon the strategic requirements of the organisation as a whole.

(2) *Licensing arrangements with other similar operators:* A wide range of budget accommodation is now available across the UK, much of which is in competition with the YHA. The organisation has therefore decided to launch YHA Enterprise which allows an operator to use the YHA name, if it adheres to certain YHA standards. In effect the YHA is looking to make more out of its brand. It is clearly concerned to maintain standards, and agreements reached with operators will be complex and rigorously enforced. However, the YHA has identified this as an effective means of expanding the network and raising revenue from the brand with relatively low outlay.

A third more generic strategy put in place to support the expansion of overnight stays is the on-line booking system. This was particularly pertinent to YHA because of the limited opening hours many of the hostels run. Receptions are often open for only a short period in the morning and afternoon, making availability to take telephone bookings difficult. The YHA is also aware that on-line booking makes it particularly accessible to international customers. This investment was considered crucial to supporting the overnight stays target.

Streamlining before growing

Property underpins the operation of the YHA generally but is also clearly fundamental to the achievement of the first of these three expansion targets. Ironically, the review of the portfolio and the implementation of the property strategy that grew from this led to a small reduction in the portfolio before any expansion took place.

The property review revealed nine hostels that were not contributing sufficiently either to income generation or charitable objectives to be retained. A strategic decision was taken to dispose of these nine hostels, in the process releasing capital to invest in expanding other areas of the network which provided more effective support to the organisation's objectives.

The decision attracted a negative response from some stakeholders. However, being made in the light of a clear management strategy and response to market demands made the decision defensible. It was made for the benefit of the network as a whole and consequently the membership, making it good strategic management.

Interestingly, making the strategic decision to dispose of these properties opened new opportunities for the YHA to bring them back into line with the organisation's objectives. Two local authorities were keen to retain the hostels within their areas and agreed to provide the necessary investment to make it viable for the YHA to continue operating them. Without a real estate strategy sufficiently developed to make a rational decision about these hostels, they would have remained an unnecessary burden to the rest of the network and would not have benefited from a hitherto unexpected injection of cash.

Expanding without spending

Achieving the expansion of the network without increasing the debt burden will require identification of more cash injections of this nature. The strategy here has been to identify organisations with objectives that can be aligned with the real estate requirements of the YHA. This has enabled the YHA to acquire new properties on long leasehold interests, without making substantial capital outlays, either on restoration for refurbishment.

The National Trust has a substantial real estate portfolio, the financial burden of which it needs to offset as far as possible, without undermining its own organisational objectives. The YHA offers the National Trust the opportunity of having a tenant with a vested interest in maintaining the building, and an active remit to make the building accessible to the public, via its membership. Consequently, the National Trust is a regular YHA landlord.

Many local authorities have similarly aligned objectives particularly with regard to the YHA's emphasis on young people and education. The YHA provides a means of retaining, or introducing a recreational use with an educational remit within a community, while the local authority avoids the burden of management and can collect rental income. A local authority will often be willing to make a substantial capital outlay on the refurbishment and redevelopment of a property which YHA will then operate.

There are also examples of private individuals or estates who identify YHA as a solution to a major property liability. The YHA is currently in the process of acquiring a historic building in Whitby that is part of a private estate. The building is listed and in need of substantial repair and refurbishment, for which the owners are liable. The YHA has agreed to take the building once it has been refurbished, which has enabled leverage of approximately £2 million of grant funding to finance the refurbishment programme. The YHA has contributed approximately £250,000 which it considers good value for money, given the property it will acquire as a result.

The benefits of these types of arrangement for the YHA are clear; acquisition of interesting properties in rural locations which directly support both their operational and charitable objectives, with little capital outlay. There is little competition for the property so long leases can be taken at low rents, allowing the network to expand without increasing the debt burden.

The institutional arrangement of the property market

The YHA is affected by the legal institutions of the property market through its decisions regarding tenure, and by the financial institutions that govern the use of property as a capital asset. As an occupier, the YHA holds 80% of its property freehold. While this represents a considerable capital investment, in a relatively illiquid form, it is entirely appropriate for a mature business that is location specific and invests heavily in the services and facilities at each site.

It also reflects the fact that the YHA in some ways is defined by its property; it can not fulfil its objectives, either business or charitable, without that property, so it must have control over it for the foreseeable future. Furthermore, it could not operate if it expected a market rate of return on the capital invested in the portfolio. The bequests and legacies that have allowed the YHA to develop such an extensive and valuable collection of real estate in effect go on donating to the movement into perpetuity as they take away the imperative to achieve a competitive rate of return on capital. It is the flexibility this gives to the operation of the business that allows the charitable objectives to be given priority over business ones where the organisation sees this as necessary.

While this is the case for the existing portfolio, expansion is more likely to involve the acquisition of long leasehold interests, through a partnership arrangement with the freeholder, than outright purchase of freehold interests. The YHA has been effective in exploiting its positive characteristics as a tenant in order to negotiate favourable terms and conditions in the form of contributions to refurbishment and fitting out costs. Its willingness to take a long lease (it sees its minimum term as 15 years), make it attractive as a tenant, as does its ability to take on management responsibilities through its infrastructure and its vested interest in maintaining the fabric of the building.

The hostels where a slightly different strategy might be adopted are the London based ones. There are a different set of factors affecting the strategy here:

- these hostels contribute substantially to the cash flow of the organisation
- they achieve 98% occupancy levels
- their asset value is the largest in the portfolio
- the conditions of the local property markets dictate the options available.

The acquisition of a long lease on one of the most lucrative London hostels was felt to be sufficiently important to make extending the debt burden a worthwhile risk. As the original lease was nearing its end, a long leasehold interest was offered. This presented the opportunity to exchange the obligation of a market rent coupled with the insecurity of a relatively short lease for a reduced rent plus interest payments on a mortgage for a limited period, and the greater security of a long lease.

One of the other London hostels is held on a standard 25-year lease on a turnover rent. While this is a risk in that capital investment has to be made and the building could be lost at renewal, occupancy levels are such that the YHA would be able to compete effectively in the open market for the property anyway. This coupled with its positive characteristics as a tenant reduces the risk within this particular tenure situation.

Three out of the seven London hostels are owned freehold. This might be seen as an inefficient use of capital, particularly given the high capital values attached to these buildings. However, it would not be possible for the YHA to fulfil its objectives without these hostels, or ones similar, so selling them is not an option. Within the markets these hostels target – the backpackers and other overseas visitors in particular – demand is for city centre locations with good transport links. Selling to purchase cheaper accommodation in the suburbs would prevent the YHA from effectively reaching its target market.

Using these properties to raise finance through a sale and leaseback arrangement might be an option but again, the unusual objectives of the business make it unfeasible. The return made by the hostels would not be attractive to a commercial investor and it would substantially increase risk within the YHA. Furthermore it would be difficult to align the charitable objectives of the YHA with a commercial investor; the partnership arrangements and grant funding opportunities YHA has identified have so far provided a much more effective and less risky means of raising capital.

The YHA utilises the institutional arrangements of the property market within its property strategy to ensure that it occupies its property in the most cost-effective, low-risk way possible. This does leave it with a large capital investment in property, but the manner in which this has been acquired makes it less of a financial burden than it might be and ultimately allows it to continue to pursue its charitable objectives.

The external world

While it has an educational remit within its objectives, the YHA is essentially a leisure and tourism operator. The rapid growth of this sector since the early 1970s has changed the operating environment beyond all recognition from that which existed when the YHA was first formed. This has impacted on the real estate through:

- the expansion of the organisation's market as people's leisure time has increased
- the development of new markets as international travel has burgeoned
- the changing demands of the markets it now serves
- the amount of competition within the industry.

The YHA has responded to these pressures from the external world through expanding and updating its real estate, capitalising on the opportunities presented by its charitable objectives and by taking a more sophisticated approach to its target markets. This response has also made the organisation as a whole more capable of withstanding the impact of less predictable shocks within the external world with which it interacts. For example, the value of having three different types of user group was critical during 2001 when the effects of both the foot and mouth epidemic and the terrorist attacks of September 11 were felt.

The foot and mouth epidemic in 2001 resulted in the closure of access to most of the countryside throughout England and Wales, effectively closing the vast majority of the YHA portfolio. The city centre hostels were thus the main generators of business during 2001. They were then affected by the reduction in overseas visitors following September 11. Having a third market of domestic families and individuals gave YHA at least some market demand to maintain a cash flow.

A third organisational factor was vital to the YHA's recovery from these very difficult market events. Taking a strategic approach to the management of the organisation as a whole encouraged a very outward looking management ethos. This opened up partnership opportunities and the organisation learned a great deal about its importance to external funders, local government and other agencies. This has also enabled it to become effective at lobbying government on issues that will affect it, the continuation of 80% rates relief, for example.

Through the development of its role in this area, YHA identified opportunities for compensation payments which a more inward looking organisation might have missed. Given that the foot and mouth epidemic cost the YHA an estimated £4.5 million in lost revenue, this has made a significant difference to its recovery. This brings out an important element of the operational strategy of any organisation: the ability to develop relationships with organisations whose objectives can be aligned with its own. As the political economic context within which organisations operate becomes more complex, the importance of understanding the organisation's position in relation to others and the negotiating strengths and weaknesses that this brings, increases.

Insurance and legislation

Other external world factors that affect the operation of the YHA portfolio include the increasing burdens of insurance premiums and legislation. Insurance premiums are an escalating cost for most business operators and the YHA has not escaped. There are a limited number of insurers willing to take on this type of business in the market at the moment (2003), making competition limited and reducing the opportunities for negotiation on premiums. The reinstatement value of the property portfolio is estimated at £150m and it is against this figure that a premium will nominally be calculated. However, looking at the insurance risk more carefully, it is unlikely that the whole portfolio would be put out of action at any one time. This reduces the risk substantially and begins to make building insurance premiums poor value for money. Strategies have been put in place to increase the level of self-insurance that the YHA carries through increasing the level of excess within a policy, which obviously reduces premiums.

The Disability Discrimination Act, which came into effect in April 2003, increases the obligations of the YHA in terms of access to its buildings. The YHA sees itself as a high performer in this area as its educational and accessibility objectives require a positive commitment to physical access to its buildings and facilities. It has also been innovative in its methods of carrying out checks on buildings to ensure they comply. Approximately 40 existing staff who routinely use the hostels in their spare time have been trained to carry out audits and have then been given mileage and subsistence expenses to gradually audit the whole portfolio.

The YHA has utilised the commitment of its staff to provide a cost-effective means of ensuring compliance with these new regulations, as far as it feels it can reasonably be expected to. The problem the YHA has with the legislation is lack of clarity as to what is 'reasonable'. The number of listed buildings and very remote buildings within the portfolio make it unlikely that every building will be capable of being made fully accessible by wheelchair, in the same way that a shopping centre or office block might be. The risk at the moment for the YHA is the uncertainty around the extent to which they will be required to comply.

Evaluation

The pursuit of charitable objectives alongside business objectives inevitably clouds issues of performance evaluation. As is evident from the discussion above there are many instances in which the performance of elements of the portfolio as operational assets is secondary to the fulfilment of the YHA's charitable objectives. However, this does not mean that performance evaluation is any less important. While one might not close a hostel because it does not break even, it is important to know that it is not breaking even in order for the property strategy as a whole to be effective.

The greatest difficulty the property management team currently face in terms of performance evaluation is finding a means of incorporating the charitable objectives into the appraisal of the portfolio. Without a systematic, consistent means of assessing performance of charitable objectives, overall performance is inevitably unclear. However, this does not make it impossible and some level of performance evaluation has to be in place for the property strategy to be effective.

Each hostel is monitored in terms of:

- usage (% occupancy)
- meal rates per overnights
- days open
- the production of surplus income.

This gives a standard data set against which performance is evaluated from year to year, which will highlight trading problems relatively quickly. This also allows the operational and property teams to build up knowledge of hostel performance generally and track the performance of individual hostels over time. The property team will incorporate this data into an appraisal and add building costs, including maintenance, rent etc., and a target rate of return on capital invested. Even where the property was a gift, the performance of that capital has to be measured against a target rate.

We have discussed above the importance of the limited capital outlay that has been made in building this portfolio, and how the bequests and legacies continue to donate in perpetuity by reducing the imperative to achieve a market return on capital. Nonetheless the opportunity cost of that capital needs to be understood if the value of the property to the operation of the YHA is to be appropriately reflected in the business strategy.

Conclusions

The uniqueness of the YHA property portfolio reflects the variety of stakeholders who have contributed to it, the length of time over which it has been built up and the unusual objectives it has been designed to fulfil. The fact that it is in such a strong position to continue to fulfil these objectives having undergone a period in which its operating environment has changed so dramatically is to some extent a result of the strategic approach it has taken to the management of its property in recent years. It would be impossible to build a portfolio from scratch now, which so accurately reflected the operational requirements of this organisation, and with such limited capital outlay. This makes the portfolio an irreplaceable operational asset, something which has to be reflected in the strategies developed for maintenance and investment. The YHA has been effective in exploiting and protecting this invaluable business resource by:

- carrying out a thorough review of the estate, allowing management and planned maintenance to be aligned with the actual needs of the estate rather than estimated needs
- utilising ground level data sources to support the planned maintenance programmes
- ensuring the tenure patterns within the estate reflect the risk profile and operational requirements of the business
- making realistic decisions regarding the level of debt burden the organisation can withstand
- establishing an outward looking management ethos that encouraged the development of relationships with organisations with sympathetic operational objectives.

These five factors have enabled the YHA to align the operational management of the property portfolio with the organisation's business and charitable objectives. They have also given it sufficient flexibility as an organisation to withstand the impact of some substantial political–economic shocks. Perhaps most importantly they have enabled the whole organisation to take a proactive approach to its future expansion.

Information for this case study was obtained directly from YHA through its Chief Executive, Roger Clark, and Senior Property Manager, Jake Chalmers.

References

Nourse, H.O. & Roulac, S.E. (1993) Linking real estate decisions to corporate strategy. *Journal of Real Estate Research*, **8** (4) 475–494.

YHA (2000) *YHA in the New Millennium*. YHA, Matlock.

YHA (2002) *YHA in London: broader horizons for young people*. YHA, Matlock.

YHA (2003) *Go YHA 2003–2004 Accommodation Guide*. YHA, Matlock.

Case Study 4
Cancer Research UK

Introduction

Cancer Research UK is the product of a merger between the two largest research charities in the UK, the Imperial Cancer Research Fund (ICRF) and the Cancer Research Campaign (CRC). The merger formed the second largest cancer research organisation in the world after the National Cancer Institute (NCI) in the US. The major difference between the NCI and CRUK is that NCI's $3 billion budget is entirely government funded, whereas CRUK's £130 million research budget relies solely on charitable donation (Rutherford, 2002). The fundraising activities of CRUK form the foundation upon which all its work rests.

Completed on 4 February 2002, the merger was the largest corporate event in the UK charity industry in recent times. It had repercussions within every area of the two organisations, from the senior management teams to the thousands of volunteers who give their time and effort to fundraising. The merger inevitably had an impact on the property portfolios of both charities.

While research laboratories are clearly fundamental to the research objectives of CRUK, its most important real estate, in terms of fundraising, is its retail portfolio. This estate has four main functions for the charity, it is through its chain of shops that:

- contact is made with customers and donors
- brand image is developed and promoted
- volunteers and staff are recruited
- funds are raised.

The shops perform other social roles such as the provision of low cost goods, recycling and reuse of unwanted items and opportunities for training and communication within a community (Horne, 1998; Parsons, 2002). These roles are important but they are secondary to the functions the shops perform for the charity itself. These central functions are the focus of this case study, in particular the strategic approach that has been taken to the management of this property portfolio, leading up to the merger that formed CRUK, and afterwards, is examined here.

Background

As a charity, CRUK has a straightforward, if ambitious, aim – the prevention and cure of all forms of cancer. The steps it takes to address this are various but tend to be targeted at supporting as much scientific research into prevention and cure, as possible. The main objectives are to:

- raise sufficient and consistent income to support their scientific ambitions
- raise awareness of Cancer Research UK and its mission
- recruit and retain high quality staff across the organisation
- create the highest quality infrastructure and support services.

Source: WWW.CRUK.ORG.UK

The charities which merged to form CRUK had both proved themselves effective in achieving these objectives. In 2000, Imperial Cancer Research Fund spent £66 million on research and Cancer Research Campaign £57 million. Of this, £25 million was raised from sales in the two organisations' charity shops. Prior to the merger with CRC, ICRF had realised that it was not managing its retail portfolio as effectively as possible. This was particularly significant as it was the biggest overhead.

Charity retailing as a sector expanded considerably during the late 1980s and early 1990s. Perhaps more significant than the expansion, however, was the simultaneous change in shop management and people's attitudes to frequenting them (Parsons, 2000; 2002). Having become more professional and organised and enjoying an expanded customer base (for donations as well as sales) the charity retailers substantially increased trade.

The downside of this expansion was a simultaneous increase in costs associated with running the stores. This was a problem ICRF was now struggling with. The Board of Trustees decided, following advice from the Head of Retail, to approach an external real estate consultant to advise them on strengthening the management of the retail portfolio. This case study is therefore different from the others we have developed for this book. It investigates not the organisation itself, but the approach taken by an external real estate consultant in advising the organisation on the strategic management of its corporate property.

This type of consultancy service is an important development for the property industry. Businesses are using management consultants with increasing regularity to advise on corporate property issues. Often this has led to other professions, legal, accountancy, etc. encroaching on traditional chartered surveyor territory, mainly because of a dearth of strategic management skills and services being offered by the profession. More recently this situation has begun to change, as real estate consultants are beginning to offer bespoke strategic property management advice to corporate clients. The setting up of the Management Consultancy Faculty within the RICS is clear evidence of the importance this element of property has to the profession as a whole. Indeed, research carried out for the Management Consultancy Faculty by Cranfield University revealed a strong belief amongst the Faculty membership that real estate management consultancy would form an increasing element of surveyors' work in the medium term (Cranfield School of Management, 2002).

We are therefore pleased to be able to incorporate within this text the opportunity to explore the rationale behind the use of an external property consultant and the approach that consultant took in advising a corporate client with an unusual business brief. The advice given and the decisions made inevitably represent just one set of solutions to a range of problems; other management consultants may have taken different decisions and offered different advice. However, this particular project was considered by the Institute of Management Consultants to be one of the top five management consultancy projects completed in 2002, so we are confident that we are presenting a case study of appropriate quality and standing.

Property user characteristics

ICRF made the decision to seek external advice regarding the strategic management of its retail portfolio before the merger with CRC to form CRUK. The Management Consultants, Corpra, have thus dealt with two different organisations; ICRF at first and then CRUK. This case study starts by focusing on the advice given by Corpra to ICRF prior to the merger.

As a business organisation ICRF was mature and focused on technology. The main business objective was the use of expertise to develop new technology and knowledge in its field. The organisation's retail property is required to directly support three elements of the overall business objective:

- awareness raising
- provision of the best possible infrastructure and support
- raise sufficient and consistant income to support scientific ambitions.

Driving force

It is difficult to identify a clear strategic driving force behind the retailing activity of a charity. Its objective is clearly profit maximisation but this is not the same as a strategic driving force. A combination of product offered and market need is perhaps the closest we can get to Nourse and Roulac's (1993) list (see Chapter 10). The charity retailer offers a certain type of product (donated goods) to a particular market. It seeks to expand that market and to offer a better variety of donated goods and is assisted by people's desire to make charitable donations. It must simultaneously maximise its chances of receiving donated goods, services and funds. The ongoing business objectives for the retail side are therefore:

- increased productivity through improved management efficiency
- maximising exposure to the target market
- maximising opportunity to receive donated goods.

The organisation is focusing on increasing productivity by improving its operational quality.

Customer base

These organisational objectives require a retail portfolio with a location pattern that reflects the demographics of the customer base. It has been a tendency of retail based charities generally to acquire property wherever and whenever it was available. In some instances this is a false economy.

Corpra found that the customer base for CRUK tends to fall predominantly within socioeconomic groups B and C. Donations come from all socioeconomic groups but A, B and C dominate. While this will differ from charity to charity, for CRUK it is important that the retail outlets are accessible to these groups. Locating in the cheapest retail units makes the stores less accessible to its largest, and most affluent, customer base.

Branding

In similar vein, as the organisation's main communication point, the retail outlet is the chief conveyor of brand image. Retailing has been host to some of the most dramatic changes in the development of branding and brand imagery over the past decade. While a charitable organisation such as CRUK won't go to the same lengths as an organisation such as Nike or Coca-Cola might to develop and protect their brand imagery, it is nonetheless an important element of their business (Hankinson, 2001; 2002).

The brand conveys the unique selling point of a charity – its efforts to resolve an issue which touches the lives of many people, in this case the quest for a cure for cancer. It is thus very important that the brand is conveyed effectively to the consumer. Without it CRUK would be any other charity on the high street. The motivation to donate or purchase here rather than somewhere else will be lost.

This was, in effect, one of the issues driving the merger of the two charities. Having two charities with similar remits in the high street was confusing for the public and undermined the efforts of either to establish a clear brand image. This has been achieved more effectively since the merger but must still be supported by the real estate. The fitting and layout of the stores has to convey the brand effectively.

Organisational objectives

The organisational objectives of CRUK are clear:

- raising funds to support its scientific aims
- raising awareness of the charity.

Both objectives rely heavily on the effective operation of the retail portfolio. However, there are significant differences between the operation of a chain of charity shops and the operation of a retail multiple. One major difference is the role played by volunteers. Charity shops tend to be staffed by volunteers, without whom the organisation would find it difficult to survive. However, the relationship an organisation has with volunteers is very different to that a retailer might have with its retail staff and this in itself can create management problems (Horne, 1998; Phelan, 1996).

The volunteers working in the shops are also often highly productive fund raisers. Their role within the business organisation is crucial and their views and reactions are important. If a change in management style is to be implemented effectively and the overall aims of the business are to remain intact the volunteers have to be positively engaged with the plan. Corpra interpreted this within their brief as having two different customers within the client base:

- *the field customer* – volunteers, store managers, regional managers and retail directors
- *the corporate customer* – the head of retail, and the board of trustees and finance and accounting functions.

Whatever strategy Corpra came up with to satisfy the requirements of the corporate customer, they also had to come up with a way of making sure it would be implemented at field level. This is not easy when staff operating the stores are often not really accountable to the management team within retail operations since they are working on a voluntary basis.

This was an important issue for Corpra. As within any retailer, the stores generate brand awareness and brand identity within the community. While stores like Gap manage this element of branding down to the detail of t-shirt stacks, ICRF, and subsequently CRUK could not get a reasonably consistent stock collection, let alone a display.

To recap, this was a corporate client with a retail operation that:

- provides substantial support to the overriding business aim
- conveys the brand identity of the organisation
- generates the supply of stock
- provides the main contact point for other, often equally significant fund-raising activities
- is staffed mainly by volunteers who play a crucial role in fulfilling the business objective but are under very little obligation or direct management control because of their voluntary status
- has limited control over the stock held within its stores.

These property user characteristics presented a unique set of problems. The property portfolio itself presented another set.

Property characteristics

Prior to the merger with CRC, ICRF had 500 shops in the UK. These stretched from John O'Groats to Land's End. The major expansion of the portfolio took place during the late 1980s when 400 shops were added to the portfolio. These tended to be in good retail pitches in high street locations.

This rapid expansion had both positive and negative results. On the positive side, ICRF had secured a large number of excellent retail pitches in good locations. This was valuable to the long-term strategy, giving ICRF, and subsequently CRUK, access to a strong passing trade and high visibility. The negative factor was that the timing was such that many units were acquired at very high rents.

However, the high rents were mostly a short-term issue. While the upwards-only rent review might have prevented rents from falling to market level at review, those rents would not have risen any further for 10, in some instances 15, years. In the longer term, having identified an exit strategy from any outlets found to be completely unsuitable, the value inherent within a quality pitch and location would outweigh the short-term rental issues.

Management systems

The organisation as a whole had developed with a relatively light management structure, so systems were limited and had not been applied to the real estate in any significant way. No demographic model had been developed as a driver for the retail location decisions. With no reliable data to work from, it was not immediately obvious which outlets were out of step with the rest of the portfolio.

The reality that Corpra had to tackle was a portfolio of good quality locations but with no identifiable plan and no reliable information about what was held, where and at what cost. The first issue they had to deal with was data collection. Corpra carried out an audit of the portfolio to provide sufficient information on the property for decisions to begin to be made. Once the data was in place Corpra began to develop a management strategy for the portfolio that would address key problems.

One of the major problems ICRF had with their property was a heavy burden of maintenance and management issues for which no plan was in place. The team was fire fighting and, with limited data, was not in a position to develop an effective management plan. Looked at in this light it is not surprising that the retail portfolio had become a financial burden to the organisation.

Many of these problems were resolved by the implementation of systematic data collection, storage and retrieval, and the use of this information in developing a planned management and maintenance programme. This provided a much clearer picture of the performance of the portfolio overall, and allowed problem areas to be identified and rent reviews and lease renewals to be planned for. This type of planning considerably reduces the burden of risk associated with leasing by preparing for rental increases within business projections, and enabling negotiations and deals to be completed relatively quickly.

Holding the majority of the portfolio in the form of leases limits exit strategies for a retailer because of the problems of surrender and assignment. Nevertheless it remains important to identify properties that might be suitable for disposal, although this has to be based on very clear evidence of business benefit.

The combined portfolio

The merger with CRC brought with it an additional 250 stores and some inevitable overlap in store locations. A non-strategic response might have been to close one store in each overlap location. If it had been possible to assign or sublet each one, this would have reduced the overall rental burden in the short term, but it would not have reduced overall liabilities, guarantees being required for such arrangements. Such a solution might also have passed up the opportunity to allow two stores to continue to trade in proximity to one another quite profitably.

By carrying out an analysis of the locations where there was overlap, Corpra was able to examine:

- retail performance of both stores
- the location of each store – they might be sufficiently far apart not to compete
- the basic costs associated with the running of both stores
- the level of demand in the area – would it be possible to sublet or assign
- the potential for the catchment area to support both stores in the longer term.

Armed with this information it was then possible to see which stores to exit from and which to retain. The merger between ICRF and CRC produced a combined portfolio of approximately 700 stores. This was gradually trimmed, reducing operating costs and avoiding an increase in liabilities while causing little negative impact on trade. The organisation's strategy now is to expand the portfolio by 50, in selected locations.

Organisational objectives in relation to real estate

The organisational objectives have been identified as increased productivity through improved management efficiency and maximising exposure to the target market both for selling and receiving donated goods. To achieve these organisational objectives, Corpra began by focusing on the presentation of the organisation's brand, particularly through the retail outlets. In practice this meant that brand values had to be reflected in:

- the customer experience
- customer service
- the overall design theme
- the merchandising and retail display
- the retail frontage
- point of sale literature and packaging
- lighting
- the electronic point of sale.

Refitting the stores

This strategy was implemented through a major refit of the retail portfolio and some minor changes to the stock. Corpra used a team of specialist commercial interior designers and fitters to develop a new image and layout for the stores and to roll it out across the portfolio. Outsourcing the process to a specialist team in this way removed any project management responsibilities from Corpra and from CRUK, placing responsibility for completion with a single contractor. This was an innovative procurement strategy that enabled 75 stores to be refitted within three months and 400 more CRUK shops to be re-branded within a six-month period.

The majority of the stock within a charity shop inevitably comes through donation, making it difficult to establish any consistency within the appearance of the store. This was overcome by buying in some ranges of goods. Having a set selection of bought in goods in each store allows some element of uniformity to be developed underpinning the brand image. Working groups were established, including the professional manager, to ensure a consistent approach across both portfolios, taking the best working practice of each organisation. This enabled CRUK to ensure some consistency of window display and a brand image to develop.

Managing the stock

While the data management had been limited, what CRUK did have was a team of people at operational level who had substantial experience of charity retailing and a valuable understanding of what made a charity shop succeed or fail. Corpra had to find a way of retrieving, organising and using this information for the benefit of the business as a whole.

Some of the most valuable information in this context relates to the demand for different types of stock. An ordinary retailer has control over the stock held and will be able to identify with some certainty which lines are going to sell in which locations. Each store is then stocked accordingly. A charity retailer has little control over the stock it holds and, traditionally, limited information about what sells well in different stores.

Some charities resolve this through centralising the supply of donated goods. All stock coming in through the stores is sent to a central sorting point and distributed out again. This allows the retail operations team to control what goes into the different stores and gain feedback on what is selling well and where. The property requirements of such a facility are fairly straightforward: a distribution centre with good access to a motorway network.

The downside of such an operation is the expense. The price for which donated goods can be sold is relatively low. Even though the initial cost of the goods to the store is zero, transporting the goods to a central supply depot, sorting them, allocating them and transporting them out again will quickly eat into profits. Once one takes into account the cost of the property, the redistribution system would have to generate substantial sales to be cost effective.

CRUK do not use a centralised supply system to stock their stores. However, it is not blind to the importance of locational stock preferences. To support this, it relies on a weekly system of feedback from the stores about which lines sell well, so using field level experience. This allows the operational retail team to identify trends in sales of particular items and capitalise on them.

Aligning the real estate with the business

The main organisational objectives of ICRF, and subsequently CRUK, are more effectively supported by the property strategy through:

- the collection, organisation and standardisation of data and data management
- the changes made to the operational management of the property portfolio
- the development of the brand image and refit of the stores
- development of understanding of the customer base
- the analysis of performance of the merged portfolio in light of demographic data and catchment area.

The retail operation is now more streamlined and cost effective. It delivers a better quality infrastructure and support service to the fund raising initiative.

The next stage of the strategy is expansion. The aim is to expand the chain in specific locations. Corpra have identified a range of locations which, based on demographics, catchment area population and existing retail mix, they consider will support a CRUK store. Whether they open in each of these locations then depends upon supply and demand within the local property market and whether an appropriate property is available. This is where we can see the property strategy aligning with the business strategy to support the overall business objective.

The institutional arrangement of the property market

Having a portfolio with a long history often means holding a variety of different title arrangements. However, in this case, the majority of the property was acquired in the late 1980s on standard institutional lease terms. In the CRUK portfolio, nine properties are held freehold.

Leasehold v. freehold

As the core business of CRUK is scientific research not real estate, or even retail, investing substantial capital sums in property is not appropriate for the organisation, making a leasehold strategy more suitable. Oxfam, by contrast holds 100 of its 800 retail stores freehold (Hill, 2002). However, property values are such that this represents a substantial capital investment which is not easily liquidated, exposing the charity to another set of risks.

Leasing also brings with it a set of risks that have to be addressed within the property strategy. Consideration must be given to issues such as:

- holding the property on the best terms possible
- reducing occupancy costs
- identifying those properties posing the greatest risk of major rental increases
- identifying underperforming properties and finding an appropriate exit strategy.

During the downturn in the property market in the early 1990s, the dearth of commercial retail occupiers wanting to take space led to some unusual deals on shop lettings. If it meant avoiding vacancies, landlords were willing to take very low rents on retail units, creating the opportunity for charity retailers to take space in locations they previously could not afford. By offering short leases the landlords retained the opportunity to benefit from a market upturn. By taking short leases the occupiers avoided being exposed to rents beyond their financial reach.

However, as a property strategy to support a retailer, this has some flaws. The rent on these units may have been low but this reflected the lack of demand for retail goods at the time. This applied to charity shops goods as much as to anything else. While one could argue that cheap goods available in the charity stores might have been in higher demand, it would require a substantial change in consumer habits to make the switch to these types of good sufficient to support these new enterprises in such a deep recession.

As a retailer, longevity of store location is important although there may be circumstances in which a short-term letting is appropriate for a retailer and aligns with a longer-term business strategy. For a mature retailer looking to establish a market presence and expand, this would be unusual. In the case of

ICRF, and now CRUK, the property strategy focuses more on identifying profitable stores and securing those sites for the longer term.

Negotiating strengths

A more effective way of aligning the property strategy with the business strategy is to take a long lease as a means of negotiating favourable terms and conditions. This is particularly pertinent in an environment where occupiers are often demanding shorter leases. CRUK are in a position to go to a landlord and, being willing to take a 25-years lease, with 5-yearly rent reviews, negotiate fitting out or refurbishment costs and good rental terms. Where a lease is coming to an end or is up for review, it may be possible to offset forecast rent increases by negotiating an early surrender and renewal. The financial liabilities a predominantly leasehold portfolio places on a retailer are substantial, and this makes effective property strategy more vital and provides the incentive to make the assets work efficiently.

Added to this, major charities are now often seen by investment institutions as being of good covenant. Whereas they were perceived as poor quality tenants, offering cheap goods in poorly designed stores, more positive characteristics are now being identified. As well as being willing to commit to longer leases, CRUK is backed by a board of trustees and has a Royal patron. They are unlikely to renege on rental obligations.

The external world

Every organisation has to respond to external world factors over which it has little or no control. From a property perspective, the main factors likely to impact on the business strategy are rent levels and demand. Strong consumer demand in recent years has kept retail rents rising, and CRUK are exposed to risk in this area through their predominantly leasehold portfolio. However, the property strategy contains a sufficiently robust management system to foresee major rent increases and take action to mitigate their impact.

Taxation

Tax issues are often a concern of charity retailers. Charity shops selling 'wholly or mainly donated goods' benefit from an 80% reduction in Uniform Business Rate and can apply for relief from the other 20%.[1] There has been some suggestion in the past that this might change (Keating 1998). While it is increasingly difficult to get the extra 20% waived by the local authority, the 80% reduction is significant, particularly for smaller retailers. CRUK would see such a change as another business cost and incorporate it into its business plans accordingly. This may result in some minor changes to the spread of its portfolio, but with sufficient management systems in place it could foresee and plan for them. This would, however, require effective negotiation on rateable values with the local authority.

VAT harmonisation through entrance to the euro would create a similar issue. The UK and Belgium are the only EU states that zero-rate donated goods for VAT purposes. Were the UK to enter the euro this would probably change, increasing costs again. The direct impact on the property portfolio would be limited, the pressure mainly coming in the form of a requirement to increase turnover and reduce operating costs without undermining performance.

Sector expansion

The number of charity retail stores in the UK is estimated to have increased from 3,480 in 1992 to 6,220 in 2002, with sales increasing over the same period from £183.3 million to £426.5 million (Parsons, 2002). This is a substantial increase which may impact on the availability of volunteer workers and on the supply of donated goods, two factors which are crucial to any charity retailer (Phelan, 1996). Evidence also suggests that costs have risen on a per shop basis as this expansion has happened, put down in part to the stores becoming more professional and having to pay staff.

The successes Corpra have had in reducing the operating costs of CRUK's retail portfolio become even more significant when seen within the context of rising costs incurred by others within the sector. Aligning the property strategy with the organisational objectives of CRUK has clearly been a helpful approach.

Evaluation

Having developed a demographic model for CRUK stores, Corpra can make an assessment of how they think each store should operate. This will take into account:

- the location of the store in terms of retail pitch
- the demographics of the area
- the size of the catchment area
- the proximity of other CRUK stores (as we established earlier there may be two in the same town)
- the retail mix in the area.

This enables management to take a more sophisticated approach to performance assessment than simply looking at store turnover or profit. The most profitable store might not be performing as well as it should be once it is measured against the demographic model. It also enables the retail operations team, and Corpra, to further develop their understanding of how the stores work.

Performance evaluation also has to be applied to the operation of the property portfolio itself. As identified earlier, across the charity sector costs associated with the retail operation having been increasing. This manifested itself within ICRF with the retail portfolio becoming the charity's biggest overhead. Corpra managed to reduce costs through the management changes we have examined. Continuing to improve on an already better position is, however, more difficult. This is akin to the 'low hanging fruit' theory common to environmental economics; the low hanging fruit represents those initial changes that are clearly needed and that bring about significant results. Once the low hanging fruit has been 'picked', finding more opportunities to improve efficiency becomes a bigger and bigger challenge.

One area where it is possible to improve property performance is through effective strategic management of the leases. Holding most of its property leasehold gives CRUK the opportunity to engineer surrenders and renewals as leases come to a close, often enabling them to negotiate better rental terms. As the investment institutions approach to charity retailers has changed to one of acceptance, this has also become easier. This type of strategic management has enabled Corpra to make year-on-year reductions in CRUK's rent obligations.

Performance evaluation also focuses on overhead costs. Apart from occupancy costs, having a retail portfolio requires a substantial management structure which creates a large overhead. This should, of course, be kept to a minimum but there is a limit to the extent to which it can be reduced. One way of reducing its impact on each store is to expand the number of stores within the chain. If each new store is successful this will reduce the overhead burden across the portfolio. However, the performance of the whole chain will then have to be re-evaluated in light of this benefit.

Conclusions

ICRF moved on from a position where its retail portfolio was a significant financial burden, and was not performing as effectively as it could, to being one of the two top charity retailers in the UK. This was only possible through a complete reappraisal of the retail and property management functions, allowing the development of a property strategy that actively supports the operational strengths of the organisation.

ICRF, and subsequently CRUK, took a strategic decision in appointing consultants to review the operation of their retail portfolio. In doing so it has succeeded in establishing CRUK as the best performing charity retailer in the UK, but, perhaps more importantly, has given the retail operation the flexibility to respond strategically to the changing environment in which all retail operations work. This has been established through:

- developing an understanding of the characteristics of ICRF, and subsequently CRUK, as charity retailers

- identifying the implications these characteristics have for the charity's use of property
- developing a detailed knowledge of the property portfolio
- developing data collection and management systems to support the property management function
- developing clear objectives for the property that support the organisation's objectives
- creating sufficient flexibility within the property portfolio to allow opportunities for cost savings and improved terms and conditions to be realised
- ensuring the retail operation has sufficient data and strategic awareness to be able to respond to changes from outside the organisation
- developing performance evaluation systems to allow consistent monitoring of the retail operation and the performance of the property portfolio.

The process has been complicated and has required considerable commitment from each team working within the organisation. Implementation has clearly been helped by use of external consultants.

Information for this case study was obtained from Paul Winter at Corpra.

References

Cranfield School of Management (2002) *Changing Times: strategic consulting for professional effectiveness*. RICS, London.

Hankinson, P. (2001) Brand Orientation in the top 500 fundraising charities in the UK, *Journal of Product and Brand Management*. **10** (6) 346–360.

Hankinson, P. (2002) The impact of brand orientation on managerial practice: a quantitative study of the UK's top 500 fundraising managers. *International Journal of Non-profit and Voluntary Sector Marketing*. **7** (1) 30–44.

Hill, N. (2002) Charity finance: property: bricks and mortar. *Guardian*, April 10.

Horne, S. (1998) Charity shops in the UK. *International Journal of Retail Distribution Management*. **26** (4) 155–161.

Horne, S. & Broadbridge, A. (1995) Charity shops: a classification by merchandise mix. *International Journal of Retail Distribution Management*, **23** (7) 17–23.

Keating, M. (1998) Charity shops: faith, hope and tax relief. *Guardian*, December 15.

Nourse, H.O. & Roulac, S.E. (1993) Linking real estate decisions to corporate strategy. *Journal of Real Estate Research*, **8** (4) 475–494.

Parsons, E. (2000) New goods, old records and second-hand suits: charity shopping in south west England. *International Journal of Non-profit and Voluntary Sector Marketing* **5** (2) 141–151.

Parsons, E. (2002) Charity retail: past, present, future. *International Journal of Retail Distribution Management*, **30** (12) 586–594.

Phelan, D. (1996) High street wars hot up. *NGO Finance*, **6** (3) 18–28.

Rutherford, A. (2002) Cancer Research UK looks to NCI for success. *Trends in Molecular Medicine*, **8** (2) 96–97.

Endnote

[1] Wholly or mainly donated goods is taken to mean at least 75%, although there is no clear definition. This has to be born in mind with regard to bought in goods.

Case Study 5
Ardtornish Estate, Morvern, Scotland

Introduction

Ardtornish Estate is a privately owned 35,000 acre (14,000 hectare) estate occupying the south east corner of the Morvern peninsula on the west coast of Scotland. The estate covers some 60 square miles. It straddles the sea loch, Loch Aline, and is located on the west coast, across from the island of Mull. It is a remote and very beautiful corner of the UK.

Like many people in Morvern, much of the population of Ardtornish was uprooted during the Highland Clearances[1] to make way for extensive sheep farming, and then a sporting deer forest. The population of Morvern in the 1840s was over 2,000; it is now around 320, but rising.

The estate has been in long-term private ownership. The present owners, the Raven family, purchased the estate in 1930 and immediately sold a large section (Fuinary) to the Forestry Commission. In 1967 the title was transferred into the name of Ardtornish Estate Co. Ltd. Shares in the company are held in trust for various members of the Raven family. Such an arrangement has had several advantages, including tax efficiency, thus helping to secure its long-term future as it is passed through the generations.[2]

The Raven family are reluctant to have Ardtornish seen as a model for other estates, and are keen to point out that it is up to individual owners to establish their own objectives for estate management. However, Ardtornish proves an effective case study in demonstrating how to maintain a large and diversified property holding within an evolving economy. In particular, the estate epitomises the practical realisation of sustainable development, economically, socially and environmentally.

Background

The assets of the Ardtornish Estate Co. Ltd consist of Ardtornish Estate and the company is self-financing. In this respect, it is similar to the case study on the Youth Hostels Association, as the sustainable management of its property is central to the achievement of the organisation's objectives. Nevertheless, the company's objectives for managing its property reflect the family's desire not only to ensure the continued ownership and well being of the property, but also the continued wellbeing of the surrounding area, in social, economic and environmental terms. The estate is run with the object of maintaining a viable community in the area, in a way that contributes to conservation of the cultural and natural heritage of the peninsula of Morvern.

The stated objectives of Ardtornish Estate are:

'To manage the estate, to the best of our abilities:
- to support the strength and prosperity of the community
- to maintain and enhance the natural and cultural heritage
- to sustainably develop the value of the estate for the benefit of both the owners and the community.'

Ardtornish Estate, 2002

This objective has been adopted with increasing success. The population of the area is rising and the environment of Ardtornish is improving (see Evaluation, p. 223). At the same time, Ardtornish is able to offer something to people who visit from outside the region, whether they are interested in the archaeological, historical or natural assets of the area. While the estate is proud of its progress to date, it is always striving to do better.

The economic profile of the estate has changed significantly since the early 1980s. It used to be overwhelmingly a sporting and livestock estate. Now the estate produces several other income streams, which not only contribute to its economic viability, but mean that the property is in better condition now than it was at the end of the 1970s. In addition, the estate has done a lot to help establish a larger viable population in the area, capable of supporting local services, such as the local shop, school, etc.

The estate is managed by a resident agent (factor), Angus Robertson. Andrew Raven works with the factor, on behalf of the directors and other family shareholders, to manage the estate year-by-year. The estate boasts no comprehensive electronic property database: the estate records are all kept in fairly traditional estate terrier form. The key constraint to management is time, and it is felt that quality of management depends upon the ability of the factor to focus on developing new enterprises on the estate. In doing so, the estate calls in consultants for advice on specialist issues, such as fish farming, farm management, forestry, etc.

Property user characteristics

While many might see the Raven family as the principal 'users' of the Ardtornish Estate, it is likely that they would think otherwise. The family's objectives for the estate reflect their belief that its management must be for the benefit of the local community. Ardtornish is an important employer in its local area and one of the main objectives of the estate is to sustain such employment.

As well as the factor, it supports the employment of some 65 people in full-time, part-time and casual work.

As well as employing local people, the estate is directly involved in economic development and social activity in the surrounding area through its management system. The principal means of doing this is through the interaction of its own employees in the local community. For example, the factor's office is involved in helping a wide variety of community organisations, and the office provides an important service in this respect. In addition, Angus Robertson is involved in Morvern Community Council, Morvern Development Company Ltd, Morvern Deer Management Group, Scottish Wildlife Trust's Rahoy Hills Committee and a host of other such local community activities.

While more traditional, informal means of developing community relationships continue to exist, in September 2002 the estate held its first planned community meeting in the local village hall. Notice of the meeting was erected on the village notice board and announced at a meeting of the community council. On the evening of the meeting, presentations were made on the estate's background, its objectives and activities, and workshops were held on the community's priorities. Several positive outcomes were achieved from the meeting, particularly in relation to housing. The availability of housing was identified as a local priority and the estate offered to fund, along with the Community Council, a housing needs survey, to bring in objective data. The project has been taken up by the Highland Small Communities Housing Association. In addition, the estate was approached by three people who wanted to create a small self-build group for housing; their initiative has been put on hold until the housing needs survey is completed.

The estate is always open to new ideas and actively encourages exchange of information among interested parties. It does so informally, through liaison with neighbouring estate and formally, through inviting representatives of land use and environmental organisations to the estate. For example, in 2001 the community hosted a visit from the Countryside Exchange Programme. The Countryside Exchange Programme exchanges professionals from all sorts of disciplines who work in the countryside (planners, land use consultants, landscape architects, economists, rangers, etc.) between the USA and Britain. The professionals meet as a bi-national group at one location in either country and are set a task to work on for a week. When based in Morvern, the professionals from the programme investigated a number of issues, including tourism, housing, Information Technology, and youth matters. Among the suggestions made by the professionals was the construction of a marine enterprise. Three options are being investigated: a summer pontoon for servicing sailing boats; summer moorings; and overwintering land facilities for boats.

The suggestions of the Countryside Exchange group were taken up by Hugh Raven, who led a lively debate at a community meeting. As a result, the Community Development Company (largely government funded) may develop the summer pontoon, which is quite capital intensive, and Hugh

Raven will investigate the development of the other two elements, where less capital development is required. It is another good example of how the estate can encourage local economic development, by both stimulating interest and, if appropriate, investing capital. As Hugh Raven says, 'It is very important that the people who live on the estate are able to help in determining the trajectory that the estate takes' (BBC, 1997). The community meetings will continue as an annual event.

Property characteristics

The estate comprises a rich diversity of different habitat types, which are summarised in Table CS5.1, which is extracted from a conservation audit of the estate. In addition, there are 578.3 km of rivers and streams on the estate, 64 km of fences and 51.8 km of dykes.

Table CS5.1   Principal habitat types on Ardtornish

Habitat	Area (ha.)	Percentage
Woodland		
Natural	468	3.2
Semi-natural	271	1.8
Conifers (small)	31	0.2
Policy	14	0.1
Conifers (large)	421	2.9
Moorland		
Heather	13	0.1
Mixed	2,194	14.9
Summit heath	26	0.2
Grassland		
Upland (unenclosed)	1,439	9.8
Lowland (enclosed)	280	1.9
Improved and arable	164	1.1
Mires (peat land)		
Blanket bog	7,599	51.7
Raised bog	121	0.8
Basin mires	513	3.4
Valley mires	304	2.1
Flushes	36	0.3
Freshwater		
Transition (swamp)	4	0.1
Lochs	282	1.9
Cliffs and rocks	428	2.9
River shingle	8	0.1
Saltmarsh/mudflats	64	0.4
Buildings and gardens	8	0.1
Grand total	14,688	100

Source: Brookes (1990)

The makeup of the estate determines, in many ways, the options that are available for its management. The table shows the majority of the land to be 'blanket bog', so, while the total acreage is impressive, the options for over 7,000 hectares of peat bog are limited. Issues such as this make the strategic use of more adaptable land within the estate even more important and, unlike many lowland estates, suggest that non-farming income streams must form a large component of the overall revenue.

In terms of built property, there are some 50 separate properties on the estate, 21 of which are listed. Ardtornish House is a Grade A listed building, 20 other properties are Grade B listed. While this is a positive characteristic for the estate in that it demonstrates the quality and heritage value inherent within the buildings, it also brings with it quite onerous obligations. The repair and maintenance of listed buildings can be significantly more expensive than non-listed ones (see Organisational objectives in relation to real estate below).

Organisational objectives in relation to real estate

Like many rural estates, Ardtornish House has variously been an asset and a liability. Currently, it would be fair to say that it is both: providing a valuable source of revenue from holiday lets, but also continuing to act as a drain on the estate's resources in terms of its maintenance demands. The annual running cost of Ardtornish House alone is around £70,000. While it is capable of bringing in an income of £35,000, this still leaves an annual operating deficit of £35,000. The estate is obliged to carry out much of the maintenance work on the estate's properties to prescribed standards because they are listed by Historic Scotland.[3] The fact that the buildings are listed also means that the insurance premiums are very high, because of the possibility that the buildings might have to be rebuilt in full historic style, at a likely cost several times the modern equivalent. Throughout history, such remote rural estates in the UK have been subsidised by owners with other sources of income, normally through their work in commerce. Nowadays, such estates still exist, although the business people that support the Scottish estates are just as likely to be Danish or Dutch, looking for a residential hideaway. Other estates must survive on a mixture of self-generated income and government grants.

Ardtornish now falls into the latter category of estate and, as such, must make its property work for the furtherance of the estate as a whole. The maintenance of its built heritage is a major burden on the estate's finances and it is crucial that the estate finds sufficient income to meet its obligations. The key to the survival of Ardtornish as a thriving business over recent years has been the estate's strategy of *diversification*. In trying to achieve its objectives, the estate is involved in a wide variety of commercial activities. The main enterprises can be summarised under 12 different management activities:

- hydro-electric generation
- tourism
- salmon farming
- mining
- forestry
- in-hand farming
- property letting
- deer management
- fishing
- gardens
- access
- nature conservation.

Some of the above operations produce important income streams for the estate. Others are provided 'freely' for public benefit, with the recognition that the receipt of government grants often produces a regulatory, and always an ethical, obligation to provide benefits for society.

Each operation can be looked at in turn. However, it is crucial to appreciate that the successful management of the estate depends upon the symbiotic relationship of each component. Perhaps, therefore, it is useful to examine the main revenue earners for the estate first, and then explain how other operations fit into the whole estate management.

Hydro-electric generation

The most recent project to be implemented on the estate is the installation of a 750 kW run-of-the-river hydro-electric scheme. This has been built to supply power to the National Grid under the government's Non-Fossil Fuel Obligation Order (NOFO). The hydro-electric project runs night and day and is critical to the long-term future of the estate. In terms of income generation, it produces around £100,000 per annum for the estate, about 20% of the estate's total turnover. This underestimates its true contribution to the estate's profitability because the costs of running the hydro-electric station are relatively small. It was, however, very capital intensive to establish, and it will be some years before the initial capital costs are recovered.

The estate would like to develop further renewable energy assets, but they must be developed in a way that is consistent with the overall objectives of sustainable development on the estate. That means ensuring that each separate enterprise complements the others. For example, at the intake of the Ardtornish hydro-electric scheme, at the top of the falls of the River Rannoch, there are two structures: a diversion weir, and a main water intake structure. Water enters the pipe of the main intake through a screen, which cleans off any debris. The intake is quite complicated because the estate must ensure that a certain amount of water stays in the river as it goes down the falls, to ensure that all ecological life in the falls is protected.

New technology helps to maintain correct water levels: a sonic echo sounder measures the water level above the screen and sends a signal down to the turbine. The signal causes the turbine guide veins that control the amount of water coming through to open or close, so maintaining the water level at a steady depth of within 0.5 cm variance. The estate is also investigating the possibility of storing water by constructing an artificial reservoir behind a dam. At the moment, the hydro scheme suffers from peaks and troughs in its energy supply, according to the flows of water in the river. Likewise, a salmon hatchery site downstream suffers from drought periods. If the hatchery were to run out of water, then 7–10 million fish could be lost in about an hour. The reservoir would allow for consistency of flow, which would benefit both the hydro scheme and the hatchery. This is a perfect example of the need for integration of separate enterprises and activities on the estate.

Tourism

The second major income stream from the estate comes from tourism. Several thousand people visit the Ardtornish Estate each year and the estate has its own tourism manager. There are twelve self-catering apartments, five of which are in Ardtornish House, and seven in former estate workers' cottages, giving a total capacity for some 90 people at any one time.

Tourism is a large and important source of income, not just for the estate, but also for Morvern, helping to bring customers to the village shop, hotel and local arts and crafts businesses. It integrates well within the estate: people on the estate understand the importance of visitors and are welcoming.

The estate's unique selling point is its remote rural location and its working, living landscape. It is a place that is popular with those wanting peace and quiet and to view wildlife, including bird watchers, sub-aqua divers, and people who just want to use and enjoy the outdoors. The estate rents mountain bikes, which can be used on the estate tracks and offers fishing, deer stalking, field courses and other activities. More recently, it has appointed travel agents in Germany and the Netherlands, which have been successful in attracting German and Dutch visitors, who seem particularly attracted to the virtually pollution-free and crime-free environment. As well as the full-time tourism manager, the tourism business keeps another 15 local people in part-time jobs.

Salmon farming

The third important income stream for the estate is the salmon fish farm. The estate does not farm salmon itself, but leases the fish farm sites to a commercial company, Scottish Sea Farms Ltd which in turn reduces the risks associated with such an enterprise. Salmon farming is a huge industry in the West Highlands and critical to the wellbeing of the communities. Although controversial because of its potential environmental problems, it has provided many jobs for local people up and down the highlands, contributing significant amounts of revenue to small coastal communities. Similarly, Scottish Sea Farms Ltd contributes to the upkeep of Ardtornish, not just through the rent paid for the salmon farm sites, but also by renting residential properties from the estate to house its staff. The estate works with the farm to mitigate potential environmental problems, such as loss of wild fish stocks, water pollution, etc., in order to further its own environmental agenda.

Mining

The fourth income stream from the estate comes from sand extraction. Silica sand, which is used for glass making, was found in the area in the 1930s. When the major supply of silica sand in Belgium was annexed by the Germans during the Second World War, Ardtornish's mine was opened to supply sand for making lenses for periscopes and binoculars. The Lochaline Silica Sand Mine (Tilcon Sand Mine) has been open ever since, supplying high quality sand to the glass making trade. The mine is operated by Tarmac (Northern) Ltd, who pay a royalty to the estate for every tonne of sand extracted. This has provided another steady income stream to help sustain the estate economically over the years.

Forestry

Forestry provides the fifth income stream from the estate, although this income stream differs from the first four in that it is principally derived from public sector support rather than private enterprise. The estate houses some 600 hectares of conifer plantations, planted in the 1960s, which are managed for timber production. However, the estate is restructuring its woodlands, adopting a more modern, sensitive approach. Originally, 7.5% of the estate was wooded, two-thirds of which was native woodlands and the rest commercial conifers. The estate is building up its stock of woodlands to 15%, or 5000 acres (2000 hectares), of which two-thirds will comprise native hardwoods and the rest more production orientated species.

The estate also has a programme of harvesting and marketing small quantities of hardwoods, which are sawn, dried and supplied to local craft workers. Originally, the native woodlands on the estate supported a charcoal burning industry. Now, in addition to the income derived from timber sales, Ardtornish is eligible for the Forestry Commission's Woodland Grant Scheme. This will result in the estate receiving nearly £1 million of subsidy for its forestry enterprise under grants paid over a period of 15 years, from 1997. When the estate joined the scheme, the initial grant payments under the Woodland Grant Scheme represented a significant tranche of the total payment. By keeping woodland establishment costs sufficiently low, a surplus of grant over costs could be made and invested into the estate. In such a way, the woodlands helped to support other enterprises on the estate by presenting a cash boost that significantly enhanced the estate's cash flow. Specifically, this short-term cash injection allowed the estate to invest in its cattle enterprise, which in turn should help finance future woodland maintenance.

In-hand farming

The in-hand farming operation supports 2,800 Blackface hill ewes and 240 hill cattle. Historically, the economy of the Highlands and islands was based on cattle rather than sheep, which were introduced after the Highland Clearances. The cattle are expensive to keep, but they are significantly less subsidy-dependent than the sheep, with trading of cattle much closer to the market economy (see The external world, p. 222). As a result, their recent financial performance is encouraging and they have managed to pay for their own keep on the estate. Nevertheless, it would be logical to question the maintenance of a herd that has often been a financial drain. The answer lies within the wider ranging organisational objectives of the estate, and in particular the social and environmental aspects of sustainability. The cattle help to maintain a local farming economy, create similar employment opportunities as the sheep, and encourage the estate to keep its arable areas in good order in order to provide feed. Perhaps more importantly, the cattle are valued for their environmental benefits. As good grazers, with larger mouths, they are less able to be selective about what they eat than sheep, and therefore useful at keeping down roughage on the hill and helping the establishment of the native woodlands.

These six enterprises represent the main revenue sources for the estate. However, other operations are equally important in contributing to the overall diversified economy of the area and therefore to the organisational objectives of the estate. These additional operations are reviewed briefly below.

Property letting

The estate has a housing policy, with priorities. The first people to be housed are current and former employees. They sit in equal priority with the self-catering enterprise, which needs to maintain a set number of units to carry its fixed costs. Any surplus housing is let at affordable rents for permanent residence. There are a few properties that are not suitable for permanent occupation, because of their size, services or remoteness, which are let as second homes.

Deer management

Recent deer counts show that there are a total of around 500 red deer hinds and 300 stags on Ardtornish. The estate culls approximately 50 stags each year, resulting in an income that averages £20,000 per annum; £10,000 from stalking rents and £10,000 from venison sales. The estate's deer management policy, in terms of number of animals culled, is agreed with the Deer Commission for

Scotland through the Morvern Deer Management Group. In this sense, the estate must integrate its deer management, not only with other enterprises on the estate, but also with other neighbouring landowners. While the deer stalking enterprise provides valuable revenue to the estate, it also complements management of the estate by helping to keep the bridges and paths open for walkers.

Fishing

Ardtornish offers salmon, sea trout and brown trout fishing to visitors. Like most west coast fisheries, its sea trout fishing has been in decline since the 1930s and its salmon fishery took a sudden decline in the 1990s. The estate is very concerned about this and the effect it has on the whole estate business. Furthermore, fishing rents should total around £10,000 per annum, but have dropped to around £1,000. Fishing should produce the added benefit of letting holiday houses to fishermen, which could mean that the fishing enterprise is financially far more important than the deer enterprise.

Gardens

The gardens at Ardtornish are extensive and support two different activities for the estate. There are 28 acres of designed landscape and gardens surrounding Ardtornish House. These are open to the public and available to visitors throughout the summer. They bring in only a very modest income stream, but also add to the attraction of renting a flat in Ardtornish House.

In addition, the estate works in a limited partnership with a local market gardener, who operates Ardtornish Kitchen Gardens, selling shrubs, plants, fruit and vegetables to visitors and the local community.

Access

There is an open access policy at Ardtornish, with only minimal restrictions on parts of the estate during the September and October stag season. Even at this time, large parts of the estate and most popular walks remain available to the public. The estate also houses Loch Tearnait Bothy, which is managed by agreement with the Mountain Bothies Association. The bothy, a one-roomed shelter originally housing labourers but now giving day and overnight shelter to walkers, is available for the Association's members and the public in general.

Nature conservation

Ardtornish is managed to try to conserve and enhance the natural heritage of the area. The estate also works in conjunction with Scottish Wildlife Trust who are responsible for managing the conservation of around 600 hectares of

Ardtornish land, neighbouring their own land and forming a part of their Rahoy Hills Nature Reserve.

In the early days of sheep stocking, there was a tendency to overstock, causing damage to vegetation, especially woodland. Now that the priority for the reserve has switched to wildlife, the objective is to try to use grazing animals as a conservation tool. In principle, a balance should be found between the forestry, farming, deer stalking and nature conservation. The estate is striving to find that balance and to further the regeneration of native woodlands while maintaining grazing livestock and a viable deer population. Cattle are used to keep unwanted vegetation in check (see the section on farming above), and there have been experiments with pigs to assist the regeneration process by turning over the soil and so preparing a good seed bed.

The institutional arrangement of the property market

The Ardtornish Estate is most affected by the legal institutions of the property market through its decisions regarding diversification. The estate is owned 100% freehold and one of the principal objectives of the owners, like many rural landowners, is to protect that ownership. However, they want do so in a manner that ensures that Ardtornish continues to contribute to the local economy, society and culture, and maintains its environmental value.

The ability to separate out legal interest in the estate enables Ardtornish Estate Co. Ltd to develop diversified income streams from the estate, which, when aggregated, sustain its wellbeing. The company has been judicious in its choice of when to establish enterprises under its own management and when to sell property rights, such as leases, to allow other businesses to develop the enterprise. Its decision to lease sites for the salmon farms, for example, rather than develop the enterprise itself, has lessened the estate's exposure to risk in this highly sensitive and sophisticated industry. There are some activities where Ardtornish is the logical entrepreneur. However, the Raven family admit that they are inclined to be risk averse. They acquired the estate in 1930 at which time it was supported by income derived from the estate. Now, two generations on, the estate must pay for itself, without the benefit of an additional private income. Any risks taken with new enterprises might, therefore, put the whole estate at risk.

Nevertheless, the estate actively works as a facilitator and catalyst, to encourage other small enterprises to establish on and around the estate. Businesses such as pony trekking, the kitchen garden, and other visitor enterprises all provide employment on a seasonal basis and help to sustain the local economy. On its management overheads and cost structure, it would simply not be viable for the estate to establish them. However, the estate is able to provide the necessary licenses and permissions to use its resources and help to market such enterprises with its visitors.

Recently, the estate has had to monitor certain changes within Scottish land tenure system, recently passed through the Scottish Parliament. The new Land Reform (Scotland) Act, which received Royal Assent on 25 February 2003 has three parts to it. Part One will provide a *freedom to roam*, whereby responsible countryside access will be granted for the general public. At the time of writing (early 2003) it is believed that this part of the Act will come into effect early in 2004. Since Ardtornish has always allowed free access over its land for walkers, the Bill will have little impact on the estate. Part Two of the Land Reform Act will grant communities first refusal on any land put up for sale. Part Three of the Act will grant crofters the right to buy land. Perhaps a more important development, however, has been the establishment of the Scottish Land Fund to facilitate such purchases. The Fund was granted £10 million by the National Lottery, which was supposed to last until 2007, but has almost been depleted. The practice of communities coming forward with proposals for buyouts is not new and certainly preceded the Land Reform Act. In 2003, North Harris was bought by the island's community (in partnership with a private individual) from cider baron Jonathan Bulmer for £4.5 million. The community was in negotiation with the Bulmer Trust before the Land Reform Bill, and it is likely that the £1.6 million received from the Land Fund did more to bolster their chances than the Bill (West, 2003). The community also received £400,000 from the Highland and Islands Community Land Trust and £100,000 from the John Muir Trust. Once it had purchased the whole estate, it sold the castle and the salmon and sea trout fishing rights to a private buyer, reducing its own expenses to £2.4 million. The Land Reform Act and the Land Fund were originally designed to secure the future of sustainable rural development in Scotland, under the control of the local communities. Many are critical of its use to facilitate expensive, high-profile buyouts. Ardtornish has no crofters and since a principal objective of the estate is to remain a going concern, the right for the local community to buy it is unlikely to arise.

Similarly, the Agricultural Holdings (Scotland) Act received Royal Assent on 22 May 2003. At one time it was thought that this might grant tenants the absolute right to buy their land. This amendment has now been overturned and changes include granting tenants the right to assign a member of their family as successor, the right to live off-farm, and developments in compensation for improvements carried out by tenants. It has been seen as a success in granting landlords and tenants a secure base from which to encourage more tenancies. The Holdings Bill is unlikely to have any significant effect on Ardtornish's future. However, both new Acts are pieces of legislation that might well impinge on similar estates in Scotland. What is striking is the way in which Ardtornish has effectively pre-empted the Acts by already operating in a manner to which both pieces of legislation aspire: especially in its allowing open access on its land and working with the local community so that it can benefit from economic development.

The external world

External influences can add much complexity to the management of the estate, especially in the form of government subsidies and grants, by altering the incentive structure, making some of the estate enterprises more attractive than others. Several changes in the external world of the Ardtornish Estate have influenced its property strategy over the last 20 years.

Common Agricultural Policy

First and foremost of these is the evolving Common Agricultural Policy (CAP). The CAP has driven the entire land use management system through its encouragement of cattle and sheep. Sheep subsidies in the UK have been funded partly by the Hill Livestock Compensatory Allowance (UK based) (HLCA) and partly by the Sheep Annual Premium, a European based scheme, both of which paid according to the number of sheep kept. This encouraged overstocking of sheep on hillsides all over the UK, since the premiums paid were worth more than the sheep. HLCA has since been replaced by the Less Favoured Area Support Scheme, which is paid according to area and so does not carry the same problems of overstocking. The Sheep Annual Premium is now quota based, but still focuses on number of sheep.

The CAP has two 'pillars' of funding for farmers. Pillar one currently provides funds for agricultural production. It is hoped that pillar one of the CAP will be reformed on the basis of 'decoupling' soon. This will mean the link between production and support is severed and payments are based on a single farm payment, with money paid to farmers on condition that they comply with statutory requirements and maintain their land in good agricultural condition. Only following such reform is a sensible grazing regime likely to be achieved. At Ardtornish, such a reform might encourage the estate to reduce its sheep flock to between 1,000 and 2,000 ewes and increase its cattle to around 300.

Pillar two of the CAP provides funds for rural development. However, it is considerably smaller in size than Pillar one, containing at most 10% of the total CAP budget. The British Government is currently seeking increased funding for the second pillar of the CAP. The Morvern peninsula has also been able to benefit from European 'structural' funding, since it is located in an area that was granted Objective 1 status. The whole of the Highlands is now designated as a post Objective 1 transition area and, as such, continues to benefit from some economic development support from Europe. However, once the European Union is expanded to include Eastern European countries, the area is unlikely to benefit from European development funds.

Tourism

The growth of the leisure industry and changes in demographics in Britain have certainly helped Ardtornish's tourism businesses. Where once it struggled to let holiday property outside the popular months of July and August, its main business now is as a second holiday destination for families who mainly take their first holiday abroad. This has extended the season and has helped the estate's cash flow considerably. The estate targets families with young children, who are attracted by the number of activities that they can undertake and, more particularly, by the remote location, free from traffic, which allows the children to roam relatively freely.

Unlike the Youth Hostels Association case study, tourism on the Ardtornish Estate did not suffer from the 2001 outbreak of foot and mouth. Although foot and mouth did not reach this part of Scotland, when the outbreak was first known, bookings to Ardtornish's holiday lettings reduced suddenly. However, once the impact of the disease was known and the Lake District was highlighted as one of the 'hot spot' areas, bookings to destinations in the Scottish Highlands increased and it enjoyed its busiest Easter period ever. Visitors encountered huge tailbacks, as traffic was made to drive through wheel washers before entering the Highlands. Nevertheless, the small boost meant that annual tourism receipts in the area finished on average, having regained lost income from the beginning of the season.

Evaluation

The estate evaluates its performance against its stated objectives on a regular basis. The objectives form the benchmark from which to assess the estate's progress. Although no formal management plan is drawn up, each separate enterprise embarked upon is evaluated fully and reports relating to each component of the estate are used in aggregation to act as an overall management plan. This allows the estate to retain a flexible, inexpensive and dynamic management framework, while providing some formal system of management planning. However, like the management planning, there is no formal mechanism for comprehensive performance monitoring. Instead, each element of the estate's activity is measured against the stated objectives.

The financial sustainability of the estate is reviewed in the annual accounts and report, which are brought to the Board of Ardtornish Estate Co. Ltd for approval. However, the estate has other objectives, which arguably pose a greater challenge in terms of monitoring their achievement.

In terms of 'supporting the strength and prosperity of the community', an annual census is conducted of all the estate houses and a record made of occupants and ages. One of the estate's major successes has been the extent to which it is able to provide local employment. To give an indication of the importance of the estate within the community, the estimated number of people gaining employment from the assets of Ardtornish are summarised in Table CS5.2.

The figures in Table CS5.2 can be compared with a total population of Morvern, recorded in 1992 as 318, of which 121 are adults in full-time

Table CS5.2 Employment on Ardtornish Estate

	Full-time	Part-time and casuals	FTE
Ardtornish Estate	9	14	10
Ardtornish farms	6	2	7
Tilcon Sand Mine	11	2	12
Scottish Sea Farms Ltd	10	5	11
Others: self-employed	2	5	4
Total	38	28	44

employment. The extent to which the estate is supporting the local community is monitored through feedback at its community meetings and informal communication channels.

In terms of 'maintaining and enhancing the natural and cultural heritage', the manner in which the diverse variety of activities that take place on the estate are planned and operated is hugely influenced by this objective. In addition, the estate has a variety of research and improvement programmes in conjunction with likeminded public bodies and grant aid agencies.

First, it is able to measure its performance through the amount of land designated as nature conservation sites. Some 12% of the land area of the estate is designated and protected as Sites of Special Scientific Interest (SSSIs) and many of the native woodlands are a candidate Special Area of Conservation (SAC) site.

Second, the estate has conducted a comprehensive conservation audit of the whole property. The audit identified and graded important habitats and allowed the estate to plan its management to protect and enhance important sites. In addition, the estate was involved in a comprehensive survey of the natural and semi-natural woodlands. This showed that all the woodlands were over-mature and declining rapidly and identified opportunities for enlarging and improving the woodlands. This in turn spurred a fencing and livestock control programme to encourage woodland regeneration. A variety of methods are being used in conjunction with Scottish Wildlife Trust, Scottish Natural Heritage and the Forestry Commission. To date, the estate has established some 700 hectares of regeneration and native woodland planting schemes, which will result in stocking of over 750,000 new trees on Ardtornish. This will result in an improvement in the age structure of the existing woodlands and an increase in the percentage of land occupied by woodlands from 7.5% to just under 15% of the total land area.

In terms of 'sustainably developing the value of the estate for the benefit of both the owners and the community', the estate has to measure each new enterprise according to social, environmental and economic benefits. The latest revenue scheme on the estate, the hydro-electric power scheme, shapes up pretty well under such scrutiny. It is economically sustainable and has not detracted from the wildlife or other ecological interests of the area. The river used is not used by any migratory fish and did not have other important species that would be affected by the scheme. Socially it has contributed by bringing in a significant revenue stream that has secured another full-time job in the area and contributes to the economic viability of the estate generally.

Conclusions

The Ardtornish Estate Co. Ltd has managed to secure the future of the Ardtornish Estate, at least in the medium term, by diversifying the income streams that the estate produces. Moreover, it has done so in a way that conserves the built and natural heritage of the area and furthers the socioeconomic development of the Morvern peninsula.

Each of the estate's separate income streams must be compatible with and complement the others, as it is the combination of the separate enterprises that furthers the objectives of the estate. The estate has been effective in exploiting and protecting its property asset base by:

- ensuring a diversified income from its asset base
- carrying out a thorough review and audit of the land, allowing different priorities to be set for different parts of the estate
- ploughing revenue back into a planned maintenance and development programme
- establishing an outward looking management ethos that encourages the development of partner relationships with organisations with sympathetic operational objectives
- making realistic decisions regarding the level of capital investment that the estate can make
- working beyond the estate boundaries to further the socioeconomic and environmental development of the area.

These six factors have enabled the Ardtornish Estate Co. Ltd to manage Ardtornish in a way that combines private enterprise with the pursuit of public benefit. Perhaps most noticeably, the estate has managed to internalise any externalities that might impinge on its business. By this we mean that the estate has been able to anticipate any threats imposed by the external world and ensure that it benefits from rather than pays for any changes in the institutional arrangement of its market. A good example of this is the freedom to roam legislation. Good walking access around the estate has always been an attraction to help market its holiday cottage business. As such, Ardtornish was in a position to channel the positive benefits of free access into its own business, well before the legislation imposed on all landowners. The size of the estate, and its location, mean that it is big enough and remote enough to carry on internalising such opportunities in a way in which other estates in popular tourism locations might not be able. For example, should eagles decide to nest on the estate, Ardtornish will not fear those people who will inevitably come to see them. Instead, it will use the birds to help market its leisure enterprises and welcome the revenue that such visitors will bring to all businesses in the area.

The estate adopts a similarly opportunistic approach to what others might see as government interference: it is happy to work in partnership with public bodies to mutual benefit. Public incentives are crucial: its hydro-electric scheme was driven by the Scottish Renewables Order, its woodlands by the Woodland Grant Scheme, and its farming by the Common Agricultural Policy. The estate recognises that the public, through public agencies, will want to have an influence over the way in which the estate is developed and managed. However, instead of resisting such influences and institutional changes, the estate seeks opportunities to capture some of the value that the public place on the estate, in the form of grants and subsidies.

The estate's interaction with the public sector is crucial at the local level as well. Ardtornish itself can suffer greatly from the area's lack of public service provision. For example, although there was excellent primary school provision in the area, until recently education facilities were very poor at the secondary level, with children having to board weekly in Fort William, or travel by ferry to Tobermory School on Mull. This resulted in several good employees on the estate opting to leave the area once their children had reached secondary school age and was an unfortunate drain of valuable resources on a vulnerable community. Similarly, there was no public transport to speak of: it took two days to get to the local government centre in Fort William, involving two ferry trips, a long bus ride and an overnight stop once there. It is one of Ardtornish's objectives to work with the authorities and the local communities to try to improve public services, with some noticeable success. A community high school opened in nearby Strontian in 2002 and a minibus to Fort William now operates three days a week.

It is this involvement in the local community and development of the local economy that most characterise Ardtornish as a twenty-first century Highland estate. 'Scottish country estates have long been playgrounds for the pursuit of private indulgence' (West, 2003b), where owners would retreat for their own relaxation and, as with any form of leisure, would be prepared to sink large amounts of their earned income to maintaining the estate. As a consequence, it was customary to build an impressive mansion house and to distance oneself from the local community. The legacy of such practice is that estates are now left with 'monumental symbols of conspicuous consumption, but vast revenue deficits' (Raven, 2003). Ardtornish, hindered by such a legacy in the form of its mansion and other listed buildings, but unsupported by any new sources of outside income, must embrace the public benefits it is capable of providing.

Not all estates are in the same position. Newly acquired estates continue today to be bought by entrepreneurs wtih extensive income sources. For example, new purchasers include Fred Olsen, the Norwegian shipping magnate; Mohammed Fayed, the owner of Harrods department store; Kirk Kristiansen, owner of Lego; the lyricist Tim Rice; and theatre impresario Cameron

Mackintosh. Even then, some find the drain on their resources too much: the average length of ownership is some 11 years (West, 2003b). By working in partnership with local, national and, effectively through the EU, international communities, the future of Ardtornish can be secured. However, this can only be achieved by adopting an inclusive rather than exclusive policy of development and operation.

Information for this case study was obtained from Andrew Raven of Ardtornish Estate.

References

Ardtornish Estate Co. Ltd (2002) *Estate Documents*. Ardtornish Estate, Morvern.

BBC (1997) *Farming Today*. Radio 4, 24 May.

Brookes, B. (1990) *Ardtornish Conservation Audit*. Ardtornish Estate Office, Morvern.

Raven, A. (2003) Interviews conducted on 12 and 13 October 2002 and 14 March 2003.

West, D. (2003a) This land is my land. *The Scotsman*, 13 March, page 15.

West, D. (2003b) Country pursuits. *The Scotsman Guide to Property*, 13 March 2003, 16–19.

Endnotes

[1] The land around Morvern was cleared by the notorious Patrick Sellar, factor of the Duke of Sutherland, who bought the Ardtornish Estate with the gains he made from clearing large areas of the west coast.

[2] Each individual member of the family (four siblings and a parent) holds a 12% life interest in the Company. The other 40% shareholdings are vested equally in two separate trusts. The establishment of the hydro-electric scheme helped to validate the company as a trading company once and for all and so secure Business Property Relief.

[3] Historic Scotland is Scotland's government agency for listing and administering historic buildings. If a property is a listed building, then all of it – the interior as well as the exterior – is protected by law. Listed building consent is needed from the local planning authority for all but the most minor works of maintenance and repair, and particularly for any demolition or alteration. More information can be found on Historic Scotland's website at www.historic-scotland.gov.uk, on the English Heritage website www.english-heritage.org.uk, or on the Welsh Historic Monuments website www.cadw.wales.gov.uk.

Bibliography

Anderson, T.L. & Leal, D.R. (1991) *Free Market Environmentalism*. Pacific Research Institute for Public Policy, Westview Press, Boulder.

Anderson, T.L. & McChesney, F.S. (2003) *Property Rights: Cooperation, Conflict and the Law*. Princeton University Press, Princeton, NJ.

Apgar, M., IV (1993) Uncovering your hidden occupancy costs. *Harvard Business Review*, May–June 124–136.

Ardtornish Estate Co. Ltd (2002). *Estate Documents*, Ardtornish Estate.

Arthur Andersen, NACORE International and CCIM (1993) *Real Estate in the Corporation: the bottom line from senior management*. Arthur Andersen and Co., Chicago.

ATIS REAL Weatherall and UCL (2002) *Land Value and Public Transport*. RICS, London.

Audit Commission (1988) *Local Authority Property: A Management Overview*. HMSO, London.

Avis, M., Gibson, V. & Watts, J. (1989) *Managing Operational Property Assets*. Department of Land Management and Development, University of Reading, Reading.

Ball, M. (1994) *London and Property Markets: a long term view*. South Bank University, London.

Baum, A. & Crosby, N. (1995). *Property Investment Appraisal (2nd Ed)*. London, Routledge.

Becker, F. & Joroff, M. (1995) *Reinventing the workplace*. International Development Research Foundation, Norcross, GA.

Behrens, A.H. (1982) Managing corporate real estate as a profit centre. *Industrial Development*, **151** (5/6) 4–8.

Bell, M.A. (1987) The importance of sound fixed asset management. *Industrial Development*, **11** (1) 11–13.

Bon, R. & Luck, R. (1999) Annual CREMRU-JCI survey of corporate real estate practices in Europe and North America: 1993–1998. *Facilities*, **17** (5/6) 167–176.

Bon, R. (1994) Ten principles of corporate real estate management. *Facilities*, **12** (4) 9–10.

Bon, R., McMahan, J. & Carder, P. (1994) Property performance measurement: from theory to management practice. *Facilities*, **12** (12) 18–24.

Bootle, R. & Kalyan, S. (2002) *Property in Business: A waste of space?* RICS, London.

Brett, M. (1990) *Property and Money*. The Estates Gazette Ltd, London.

British Broadcasting Corporation (1997) *Farming Today*, Radio 4, 24th May, 1997.

Bromley, D.W. (1985) Resources and economic development: an institutionalist perspective. *Journal of Economic Issues*, **19**(3) 779–796.

Bromley, D.W. (1989) *Economic Interests and Justifications: the conceptual foundations of public policy*. Blackwell, Oxford.

Bromley, D.W. (1991) *Environment and Economy: Property Rights and Public Policy*. Blackwell, Oxford.

Brookes, Brian (1990). *Ardtornish Conservation Audit*, Ardtornish Estate Office, Morvern.

Brown, R.K., Lapides, P. & Rondeau, E. (1994) *Managing Corporate Real Estate: Forms and Procedures*. Wiley Law, New York.

Brown, R.K. & Arnold, A.L. (1993) *Managing Corporate Real Estate*. Wiley, Chichester.

Byrne, P., Lizieri, C. & Worzala, E. (2001) *The Location of Executive Suites and Business Centres: an exploratory analysis, Final Research Report*. Real Estate Institute, Bloomington, Indiana.

Callon, M. & Law, J. (1995) Agency and the hybrid collectif. *South Atlantic Quarterly*, **94** 481–507.

Cao, J. & Edwards, V. (2001) Why China has awakened: an institutional analysis of the office market in Beijing and Shanghai. *Briefings in Real Estate Finance* **1**(4), 302–318.

Cao, J. & Edwards, V.M. (2002) The Beijing office market: its current status and opportunities for international developments and investment financiers. *Briefings in Real Estate Finance*, **2**(1), 42–60.

Carn, N., Black, R. & Rabianski, J. (1999) Operational and organisational issues facing corporate real estate executives and managers. *Journal of Real Estate Research*, **17**(3) 281–99.

CIPFA (1992) *Capital Accounting by Local Authorities – Report of the Implementation Studies*. Chartered Institute of Public Finance and Accountancy, London.

Coase, R. H. (1960) The problem of social cost. *Journal of Law and Economics*, **III**: 1–44.

Cohen, N. & Hollinger, P. (2000) Sainsbury in move to add value to sites. *Financial Times*, 12 September, p. 28.

Commons, J. R. (1961) *Institutional Economics*. University of Wisconsin Press, Madison.

Cranfield School of Management (2002) *Changing Times: strategic consulting for professional effectiveness*. RICS, London.

Currie, D. & Scott, A. (1991) *The Place of Commercial property in the UK Economy*. London Business School, London.

Debenham Tewson Chinnock. (1992) *The role of property: managing cost and releasing value*. Debenham Tewson Chinnock, London.

DETR (2000) *Draft Good Practice Guidelines for Property Management in Local Government*. Department of Education, Transport and the Regions, London.

Dicken, P. (1998) *Global Shift: transforming the world economy*. Paul Chapman Ltd, London.

Disability Discrimination Act (1995) (c.50) The Stationery Office, London.

Dubben, N. & Sayce, S. (1991) *Property Portfolio Management*. Routledge, London.

Duckworth, S.L. (1993) Realizing the strategic dimension of corporate real property through improved planning and control systems. *Journal of Real Estate Research*, **4** 495–509.

Edington, G. (1997) *Property management: a customer focused approach*. Macmillan, London.

Edward Erdman & Co. (1992) *Property Asset Registers – A National Survey of the Local Authority Response to Implementation*. Edward Erdman, London.

Edwards, V.M. & Seabrooke, W. (1991) Proactive property management briefing. *Property Management*, **9** (4) 373–385.

Edwards, V.M. & Steins, N.A. (1998) Developing an analytical framework for multiple-use commons. *Journal of Theoretical Politics*, **10**(3) 347–383.

Edwards, V.M. & Steins, N.A. (1999) A framework for analysing contextual factors in common pool resource research. *Journal of Environmental Policy and Planning*, **1**(3): 205–221.

Eggertson, T. (1990) *Economic Behaviour and Institutions*. Cambridge University Press, Cambridge.

Elphick, R. & Wright, J. (2002) Assets that are leaking money. *Estates Gazette*, 2 February.

Estey, R. (1988) How corporate real estate departments contribute to the bottom line. *Industrial Development*, July/August 4–6.

Evans, M. & Weatherhead, M. (1999) *Think Profit Act Property*. RICS Corporate Property Users Group, London.

Evans, M., French, N. & O'Roarty, B. (2000) A briefing on current and proposed provisions relating to UK corporate real estate. *Journal of Property Investment and Finance*, **19** (2) 211–223.

Forestry Commission (2001) *New software brings the future on screen*. Press release no. 3748, 14 March.

Fraser, W.D. (1993) *Principles of Property Investment and Pricing*. Macmillan, Basingstoke.

Gale, J. & Case, F. (1989) A study of corporate real estate resource management. *Journal of Real Estate Research*, **4** (3) 23–33.

Galjart, B. (1992) Cooperation as pooling: a rational choice perspective. *Sociologia Ruralis*, **XXXII** 389–407.

Gibson, V., Hedley, C., Procter, A. & Fennell, B. (2000) Evaluating Office Space Needs and Choices. MWB Business Exchange and University of Reading, Reading.

Gibson, V. and Barkham, R. (2001) Corporate real estate management in the retail sector: investigation of current strategy and structure. *Journal of Real Estate Research*, **22** (1/2) 107–27.

Gibson V. & French, N. (2002) *Whose property is it anyway?* RICS, London.

Gibson, V.A. (1994) Strategic property management: how can local authorities develop a property strategy? *Property Management*, **12** (3) 9–14.

Gibson, V.A. (2000) Property portfolio dynamics: the flexible management of inflexible assets. *Facilities*, **18** (3/4) 150–154.

Gibson, V.A. & Lizieri, C. (1999) New business practices and the corporate property portfolio: how responsive is the UK property market? *Journal of Real Estate Research*, **16** (3) 201–218.

Gibson, V. & Lizieri, C. (2001) Friction and inertia: business change, corporate real estate portfolios and the UK office market. *Journal of Real Estate Research*, **22** (1/2) 59–79.

Goodhart, C. (2000) Keynote speech at RICS Cutting Edge Conference, London.

Guyat, R. (2003) The Planning and Compulsory Purchase Bill: proposed changes to the development control regime. *Planning Law Journal*, 10 February.

Hankinson, P. (2001) Brand orientation in the top 500 fundraising charities in the UK. *Journal of Product and Brand management*, **10** (6) 346–360.

Hankinson, P. (2002) The impact of brand orientation on managerial practice: a quantitative study of the UK's top 500 fundraising managers. *International Journal of Nonprofit and Voluntary Sector Marketing*, **7** (1) 30–44.

Hanson, M. (1990) Estate doubles its asking price. *Financial Times*. 14/15 July.

Harvey, D. (1985) *The Urbanisation of Capital*. Blackwell Publishing, Oxford.

Healy, P. (1991) A model of the land development process. *Journal of Land Development*.

Heighton, M. (2002) Turn over the issues. *Estates Gazette*, 2 March 214–215.

Hertz, N. (2001) *The Silent Takeover: Global Capitalism and the Death of Democracy*. Heinemann, London.

Hiang, L.K., Leong, J., Ebrahim, M. & Brown, G. (2001) Performance measurement in corporate real estate: issues, evidence and research agenda. *Journal of Financial Management of Property and Construction*, **6** (2) 71–79.

Hill, N. (2002) Charity finance: property: bricks and mortar. *Guardian*, April 10, 4.

Hines, M.A. (1990) *Global Corporate Real Estate Management: A handbook for multinational business organisations*. Quorum Books, London.

Hodges, N.W. (1996) *The Economic Management of Physical Assets*. Mechanical Engineering Publications Ltd, London.

Hoesli, M. (2000) *Property Investment: principles and practice of portfolio management*, Longman, Harlow.

Hoffman, J.J., Schiederjans, M.J. & Sirmans, G.S. (1990) A multi-criteria model for corporate property evaluation. *Journal of Real Estate Research*, **5** (3) 285–300.

Horne, S. & Broadbridge, A. (1995) Charity shops: a classification by merchandise mix. *International Journal of Retail Distribution Management*, **23** (7) 17–23.

Horne, S. (1998) Charity shops in the UK. *International Journal of Retail Distribution Management*, **26** (4) 155–161.

Hurtt, S.M. (1988) Real estate: liability or asset? *Real Estate Finance Journal*, Winter, Winter, 61–71.

IDRC (1999) Corporate infrastructure resources management: an emerging source of competitive advantage. *Research Bulletin No. 22*, IDRC, Atlanta.

Isaac, D. (1998) *Property Investment*. Macmillan, Basingstoke.

Johnson, L. & Keasler, T. (1993) An industry profile of corporate real estate. *Journal of Real Estate Research*, **8** (4) 455–473.

Joroff, M., Louargand, M., Lambert, S. & Becker, F. (1993) *Strategic Management of the Fifth Resource: Corporate real estate*. Industrial Development Research Foundation, Norcross GA.

Joroff, M. (1992) *Management Strategies for the Next Decade*. Corporate Real Estate 2000 White Paper, Industrial Development Foundation. Norcross, GA.

Kasper, W. & Steit, M.E. (1998) *Institutional Economics*. Elgar, Cheltenham.

Keating, M. (1998) Charity shops: faith, hope and tax relief. *Guardian*, December 15.

Kinsella, P. (1999) Rough road to easing traffic. *Property Week* (Supplement) February 1999, p. 27.

Kiser, L.L. & Ostrom, E. (1982) The three worlds of action: a metatheoretical synthesis of institutional aproaches. In *Strategies of Political Inquiry* (ed. E. Ostrom). Sage, Beverly Hills.

Lipsey, R. (1997) *An Introduction to Positive Economics*. Oxford University Press, Oxford.

Livingston, M. L. (1987) Evaluating the performance of environmental policy: contributions of neoclassical, public choice and institutional models, *Journal of Economic Issues* vol. **XXI**, no.1.

Lizieri, C., Crosby, N., Gibson, V.A., Murdoch, S. & Ward, C. (1997) *Right Space, Right Place? A study of the impact of changing business practices on the property market*. RICS, London.

Lizieri, C. (2001) New players, new markets: has the property industry really changed? IPD/IPF Property Investment Conference, 29–30 November, Brighton.

Lloyd, B. (1992) An effective property strategy: they key facilities challenge for the 1990s. *Facilities*, **10** (12) 9–12.

Long, N. (1989) *Encounters at the Interface: A Perspective on Social Discontinuities in Rural Development*. Wageningen Sociological Studies No. 27, Wageningen Agricultural University, Wageningen, Netherlands.

Love, J.F. (1986) *McDonald's: Behind the Arches* (pp. 151–187). Bantam Books, New York, 151–187.

Lyne, J. (1995) IDRC's real estate revolution: occupancy costs plummet, productivity crests. *Site Selection*, April 198–212.

Manning, C. (1991) Leasing versus purchase of corporate real property: leases with residual equity interests. *Journal of Real Estate Research*, **6** (1) 79–85.

Manning, C., Rodriguez, M. & Roulac, S. (1997) Which corporate real estate management functions should be outsourced? *Journal of Real Estate Research*, **14** (3) 259–274.

Manning, C.A. & Roulac, S.E. (1996) Structuring the corporate real property function for greater bottom line impact. *Journal of Real Estate Research*, **12** (3) 383–396.

Manning, C.A. & Roulac, S.E. (1999) Corporate real estate research within the Academy. *Journal of Real Estate Research*, **17** (3) 265–279.

Manning, C.A. (1986) The Economics of real estate decisions. *Harvard Business Review*, **86** (6) 12–22.

March, J. G. & Olsen, J. P. (1988) The New Institutionalism: organizational factors in political life. *American Political Science Review*, **78** 734–749.

McIntosh, A.P.J. & Sykes, S. (1985) *A Guide to Institutional Property Investment*, Macmillan, London.

Mintzberg, H. (1990) The design school: reconsidering the basic premises of strategic management. *Strategic Management Journal*, **11**, 171–195.

Monbiot, G. (2001) *Captive State: the corporate takeover of Britain*. Pan, London.

Noha, E.A. (1993) Benchmarking: the search for best practices in corporate real estate. *Journal of Real Estate Research*, **8** (4) 511–524.

North, D.C. (1990) *Institutions, Institutional Change and Economic Performance*. Cambridge University Press, Cambridge.

Nourse, H.O. (1992) Real estate flexibility must complement business strategy. *Real Estate Review*, **4** 25–29.

Nourse, H.O. & Roulac, S.E. (1993) Linking real estate decisions to corporate strategy. *Journal of Real Estate Research*, **8** (4) 475–494.

Nourse, H.O. (1986) Using real estate asset management to improve strategic performance. *Industrial Development*, June/July 1–7.

Nourse, H.O. (1990) *Managerial Real Estate: Corporate Real Estate Asset Management*. Prentice Hall, Englewood Cliffs, NJ.

Nourse, H.O. (1994) Measuring business real property performance. *Journal of Real Estate Research*, **9** (4) 431–444.

Oakerson, R. J. (1986) A Model for the Analysis of Common Property Problems. In *Proceedings of the Conference on Common Property Resource Management*, National Research Council, pp.13–30. National Academy Press, Washington, D. C.

Oakerson, Ronald J. (1992) 'Analyzing the Commons: A Framework', in Daniel W. Bromley et al. (eds.) *Making the Commons Work: Theory, Practice and Policy*, pp. 41–59. Institute for Contemporary Studies Press, San Francisco, CA.

Olson, M. (1965) *The Logic of Collective Action: public goods and the theory of groups*. Harvard University Press, Cambridge, Massachusetts.

O'Mara, M.A. (1997) Corporate real estate strategy: uncertainty, values and decision making. *Journal of Applied Real Property Analysis*, **1** (1) 15–28.

O'Mara, M. (1999) *Strategy and Place: Corporate Real Estate and Facilities Management*. Free Press, New York.

Planning and Compulsory Purchase Bill (2002) The Stationery Office, London.

Ostrom, E. (1986) An agenda for the study of institutions. *Public Choice*, **48** 3–25.

Ostrom, E. (1990) *Governing The Commons: The Evolution of Institutions for Collective Action*. Cambridge University Press, Cambridge.

Ostrom, V. (1976) John R. Common's Foundations for Policy Analysis. *Journal of Economic Issues*, **10**(4) 839–57.

Parsons, E. (2000) New goods, old records and second-hand suits: charity shopping in south west England. *International Journal of Non-Profit and Voluntary Sector Marketing*, **5** (2) 141–151.

Parsons, E. (2002) Charity retail: past, present, future. *International Journal of Retail Distribution Management*, **30** (12) 586–594.

Paulson, M.F. & Rooney, J.M. (1991) *Benchmarking in the Corporate Real Estate Function: a prime*. Industrial Development Research Foundation, Atlanta.

Pavan, M. (1996) Marketing benchmarking in professional firms. *Professional Practice Management*, **14** (4) 50–52.

Phelan, D. (1996) High street wars hot up. *NGO Finance*, **6** (3) 18–28.

Pitman, R.H. & Parker, J.R. (1989) A survey of corporate real estate executives on factors informing corporate real estate performance. *Journal of Real Estate Research*, **4** (3) 107–19.

Porter, M. (1998) *Competitive Strategy: techniques for analysing industries and competitors*. Free Press, New York.

Pottinger, G. (2000) *Occupational futures: corporate real estate restructuring and refinancing*. The College of Estate Management, Reading.

Pottinger, G. (2002) Occupational futures? Divesting real estate and corporate PFI. *Property Management*, **20** (1) 31–48.

Prudential Property Investment Managers (2002) *Environmental and Social Report 2002*, Prudential, London.

Raney, D. (1990) Managing international real estate at Hewlett Packard. *Industrial Development*, April 14–16.

Rappaport, A. (1986) *Creating Shareholder Value*. Free Press, New York.

Ratcliffe, J. (1978) *An Introduction to Urban Land Administration*. Estates Gazette, London.

Redman, A.L. & Tanner, J.R. (1991) The financing of corporate real estate: a survey. *Journal of Real Estate Research*, **6** (2) 217–240.

RICS (1995) *Valuation and Appraisal Manual*. RICS Business Services, London.

RICS (1997) *Right Space Right Price; a study of the impact of changes in business patterns on the property market*. RICS, London.

RICS (2001) *Lease Structures, terms and lengths: does the UK lease meet current business requirements?* RICS, London.

RICS (2002) A Code of Practice for Commercial Leases in England and Wales. RICS, London.

Roberts, S. (1991) How property can help organisations achieve their objectives. *Facilities*, **9** (3) 7–12.

Rodriguez, M. & Sirmans, C.F. (1996) Managing corporate real estate: evidence from the capital markets. *Journal of Real Estate Literature*, January, 13–33.

Rooney, J.M. (1989) Benchmarking corporate real estate at Xerox. *Site Selection*, October 198–205.

Roulac, S. (2001) Corporate property strategy is integral to corporate business strategy. *Journal of Real Estate Research*, **22** (1/2) 129–152.

Runge, C. Ford (1981) Common property externalities: isolation, assurance, and resource depletion in a traditional grazing context. *American Journal of Agricultural Economics*, **63**, 595–607.

Rutherford, A. (2002) Cancer Research UK looks to NCI for success. *Trends in Molecular Medicine*, **8** (2) 96–97.

Rydin, Y. (1993) *The British Planning System: An Introduction*. Macmillan, Basingstoke.

Sayce, S., Cuthbert, M., Iball, H. & Parnell, P. (2000) The business case for sustainable property: initial findings of the research team. Presentation to The Sustainable Construction Conference, London, 12 July.

Schaefers, W. (1999) Corporate real estate management: evidence from German companies. *Journal of Real Estate Research*, **17** (3) 301–320.

School of Estate Management, Oxford Brookes University and Department of Land Management and Development, University of Reading (1993) *Property Management Performance Monitoring*. GTI, Oxford.

Scott, P. (1996) *The Property Masters: a history of the British commercial property sector*. E & F.N. Spon, London.

Silverman, R.A. (1987) *Corporate Real Estate Handbook: Strategies for improving bottom line performance*. McGraw Hill, New York.

Simons, R.A. (1992) Public real estate management – adapting corporate practice to the public sector: the experience in Cleveland, Ohio. *Journal of Real Estate Research*, **8** (4) 639–654.

Steins, N.A. (1995) Securing access to the sea: the creation of an artificial common property resource. Paper presented at the 5th International Conference of the International Association for the Study of Common Property, May 24–28 Bodoe, Norway.

Sugden, R. (1984) Reciprocity: the supply of public goods through voluntary contribution. *Economic Journal*, **94** 772–787.

Teoh, W.K. (1993) Corporate real estate asset management: the New Zealand evidence. *Journal of Real Estate Research*, **8** (4) 607–23.

Then, S.S.D. (1997) A model for considering operational property as an enabling resource to business. RICS COBRA Conference. 10–12 September, University of Portsmouth.

Tregoe, B.B. & Zimmerman, J.W. (1980) *Top Management Strategy: what it is and how to make it work*. Simon and Schuster, New York.

Veale, P.R. (1989) Managing corporate real estate assets: current executive attitudes and prospects of an emergent management discipline. *Journal of Real Estate Research*, **4** (3) 1–22.

Weatherhead, M. (1997) *Real Estate in Corporate Strategy*. Macmillan: London.

Weimer, A.M. (1966) Real estate decisions are different. *Harvard Business Review* November/December, 110–112.

West, D. (2003a) This Land is My Land. *The Scotsman*, 13th March 2003, page 15.

West, D. (2003b) Country Pursuits. *The Scotsman Guide to Property*, 13th March 2003, pages 16–19.

Williamson, O.E. & Masten, E.E. (eds) (1999) *The Economics of Transaction Costs*. Elgar, Cheltenham.

World Bank (2002) *World Development Report 2002: Building Institutions for Markets*. Oxford University Press, New York.

YHA (2003) Go YHA 2003–2004 Accommodation Guide. YHA, Matlock.

YHA (2000) *YHA in the New Millennium*. YHA, Matlock.

YHA (2002) *YHA in London: broader horizons for young people*. YHA, Matlock.

Zeckhauser, S. & Silverman, R. (1983) Rediscovering your company's real estate. *Harvard Business Review*, **61** (1) 111–117.

Index